The
Great Rights of Mankind

The
Great Rights of Mankind

A History of the American Bill of Rights

BERNARD SCHWARTZ

New York
Oxford University Press
1977

First printing, May 1977
Second printing, August 1977
Copyright © 1977 by Bernard Schwartz
Library of Congress Catalogue Card Number: 76-42646
Printed in the United States of America

For Aileen
without whom nothing would be possible

It cannot be a secret to the gentlemen in this House, that, not-withstanding the ratification of this system of Government . . . yet still there is a great number of our constituents who are dissatisfied with it . . . .We ought not to disregard their inclination, but, on principles of amity and moderation, conform to their wishes and expressly declare the great rights of mankind [*emphasis added*].

James Madison

House of Representatives
June 8, 1789

preface

The now-classic inventory of governmental restrictions that Madison termed "the great rights of mankind" are today for most of us synonymous with The Federal Bill of Rights. Yet at the time of their adoption, the Bill of Rights represented the high point of a courageous struggle to pass on the relatively new idea that rule of law must forever stand as a check upon governmental power. In a broad sense, then, the history of the Bill of Rights is the history of liberty itself, as we have come to know it in the Western World. A history of that larger subject would be, however, as chimerical an accomplishment as the monumental history of freedom Lord Acton was never able to write.

Fortunately, the scope of this volume is more limited. It seeks to present the background and history of the first amendments to the United States Constitution. The approach is chronological, starting with the great Charters of English liberty, continuing with the colonial and Revolutionary antecedents, then onto the movement that led to the Bill of Rights, and finally, in summary form, to the legislative history of that document. There is also a concluding chapter with an overview of the Bill of Rights in operation, now, close to two hundred years later.

Seven years ago I edited two volumes entitled *The Bill of Rights: A Documentary History*. The present book treats in narrative form that same story. In publishing this second work, I am guided by the example of Bernard Bailyn, whose

Ideological Origins of the American Revolution followed his
earlier documentary volumes, *Pamphlets of the American Revolution*. Even if I cannot hope that the result of my work will
equal that of the acknowledged master of early American history, I trust that the grandeur of the theme will justify my
efforts. The American Bill of Rights is (to paraphrase Justice
Oliver Wendell Holmes) a magic mirror, wherein we see reflected not only our own lives, but the whole pageant of
Anglo-American constitutional development and all that
those struggles have meant in the history of freedom. When I
think on this majestic theme, my eyes dazzle. If only a part of
my feelings on the matter is communicated to the reader, I
will be more than amply rewarded for my labors.

New York, New York   Bernard Schwartz
October, 1976

contents

The
Great Rights of Mankind

one
english antecedents

The bill of rights concept is primarily American in origin. The prior existence of the English Bill of Rights of 1689 [1] tends to obscure this fact. Except for the name, however, the 1689 enactment has little in common with the later American document. In the first place, the English bill was passed as a statute by Parliament and was thus, legally speaking, forever subject to amendment or repeal at the discretion of the creating legislature. The American notion of a bill of rights incorporates guarantees of personal freedom into a constitutional document in which articles define and limit the areas of legitimate legislative action. In this sense the Virginia Declaration of Rights of 1776 [2] was the first modern bill of rights, since it was the first to use a written constitution to insulate individual rights from the changing winds of legislative fancy.

In addition, the English Bill of Rights was a rudimentary document in those individual rights it did choose to guarantee. The 1689 enactment intended to block those methods by which the last two Stuart kings had sought to control Parliament, as well as to constrain future abuses of the royal prerogative. The only sections relevant to a bill of rights in the American conception dealt with prohibitions against excessive bail, fines, and punishment. These sections would later find their way into the United States Constitution, in the Eighth Amendment.

Moreover, by the time the English Bill of Rights was adopted, at least two American colonial settlements had already enacted local governing compacts providing far more complete protection of individual rights—notably the Massachusetts Body of Liberties, 1641 [3] (containing at that early date detailed guarantees that anticipated many of the fundamental liberties protected in the Federal Bill of Rights), and the Pennsylvania Frame of Government, 1682. [4]

It would be seriously erroneous, nevertheless, to assume that only American enactments were the precursors of the Federal Bill of Rights. Madison and his colleagues were able to draw up in 1789 the classic inventory of basic rights because they were the heirs of the constitutional struggles of their English forbears. Modern Americans may fail to recognize the extent to which our modern liberties are based upon the outcomes of battles waged in seventeeth-century Britain. But the men who established our constitutional system were fully aware of the significance of these victories of Parliament over the English Crown.

Consequently, the roots of American freedom must be sought in English constitutional history. For our purposes, this means a tracing of the Anglo-American antecedents of the Bill of Rights. The constitutional amendments proposed by Madison represented a logical progression from what had gone before both in England and America. The Federal Bill of Rights, then, as new as it seems in genre, was based directly or remotely upon the great charters of English liberty, back through history to the Magna Carta. Without the English precedent of the two-sided compact—between king and peers, and later, king and Parliament—one might wonder if the American colonists, revolutionaries, and constitution-makers would have or indeed could have come up with their novel conception of a strictly defined relationship between all those governed and all those governing.

MAGNA CARTA

To an American interested in the English antecedents of the Federal Bill of Rights, the obvious starting point is Magna

Carta itself. In it one sees for the first time in English history a written instrument exacted from a sovereign ruler by the bulk of the politically articulate community that purports to lay down binding rules of law that the ruler himself may not violate. In Magna Carta is to be found the germ of the root principle that there are fundamental individual rights that the State—sovereign though it is—may not infringe.

Traditional theory makes Magna Carta the direct descendant of the Coronation Charter of 1100 issued by Henry I upon seizing the throne.[5] Yet, if the Magna Carta secured at Runnymede in 1215 from John is derived from the Henry I Charter, it went far beyond the earlier document both in wording and implication. More significant possibly were the differing circumstances under which the two charters came into being. Henry issued his Coronation Charter to obtain support for his accession to the throne, but the instrument itself was a unilateral act on the part of the monarch—a promise by the king given as a matter of grace and not as the result of external coercion.

John's Charter also, it is true, is in its terms only a grant by the sovereign to his subjects. "John, by the grace of God," it starts, and, after reciting his titles and his formal greeting to his subjects, goes on to state, "Know that . . . we have also granted to all free men of our kingdom, for us and our heirs forever, all the liberties hereunder written, to be had and held by them and their heirs, of us and our heirs." After listing the various liberties granted, it concludes with the traditional words of royal grant: "Given by our hand in that meadow that is called Runnymede between Windsor and Staines, June 15, in the seventeenth year of our reign." The actual giving, by John's hand, was effected by the imprint of his great seal.

But if Magna Carta was thus cast in the form common to royal charters of the period—announcing in the pious legal formula of the day that the king has been pleased to make certain unilateral grants, by the advice of certain counsellors who are named—how different was its reality! The reasons stated for the grant of the Charter were quaintly paraphrased by Sir Edward Coke, the great British jurist and parliamentarian, four centuries later: "Here be four notable causes of the making of this great charter rehearsed. 1. The honour of God. 2. For the health of the King's soul. 3. For the exaltation of holy church, and fourthly, for the amendment of the Kingdom." [6] But the most powerful argument is to be found in the army opposing the king. The quid pro quo John received for the grants was renewal of homage and fealty by his former opponents.

Seen in this light, what can we say is the true legal nature of the Great Charter? This is a question on which countless scholars have disagreed. As already indicated, the document's form as a unilateral grant—a mere act of grace—on the part of the Crown does not give the answer.

Although constitutional historian William Stubbs's famous characterization of Magna Carta as "really a treaty between the King and his subjects" [7] has now been rejected, it is not as far from the truth as recent historians contend. Bear in mind that, unlike the more common treaty between independent states, this was a concord worked out between ruler and subjects of the same state. To the modern American, such an agreement (1) drawn up by the different estates of the realm, (2) accepted by the king as the price of the continued obedience of his subjects, and (3) for the purpose of setting limits to the powers of government, has many of the earmarks of the constitutional documents with which he is familiar. Even the charter form—a grant of franchises freely made—does not seem out of place to one cognizant of the constitutional role played by documents cast in a similar form in the American colonies.

What took place at Runnymede was essentially a bargain struck between the king and the nation. The result of this bargain was a document enumerating what were deemed the basic liberties of Englishmen of the day.

The enumeration may strike us as brief, contained as it is in sixty-three short chapters. For its date, nevertheless, it is a rather lengthy document. It was natural for the men of the day to resort to the legal form invariably used for all irrevocable grants: the feudal charter authenticated by the grantor's seal. The analogy was that of a grant of land and much of the language employed was that appropriate to such a grant.

In a provocative passage, Frederic William Maitland, perhaps the greatest of legal historians, asks, "Have you ever pondered the form, the scheme, the main idea of Magna Carta? If so, your reverence for that sacred text will hardly have prevented you from using in the privacy of your own minds some such words as inept' or 'childish,' etc." [8] Certainly, Magna Carta is an unrewarding document for the non-specialist. "If we set aside the rhetorical praise which has been so freely lavished upon the Charter, and study the document itself, we may find it rather surprising." [9] The Great Charter is a feudal grant, abounding in the technicalities of feudal law and, when these are out of the way, dealing mainly with mundane and petty aspects of the relations between the king and his barons. There is in it no broad statement of principle or defined political theory. It is not what we would accept as a declaration of constitutional rules. It is, finally, only a practical document to remedy then-current feudal abuses. Most surprising is that most of what we now consider the safeguards of Anglo-American liberty are conspicuously absent from the first Great Charter of English liberties.

Yet if we analyze the Magna Carta on its own terms, there is much in it that is notable. It is of great significance, for instance, that the custom of feudal tenure is here stated as a defined component of English law, with precise limits set in strict terms of money, time, and space to royal claims. The questions of scutage, feudal reliefs, wardship, and the like are regulated in legally enforceable terms against a king who had claimed to be all but a law unto himself.

More important is the fact that while Magna Carta was primarily a feudal document directed to specific feudal abuses committed by the king against his tenants-in-chief, its important provisions were cast in broader terms. Although true that the barons were concerned with their own grievances against John, when the original Articles of the

Barons were being refined, the words "any baron" were changed in important provisions to "any free man" (*liber homo*).[10] This change in phraseology may have seemed of lesser significance at the time (certainly "free man" was a technical feudal term with far more restricted meaning than we should give it today), yet it turned out to be of momentous importance; for it meant that key chapters of the Charter would be continually capable of construction to fit the needs of later ages seeking precedents to protect developing liberties. The royal assaults on the rights of the barons may have been the direct impetus for the Magna Carta, but the language used was to prove through time broad enough to protect the entire nation.

This was particularly true of what history has come to consider the two key provisions of the Great Charter: 1) Chapter 12, under which "Scutage or aid shall be levied in our kingdom only by the common counsel of our kingdom"; and 2) Chapter 39, which declares, "No free man shall be captured or imprisoned or disseised or outlawed or exiled or in any way destroyed . . . except by the lawful judgment of his peers and by the law of the land." The first of these may have been intended by the barons only as an assertion of their right not to have their feudal obligations unilaterally altered by the king. But the language is more sweeping than that of a mere declaration of feudal right. Without undue stretching, it can readily be construed as the "no taxation without representation" of the 1760's, albeit in primitive form.

Chapter 39 has been even more consequential in the evolution of constitutional liberty, although it was probably intended merely as written confirmation of the baronial right, recognized by feudal custom, not to be tried by inferiors. The breadth of the language used has made it serve a far wider purpose. Sir Edward Coke, in his seventeenth-century commentary on Magna Carta, could read it as a guaranty of trial by jury to all men; as absolutely prohibiting arbitrary arrest; and as solemnly undertaking to dispense to all, full, free, and speedy justice—equal to all. Even more suggestive for an

American, in Coke's commentary the crucial phrase at the end of the chapter, "by the law of the land," is read as an equivalent to "due process of law" [11] (a connotation it had begun to acquire as early as the time of Edward III), thus providing the link between the Great Charter and perhaps the most important clause of the American Bill of Rights.

Of course, by reading our own conceptions into the document sealed at Runnymede we make of it an organic instrument designed to "protect the personal liberty and property of all freemen by giving security from arbitrary imprisonment and arbitrary spoliation." [12] Yet, whether intended so broadly or not by its framers, Magna Carta did, without doubt, ultimately have such an effect. What is significant for us, as J. W. Gough points out, is that, irrespective of the Charter's original purpose, this was its value for later generations. [13] If later, men came to worship the words of Runnymede only because they misunderstood those words, the significant thing, after all, is that the words were written in a way that could be "misunderstood" so as to serve the needs of later ages. Because of this the "document becomes and rightly becomes a sacred text, the nearest thing to a 'fundamental statute' that English law has ever had." [14]

The significance of Magna Carta lies then in its potential for meaning different things to different ages. Thus it is that a document, itself a product of feudal class selfishness only, was able to serve as the basis for molding the foundation of a Parliamentary monarchy over the next two centuries, and then as the vehicle by which Parliamentary leaders would resist the Stuart kings four centuries later. Even later it would become the core of the body of rights of Englishmen that American colonists claimed as inherently their own. Those who look at Magna Carta with only the pedantic rigor of the thirteenth-century specialist are bound to miss the mark. The mere existence of such a document, extorted from the king as it was, remained as a standing condemnation of governmental absolutism. As the Charter tells us, "[t]here is a law which is above the King and which even he must not break.

This is a reaffirmation of a supreme law and its expression in a general charter is the great work of Magna Carta; and this alone justifies the respect in which men have held it." [15]

COKE AND PETITITION OF RIGHT

The 1628 Petition of Right is the next documentary antecedent of the American Bill of Rights. Much of its creativity and distinctiveness emanates from the mind of the man who played the all-important part, Sir Edward Coke. In many ways, Coke is the juristic progenitor of the men who made the American Revolution. James Otis, John Adams, Thomas Jefferson, to name but a few, were all nurtured upon Coke's writings and the example of his three-fold career in the law, each part of which left its imprint on both the English and American Constitutions. As a writer and as a judge, Coke furnished a doctrinal foundation for the American constitutional edifice whose first stone was laid in 1761 by James Otis with his argument against general writs of assistance. As a Parliamentary leader, Coke was the catalyst in the struggle that culminated in the Petition of Right, itself a guiding precedent for the American colonists in their struggle with the mother country.

In 1616, Coke was discharged from his three-year position as Chief Justice of King's Bench, the highest judge of the realm. He had been removed because of his consistent judicial efforts to frustrate royal attempts to place the power of the Crown above the law and, at the age of sixty-five, appeared to be at the end of his public career. In 1620, however, he was elected to the House of Commons. With it came the third and in some ways most admirable part of his career.

In Parliament, Coke gravitated toward the growing forces in opposition to the Crown. His reputation, learning, and passionate belief in the common law and a balanced Constitution—he was termed that great *"Monarcha Juris"* by no less a Parliament man than John Selden [16]—made him a natural leader in the Commons almost immediately.

On the bench, Coke had been conspicuous in his refusal to accede to the Stuart theory of absolutist government. In fact, his influence there was so great that with his removal from the bench, the struggle against that theory was also to shift, from the law courts to the Parliament. Coke's reappearance in public life as a Parliamentary leader was then a natural development. Thenceforth, opposition to the Crown would be centered almost entirely in the House of Commons, which ultimately would lead the nation in arms to vindicate the principle that even the king is subject to rule by law.

Coke's emergence as a Parliament man was also of primary significance in directing that Parliamentary conflict along legal lines. Both contemporaries and subsequent historians have stressed the role of the common lawyers in Parliament. At the beginning of the Long Parliament there were some seventy-five lawyer M.P.'s. Like the country itself, it is true, their allegiance was divided: when war came forty-two lawyers would side with Parliament, thirty-three with the king. But it is fair to say that the Parliament lawyers included most of those pre-eminent in legal talent. As the leading study has put it, "Nor was the government particularly strong since its available talent was few in numbers and had to be split between the two Houses." [17]

Without the support of the lawyers, Parliament would have appeared only as a group of revolutionaries, seeking to tear down the established order. Instead, Coke and his confreres were able to enlist for the opposition that almost superstitious reverence Englishmen feel for their law and to give to their struggle that note of legal conservatism that was at once its distinguishing characteristic and the cause of its successful issue. It was the common lawyers who rewrote history on Parliamentary lines in the House of Commons and who built up the body of rights and precedents alleged to be the immemorial heritage of the English people. [18]

During the reign of James I, the growing struggle between the legislators and the pretensions of the Crown eventuated in the Parliament of 1621. The House of Commons had already sent two petitions to the king, calling attention to the alarming spread of Popery and expressing their desire for a Protestant marriage for the Prince of Wales. The king replied that the matters mentioned were not fit subjects for Parliaments to consider. The privileges of the Commons themselves, James asserted, "were derived from the grace and permission of our ancestors and us, for most of them grow from precedents which show rather a toleration than inheritance." At this, Coke delivered an impassioned address: "The privileges of this House is the nurse and life of all our laws, the subject's best inheritance. . . . When the King says he cannot allow our liberties of right, this strikes at the root. We serve here for thousands and ten thousands." As the representative of "thousands and ten thousands," the Commons could scarcely remain silent in the face of the royal rebuke. Instead, Coke suggested, "Let us make a *Protestation*, enter it in the Journals and present the Journals to the King—but not as requiring an answer." [19]

By candlelight, with Coke's guidance, the Commons drafted their famous protest, which was an unequivocal declaration: "That the liberties, franchises, privileges and jurisdictions of Parliament are the ancient and undoubted birthright and inheritance of the subjects of England; and that the arduous and urgent affairs concerning the King, state and defence of the realm, and of the Church of England, and the maintenance and making of laws and redress of mischiefs and grievances which daily happen within this realm, are proper subjects and matter of counsel and debate in Parliament." [20] In addition, there was a categorical assertion of the privileges of Parliament, particularly that of freedom of speech.

A late nineteenth-century history of Parliament calls the 1621 Protestation "one of the landmarks in our constitutional history." [21] The king himself realized what the Commons action portended. Sitting in Council Chamber, he sent for the *Commons Journals* and in the presence of the Lords and judges tore out the page upon which the Protestation appeared. Coke and two other Commons leaders were sent to the Tower—Coke to remain there for nearly seven months in close confinement, the penalty customary for traitors and murderers.

Mere declaratory protest, however solemnly resolved by the people's representatives, can have no coercive legal effect. The 1621 Protestation laid down mere maxims of political morality that could be transgressed by the Crown with impunity. The violations of rights and liberties that occurred after 1621 led to the enactment of the Petition of Right by the last Parliament in which Coke would sit, that of 1628. Coke's "labours in that Parliament were destined to be a fitting conclusion to his career. They were to result in adding to the statute book the first of those great constitutional documents since Magna Carta, which safeguard the liberties of the people by securing the supremacy of the law." [22]

Much had happened since 1625 when Charles I acceded to the throne. Under Charles, the Stuart theory of prerogative was pushed to the extreme. By 1628, Englishmen had suffered serious attacks upon their liberties. In the two years that had intervened since the dissolution of the previous Parliament, a forced loan had been demanded; men who refused to pay had been punished; the judges who refused to enforce it had been dismissed. Soldiers had been billeted on the people and men committed to prison by the summary command of the king, without a trial and with bail refused. Well might Coke plaintively ask the 1628 session, "Shall I be made a tenant-at-will for my liberties, having property in my own house but not liberty in my person?" [23]

The members of the 1628 Commons were confronted with the question of what they should do about the situation. Coke rose to declare that it was the law of the realm that counted, not mere gracious promises from the throne. "Messages of love," he urged, "never came into a parliament. Let us put up a Petition of Right! Not that I distrust the King; but that I cannot take his trust, but in a Parliamentary way." [24]

The Petition of Right, passed in response to Coke's plea, was enacted as a statute. It declared the fundamental rights of Englishmen as positive law. Nor was the declaration weakened by any ambiguous saving of prerogative right. The

Lords had proposed an amendment that the petition "leave entire that Sovereign Power, wherewith your Majesty is trusted for the Protection, safety and happiness of the People." But Coke and the Parliamentary leaders saw that the Lords' amendment would explicitly safeguard the royal prerogative [25] and thus virtually nullify their Petition. "To speak plainly," said Coke, "it will overthrow all our Petition. . . . And shall we now add it, we shall weaken the foundation of law, and then the building must needs fall; let us take heed what we yield unto; Magna Charta is such a fellow, that he will have no sovereign. I wonder this sovereign was not in Magna Charta. . . . If we grant this, by implication we give a sovereign power above all these laws." [26]

The Petition of Right was aimed directly at the violations of rights and liberties that characterized Charles I's reign. In particular, it sought to restrict the arbitrary power of imprisonment, which had been at issue in the 1627 *Five Knights' Case*.[27] The five knights had been imprisoned without trial by order of the king after they had refused to contribute to a forced loan. The Court of King's Bench ruled in favor of the Crown, stating that, "if a man be committed by the commandment of the King, he is not to be delivered by a Habeas Corpus in this court, for we know not the cause of the commitment." [28] Under the decision, any writ of habeas corpus could be rendered ineffective by the simple statement that the individual concerned was being detained by special command of the king.

The popular feeling against the *Five Knights' Case* was a primary factor in the Parliamentary movement to enact the Petition of Right. In the Parliament of 1628, Coke pointed out just what the *Five Knights'* decision meant to the nation. "This draught of the judgment," he proclaimed, "will sting us. . . . What is this but to declare upon record, that any subject committed by such an absolute command may be detained in prison for ever? What doth this tend to but the utter subversion of the choice, liberty, and right belonging to every free-born subject in this kingdom." [29] Then, summing up in a phrase that illumined the impact of the judgment,

Coke affirmed that its effect was to "make men tenants at will of their liberties." [30]

The Petition of Right starts by seeking to "Humbly shew unto our sovereign lord the king" the various laws that have established the essential liberties of the subject, notably with regard to freedom from illegal exactions and arbitrary imprisonments. It goes on to enumerate violations of such liberties in the forced-loan procedure and by imprisonments "without any cause shewed." In conclusion, the petition asks the king, "That no man hereafter be compelled to make or yield any gift, loan, benevolence, tax, or such like charge, without common consent by act of parliament; . . . and that no freeman in any such manner as is before mentioned, be imprisoned or detained."

When the king finally gave the royal assent to the Petition of Right in the traditional form—he had tried in vain to put the Commons off with a different form of assent—members broke into loud acclamations as soon as the clerk pronounced the ancient formula, *"Soit droit fait comme il est desiré."* When these words were spoken, "the Commons returned to their own House with unspeakable joy, and resolved . . . to express their thankfulness." [31]

The thanksgiving was, however, premature. The Petition of Right, though voted by Parliament and not as the mere protestation that had been passed in 1621, was still only a declaratory document. It did not provide for any enforcement machinery or, as it turned out, really alter the constitutional balance between Crown and Parliament. As put by the Attorney General in a 1629 case, "the law is not altered by it, but remains as it was before. . . . A Petition in parliament is not a law." [32]

Before giving his assent, King Charles had asked the judges if the Petition would, indeed, "exclude himself from committing or restraining a subject for any time or cause whatsoever without showing a cause." The judges answered that, "although the petition be granted, there is no fear of conclusion as in the question is intimated." [33]

Armed with this judicial advice, the king proceeded to act

as though the Petition of Right had never been added to the statute book. During the next decade of Charles's reign, "the provisions of the Petition of Right were violated by him, not occasionally, but constantly, and on system; . . . a large part of the revenue was raised without any legal authority; and . . . persons obnoxious to the government languished for years in prison without ever being called upon to plead before any tribunal." [34] And the judges, in their decisions on the bench, proceeded to give official confirmation to the advisory opinion they had earlier given Charles that the Petition of Right was a mere declaration of principle, not binding as a practical restriction upon the royal prerogative. To us the Petition of Right may mark a vital stage on the journey that was to end in the defeat of the royal claims, but to contemporaries it must have seemed to have achieved little or nothing.[35]

The king and his counselors treated the Petition as nonexistent during the years between its passage and the summoning of the Long Parliament in 1641. Statutory declaration, without enforcement machinery, is scarcely sufficient to restrain an executive determined to operate as the sole source of governmental authority. The right against arbitrary imprisonment exists as a legal right only when it is enforceable in the courts. That was emphatically not the case with the Petition of Right; the judges were willing, even after the 1628 enactment, to recognize almost unlimited powers in the king to commit his subjects to prison.

COMMONWEALTH CONSTITUTIONS

The brief period (1649–60) during which Britain, for the first and only time in her history, possessed a republican polity was one of vigorous speculation and experiment within political, legal, and social realms. The activity in these areas, particularly in governmental experimentation, was to influence American constitutional development directly, although it played no comparable part in Britain once the old institutions were restored with the accession of Charles II.

One who looks at the period that followed the death of Charles I through the lenses of American constitutional experience is bound to find striking parallels between the situation of Englishmen who had executed their king and that of the colonists almost a century and a half later who declared their independence. In both cases, there was the overriding need to mend the tattered fabric of government. In both cases, too, the need was met in similar fashion. When in May, 1776, the Second Continental Congress adopted a resolution urging the various colonies to set up governments of their own, the latter acted by drawing up written constitutions establishing the new governments called for.[36] In so doing, they were following the example of Englishmen who had acted to fill the constitutional vacuum caused by the death of Charles I.

Even before the execution of the king, the constitutional ferment had begun. The radicals among the Parliamentary party—the so-called Levellers—urged a complete remaking of the polity. The idea of limiting government by law had been in the air throughout the first half of the seventeenth century.[37] The failure of declaratory protestations and enactments, such as those passed in 1621 and 1628, led men to look for more effective legal safeguards by 1649. New constitutional machinery was necessary if those safeguards were to be secured.

The Levellers asserted that the people had a constituent power superior to that of Parliament itself: "The only and sole legislative law-making power is originally inherent in the people, and derivatively in their Commissions chosen by themselves by common consent." [38] To the overweening claims of Parliamentary power, the Levellers replied, "Wee are your Principalls, and you our Agents." [39] Implicit was the notion that the "Principalls" could "by common consent" exercise their constituent power to reestablish the Constitution in such a form that it could not again be set aside arbitrarily.

This meant something very close to a written constitution. "We know," declares a 1647 Leveller pamphlet, "that it is better to live under an hard and harsh known written law . . . than under the mildest arbitrary government." [40] Only by a written organic document—"a Law against all Kinds of *Arbitrary Government*" [41]—would the powers of both Parliament and Crown be effectively curbed: it must "be positively and resolvedly insisted upon, that a law paramount be made, enacting it to be unalterable by Parliaments." [42]

The Leveller agitation culminated in the Agreement of the People, presented as a new social contract with which to refound the political order disturbed by the Civil War. The Agreement was originally drawn up in 1647 by the Leveller agents of the Army. "The document they framed . . . was the first rough draft of a written constitution in the history of democracy. These troopers were the pioneers who blazed the trail the Founding Fathers were to follow." [43] The Agreement of the People was to constitute the basic platform of the Leveller party for the next two years and was improved and expanded by them in 1648 and 1649 drafts.

The great Leveller contribution to republican theory was the notion of limiting the power of Parliament and doing so through a written document agreed to by the people. With the disappearance of the monarchy, misuse of power by a legally omnipotent legislature was the greatest threat. To meet that threat, the Levellers argued that the people must adopt a written agreement, which would lay down limits that even Parliament would be legally powerless to violate.[44] Such limits were prescribed expressly in the agreement in a manner that anticipated the prohibitory provisions of American constitutions.

At the beginning of 1649, the Council of Officers of the Army presented to the House of Commons a "Petition . . . concerning the Draught of an Agreement of the People, by them framed and prepared." [45] The officers' agreement accepted the leading Leveller principles. The Levellers themselves were nevertheless far from satisfied. They resented changes the officers had made in the agreement, particularly three: one that weakened the clause on freedom of religion, another that provided for Parliamentary power to create special courts, and a third that omitted the provision barring titles and special privileges. Even more important, they were displeased with the Army's action in presenting the agreement to the Commons; [46] their view of political organization was such that the agreement did not need Parliamentary ratification. It should "take its rise from the people"; "common consent" would bring it into effect as the fundamental law. [47] Their opposition induced the Leveller army leaders, led by John Lilburne, to issue a refined third draft of their agreement in May 1649. [48]

The officers' agreement may, however, be considered the nearest thing to a British version of the American-type constitution. In looking at its provisions, we should bear in mind that although the agreement is not a written constitution, it is the forerunner of constitutions and bills of rights in the American colonies and subsequently the Federal Constitution and Bill of Rights. [49] Unlike the American Constitution, it is, however, far from a complete frame of government. Yet it clearly rests upon the notion of restrictions to governmental power, a notion that was to be so important, key, in fact, to the development of American constitutionalism.

The officers' agreement provided for a Parliament of one House and a system of election based upon an expanded franchise and a more equal apportionment of legislative seats; in both aspects, the suggested electoral reform was not to be undertaken in Britain until the nineteenth century. It then went on to set forth six fundamental "points in the Reserve." These were to be matters beyond the power of the Parliament itself to alter. Although not so recognized at the time, this was, in effect, a list of fundamental rights. [50] Included in it were matters of religion, (except for "Popery or Prelacy"); military conscription; indemnity "for any thing said or done in relation to the late wars or public differences"; sanctity of the public debt; no punishment "where no law hath before provided"; and equality before the law. [51]

In addition, during the debates held by the army officers

before the final draft of the agreement was submitted, other "Particulars were offered to be inserted in the Agreement" as additions to the reserved points beyond the power of Parliament. They included guarantees of the right against self-incrimination, against imprisonment for debt, against restraints of trade, of "punishments equall to offences," of trial by jury, against usury, and against religious disabilities. The Levellers' "third draft" agreement expressly provided for each of these guarantees.[52]

The Commonwealth constitutional experience developed, therefore, many of the notions Americans associate with constitutions and bills of rights. In particular, there was the basic conception of a written constitution as a fundamental law drawn up by the people as a constituent power. John Lilburne tells how, in 1648, prior to the second draft of the Agreement of the People, the two leading factions, the Levellers and the Independents met "at the NagsHead Tavern" and agreed that,

"The onely way of Settlement is,

1. That some persons be chosen by the Army to represent the whole Body: and that the well-affected in every County (if it may be) chuse some persons to represent them. . . .

2. That those persons ought . . . to draw up the foundations of a just Government, and to propound them to the well-affected people in every County to be agreed to: Which Agreement ought to be above Law."[53]

The fundamental distinction between the legislative and the constituent power, upon which the various Agreements of the People were based, was stated in almost its modern terms in the pamphlet, *A Healing Question*, published by Sir Henry Vane in 1656.[54] Vane is known to Americans as a colonial governor of Massachusetts, but his main role was in English politics where "he was that within the House of Commons that Cromwell was without."[55] Although an early leader of the Commonwealth government, he broke with Cromwell over the forcible dissolution of the Rump Parliament. On that occasion Cromwell is said to have exclaimed, "O Sir Henry Vane! Sir Henry Vane! The Lord deliver me from Sir Henry Vane." [56] His conflict with Cromwell did not prevent Vane from being executed for treason after the Restoration.

In his pamphlet Vane sought to expound the basic principles of civil and religious liberty. In it he proposed the method of drawing up a constitution through a convention called by the people for the purpose. This was, of course, precisely the method subsequently used by Americans during the Revolution, when conventions in the newly independent states enacted constitutions and bills of rights. Exercise of the constituent power through a "convention of faithful, honest, and discerning men, chosen for that purpose by the free consent of the whole body" of the people would enable the "fundamental constitutions[to] be laid and inviolably observed as the conditions upon which the whole body so represented doth consent to cast itself into a civil and politic incorporation." [57]

It should not, however, be thought that the later American achievement was no more than the mere refurbishing of a constitutional edifice erected by Interregnum Englishmen. The concept of constitutionalism embodied in the Agreement of the People was rudimentary compared with that upon which American constitution-makers were to act. Covenants without the sword, says Hobbes, are but empty words. The same is true of a constitution written in hortatory terms. The American Framers knew it was not enough to declare fundamental rights and limitations in an organic document; just as important was enforcement machinery. The great contribution of the Framers was the establishment of a polity based upon a system of checks and balances as well as on a power in the courts to control the constitutionality of governmental action. Thus, judicial review, the concept essential to the maintenance of restrictions on governmental power, was made possible. No comparable enforcement machinery was suggested in the rudimentary constitutional documents drafted in Interregnum England. The various Agreements of the People were, by their own terms, intended as "Fundamental to our common Right, Liberty, and Safety." [58] The

Levellers' third draft went even further, providing expressly that "all Laws made, or that shall be made contrary to any part of this Agreement, are hereby made null and void." [59] This germ of the Federal Constitution's Supremacy Clause and judicial review was to remain stillborn, for the Leveller movement itself was soon to be crushed by military repression. [60]

The conclusion of the Commonwealth constitutional experience may be briefly stated. The Agreement of the People never went into effect as a working constitution. In 1653, Cromwell announced his intention of ruling according to an organic document known as the Instrument of Government. It provided for a government carried on by a Lord Protector and a single House, as well as a Council of State to advise the Protector. It sought to apportion governmental power between the executive and legislative branches, but in effect established a limited monarchy without a king in name. In practice, however, the Instrument in operation quickly revealed the basic defect referred to above—the lack of machinery for effective enforcement. A key provision of the Instrument did provide that legislative acts were to "contain nothing in them contrary to the matters contained in these presents." [61] But there was no means of enforcing this provision.

When the Parliament elected under the Instrument met in 1654, it immediately refused to accept the binding force of the Instrument itself. Instead, Parliament sought to enact a wholly new constitutional scheme, imposing legislative control far greater than that provided for in the Instrument. The result was a speedy dissolution of the House by the Protector. Thereafter, Cromwell governed by military force, setting up a system of military govenment by major-generals throughout the country. Funds were obtained by vote of the Council of State alone, including the imposition of a tithe on the property of royalists. All this was, of course, wholly contrary to the scheme of government set up by the Instrument of Government and, in the modern American sense, plainly unconstitutional. Yet no legal method had been provided for by which the question of constitututionality could be determined and hence nothing existed to prevent first the legislature and then the Executive from violating the organic document with impunity.

We can consequently say that the English age of written constitutions, which began with striking precedents for the American conception of government by law, ended in the very negation of that concept. Although Cromwell's desire may have been "to govern constitutionally, and to substitute the empire of the laws for that of the sword," [62] he soon decided that only by using the latter could he govern effectively. The result was that "the government, although in form a republic, was in truth a despotism, moderated only by the widsom, the sobriety, and the magnanimity of the despot." [63]

BILL OF RIGHTS, 1689

To eighteenth-century Americans the Bill of Rights of 1689 was "that second Magna Carta." [64] Its technical title was "An act declaring the rights and liberties of the subject and settling the succession of the crown." To understand the popular title by which it has always been known and by which the standard, as well as the name for the American Bill of Rights came about, one must know something of the historical events that led to the 1689 enactment.

The Bill of Rights was the culmination of what has since been termed the Glorious Revolution of 1688. The mildness of that event may lead modern observers to find hyperbole in the characterization of it as revolution. From a constitutional point of view, however, the events that terminated in the Bill of Rights did constitute a true revolution, one that John Holt could characterize in a 1774 New York newspaper as "the Work of Ages which is the Envy and Admiration of the Universe, the Glory of the English Nation." [65]

When James II ignominiously fled from his kingdom to spend the rest of his days (after a brief incursion into Ireland) as the pathetic figure we meet in the pages of Saint-Simon, he did what he could to disrupt civil government and plunge the realm into anarchy. Even the Great Seal, that almost mystic symbol of constitutional continuity, was cast into the Thames by James on December 11, 1688, and from that day until February 13, 1689, when William and Mary accepted the Crown, there was no legal government. Not only was there no king, but no Parliament, since James's only Parliament had been finally dissolved in July, 1688. Without a king it was impossible to assemble a lawfully constituted Parliament, and without the Houses a legal solution of the problem posed by James's flight seemed just as impossible.

The dilemma was resolved, as it had to be, by extra-legal methods. Recourse was had to the calling by William of an assembly composed of the peers and members of the Commons during the reign of Charles II, as well as the magistrates of London. From a legal point of view, this assembly was quite irregular. Yet even the lawyers recognized that this was an occasion when legal niceties would have to yield to the exigencies of the political crisis. The assembly called by William advised him to summon a convention Parliament. It met on January 22, 1689, and soon thereafter passed its celebrated resolution announcing that James II had abdicated "and that the throne is thereby vacant." After the Crown was settled on William and Mary, the convention passed an act declaring itself to be a true Parliament, notwithstanding the want of proper writs of summons.

The throne had been offered to William and Mary subject to the conditions laid down in an instrument known as the Declaration of Right, which had been drawn up by a committee of the convention. After that body had declared itself to be a Parliament, it turned its declaration into a regular Act of the legislature enacted as a statute in 1689. Hence, the name Bill of Rights itself is the result of the fact that the original declaration was introduced as a bill—i.e., the first step in enactment of a statute—in the new Parliament.

The 1689 Bill of Rights [66] served notice on the king that royal efforts to dominate Parliament must thenceforth cease. It declared that the election of members of Parliament ought to be free; that freedom of speech and debates in Parliament ought not to be questioned in any court or other place; and that Parliament ought to be held frequently (a provision made more specific by the Triennial Act, 1694, which prohibited the intermission of Parliament for more than three years).

In addition, the Bill of Rights specifically condemned the abuses of the prerogative by James II. It declared "that the pretended power of suspending of laws or the execution of laws by regal authority without consent of the parliament is illegall." A similar provision outlawed the dispensing power "as it hath been assumed and exercised of late." Another royal abuse was dealt with in a provision prohibiting the raising or keeping of an army in time of peace, "unless it be with consent of Parliament," and there is a rudimentary statement of the right of the people to bear arms, as well as a complaint against the quartering of soldiers.

Those sections of the Bill of Rights that deal with the perversions of justice by the last Stuart kings are of particular interest, for they served as the models for similar provisions in subsequent colonial bills of rights in America. These sections provide that "excessive bail ought not to be required, nor excessive fines imposed, nor cruel and unusual punishments inflicted" (the direct ancestor of the Eighth Amendment to the Federal Constitution); that jurors should be duly impaneled; and that grants and promises of fines and forfeitures by particular persons before conviction are illegal.

UNWRITTEN VERSUS WRITTEN LAW

Alexis de Tocqueville once compared the Switzerland and the England of the 1830s: "In . . . England there seems to be more liberty in the customs than in the laws of the people. In Switzerland there seems to be more liberty in the laws than in the customs of the country." [67] One who looks only at the written law in tracing the history of English liberty is bound to obtain an incomplete and distorted picture. If "it is impossible to think of the English as living under any but a free government," [68] that is not because the rights of Englishmen are based upon anything like constitutional guarantees in the American sense.

The true English antecedents of the Federal Bill of Rights are not documentary, but customary. By the time of the American Revolution, many of the rights guaranteed by the Federal Bill of Rights were recognized or coming to be recognized in English law. These included the rights *of* free speech and free press, petition; *against* unreasonable searches and seizures, double jeopardy, excessive fines and cruel and unusual punishments, self-incrimination; *to* a grand jury indictment, and jury trial. By later American standards, these rights were but imperfectly recognized, and their basis was tradition rather than written law. As a leading English text puts it, "The security which an Englishman enjoys for personal freedom does not really depend upon or originate in any general proposition contained in any written document." [69] The same is true in England with regard to the other rights guaranteed by the Federal Bill of Rights.

Freedom of the press is a typical example of the growth of rights in the English system. Control of the press was originally exercised through the Star Chamber. Although that tribunal was one of the first victims of the Long Parliament in 1641, its abolition did not mean press freedom. Censorship survived the Civil War and was given a statutory foundation by the Licensing Act of 1662. [70] Still, even that law was an important step forward, since the licensing power now depended, not on any claim of inherent executive authority, but on statute law. [71] Then, in 1695, the House of Commons refused to renew the Licensing Act. Consequently, the system of compulsory licensing of all publications, rigorously enforced since Tudor times, expired, and the English press has since been legally free from prior restraints. In Macaulay's phrase, the press "was emancipated from the censorship soon after the Revolution; and the government immediately fell under the censorship of the press." [72] Yet this was brought about, not by ringing constitutional declaration, but by the simple fact that the Parliament failed to renew a statute.

Certainly, without the prior English development, individual rights could scarcely have evolved to the level they did in American law. The development in this country has, however, had a different basis from that in the English system. The charters of English liberty discussed in this chapter are records of the existence of rights rather than enactments to confer them.[73] They stimulated American history more by their fame than their substance. The American constitutional experience emphasizes the substance of written guarantees. American constitutions and bills of rights are the legal source, not merely the records, of basic rights. To understand the development in this respect, one must turn to the American experience during the Colonial period.

two
colonial charters and laws

CHARTERS AND SELF-GOVERNMENT

In assessing the impact of our colonial heritage upon the development of the Bill of Rights, the most important thing to bear in mind is that the American colonies were *British* colonies. From a constitutional point of view, the colonies settled by Great Britain were unique—utterly unlike those of Spain or France or the nations of antiquity. When Englishmen migrated, they took with them, as it was later put in Parliamentary debate, "all of the first great privileges of Englishmen on their backs." [1] "Let an Englishman go where he will" said Richard West, counsel to the Board of Trade, in 1720, "he carries as much of law and liberty with him, as the nature of things will bear." [2] So armed, Patrick Henry would later claim, in his 1765 resolves passed by the Virginia Assembly, that the people of that colony possess "all the liberties, privileges, franchises and immunities that at any time have been held, enjoyed and possessed by the people of *Great Britain*." [3] A similar claim could hardly have been asserted by the ancient Romans, or eighteenth-century Frenchmen or Spaniards who had settled overseas.

Thomas Pownall, perhaps the best of the Massachusetts colonial governors, argued that the right of self-government was preserved to the American colonists because the Island of Jersey had, by its constitution, "a shadow and semblance of an English parliament." [4] This precedent, he said, made it easy to put the same idea into early American charters.

The earliest instrument to play a part in the constitutional training of Americans was the colonial charter. Colony-founding by royal charter was a natural development in an age when property, powers, and immunities were commonly granted through such instruments. Armed with the first of these, the 1606 charter granted by James I, the colonists to Virginia were authorized "to make Habitation, Plantation, and to deduce a Colony of sundry of our People into that part of America, commonly called Virginia." The Virginia Charter states—at the outset of colonization—the fundamental principle that the colonists had brought with them all the rights of Englishmen; they were to "Have and enjoy all Liberties, Franchises, and Immunities . . . to all Intents and Purposes, as if they had been abiding and born, within this our Realm of England." [5]

The Virginia Charter thus established the precedent that the American colonists were entitled to all the "rights of Englishmen." Had that principle not been so established, the history of British North America might have been far different. Patrick Henry's 1765 resolves relied directly upon the 1606 charter provision, resolving that by it "the colonists aforesaid are declared entitled to all liberties, privileges, and immunities . . . as if they had been abiding and born within the realm of England." [6]

The Virginia Charter was only the first of a series of colonial organic documents that guaranteed the colonists all the rights of Englishmen. The same guaranty would appear in the Charter of New England, 1620; the Charter of Massachusetts Bay, 1629; the Charter of Maryland, 1632; the Charter of Connecticut, 1662; the Charter of Rhode Island, 1663; the Charter of Carolina, 1663; and the Charter of Georgia, 1732. [7] But much more sophisticated protections would have to be evolved before American constitutional history would bring forth a Federal Bill of Rights. The 1606 charter, for instance, contained only the bare declaration that the colonists possessed all the rights of Englishmen. It made no attempt to define what the rights of Englishmen were, even in rudimentary form. Admittedly, at the beginning of the seventeenth century, such a definition would have been premature. It would take the constitutional struggles of the seventeenth and eighteenth centuries on both sides of the Atlantic before specific content could be given to the notion of fundamental rights, of which the Federal Bill of Rights itself would eventually become the classic inventory.

A second essential step was the establishment of representative government on the western side of the Atlantic. Self-government was not secured under the first Virginia Charter. The government provided by the 1606 instrument was under a Royal Council of Virginia, whose thirteen members were appointed by the Crown and sat in London. In Virginia there was to be a Colonial Council appointed by the Royal Council and under the direction of that body. It soon became clear, nevertheless, that government wholly under the control of London was not proving itself effective. In 1618 Ordinances for Virginia were issued by the Crown, which provided for direct participation by the colonists in their government through a representative legislative assembly. The House of Burgesses, first elected in 1619, was the first American legislature and the progenitor of similar assemblies in all the colonies.[8]

As other colonies came to be settled, representative assemblies were set up elsewhere as well, either, as in the case of Virginia, through decrees from London or through the voluntary action of the colonists themselves. The first example of the latter was the Fundamental Orders of Connecticut, 1639,[9] which James Bryce characterized as "The oldest truly political Constitution in America." [10] The Fundamental Orders was framed by the inhabitants of the Massachusetts Bay Colony who left in 1635 and founded settlements at Hartford, Windsor, and Wethersfield along the Connecticut River. Those settlers, led by Reverend Thomas Hooker, had no royal charter and, thus unencumbered, provided for their own self-government from the beginning, setting up a General Court,[11] modeled upon that of Massachusetts, which first met in 1637. The Fundamental Orders was drawn up as an instrument to set forth and define the organs of government and their powers. Based upon the Puritan principle of a covenant between the settlers, it dealt with both religious and civil affairs. But unlike the earlier Massachusetts covenant concept, it was far more specific with regard to the government formed.[12] The Fundamental Orders bears a closer resemblance, in fact, to later constitutions than to earlier models like the Mayflower Compact.

Although the Connecticut enactment did not contain any guarantees of individual liberties, its adoption was an important step in American constitutional development. The Fundamental Orders was the first constitutional document in the colonies. To be sure, compared with later constitutions it was still an elementary document, not providing for any enforcement machinery, for example. Yet in its application of the principles developed in covenants, charters, and practice to the conscious organization of a new government, it was ground-breaking.

Nevertheless, the early colonial documents—both those evolving from royal charters and those evolving spontaneously in the colonies—hardly possessed anything like the legal status subsequently attained by later American constitutions. The colonial charters received from London, like all royal charters, were accorded as a matter of privilege. They could be amended or revoked at will and were legally similar to medieval grants, subject to the will of the grantor, even when they began to regulate the lives and property of ever-increasing thousands of Americans. There was no answer in British law to Lord Mansfield's assertion that the American governments set up by charter were "all on the same footing as our great corporations in London." [13] The same was true of the fundamental laws drawn up by the colonists themselves. These, too, were legally subject to the overriding authority of the British government.

The letter of the law did not, however, control the manner in which colonial charters or fundamental laws were viewed by the bulk of Americans. "Who, then," asked John Adams in 1818, "was the author, inventor, discoverer of independence? The only true answer must be the first emigrants, and the proof of it is the charter of James I." Strict legal rule might make of the charters mere matters of royal grace. But the colonists looked upon them as much more. The first charter, that of James I to Virginia, said Adams, "is more like a treaty between independent sovereigns than like a charter or grant of privileges from a sovereign to his subjects." [14]

Americans came to regard their charters as defensive bulwarks against the misuse of power [15] by those with governing privileges, and were quick to oppose all infringements upon their charter rights. The Massachusetts Charter, said Cotton Mather, was a "Hedge, whereby our Titles to our properties, and possessions, once questioned, are at once Confirmed." [16] As early as 1664, the men of Massachusetts resisted an attempt to replace their charter with commissioners sent from London to "regulate" New England. The colonists, we are told, put their charter in safe hands, manned the harbor fort, and petitioned the king to let their "laws and liberties live." When, in 1681, Massachusetts Charter rights were again attacked, the colonists asserted that it was their undoubted duty "to abide by what rights and privileges the Lord our God in his merciful providence hath bestowed upon us." [17]

In 1684, the Massachusetts Charter was actually withdrawn and the Dominion of New England governed in accordance with Sir Edmund Andros's notions of Stuart prerogative. But the continued resistance of the colonists led in 1691 to the granting of a new charter. In the other colonies, the situation was similar. The charters were regarded as the fundamental basis of the rights and liberties colonists enjoyed, and when colonial charters were restricted or modified, the loss to the colonists was as deeply mourned as the loss of Magna Carta would have been by Englishmen.

Attachment to the colonial charters continued until the end of the colonial period. As late as 1771, Thomas Young of Boston referred in a speech to "the Threats of the British Ministry to take away the Massachusetts Charter." [18] And in 1774, when the Massachusetts royal judges were impeached by that colony's House of Representatives, they were charged with "high crimes and misdemeanors, and . . . a conspiracy against the charter liberties of the people." [19]

As significant as the purposes to which the colonists put their charters was the training in self-government afforded by such usage. "Englishmen hate an arbitrary power," wrote John Wise of Massachusetts in 1710, ". . . as they hate the devil." [20] The political history of the colonies shows that the hatred did not diminish with the migration to North America.

From the beginning, colonial legislatures looked upon themselves as direct descendants of the House of Commons, vested with the privileges and powers won by that body in its struggles against the Crown. This was apparent from the first sitting of the first colonial assembly, the Virginia House of Burgesses. When the Speaker took exception to the qualifications of two members, the House, in imitation of the English Commons, proceeded to exercise the sole right to judge the qualifications of its own members.[21] In this way and others, then, the constitutional history of the colonies in the century before the Revolution repeated that of seventeenth-century England. That very claim for which one Stuart king lost his life and another his throne was again put forward in lesser form by the royal governors. A period of constant conflict between the popular assemblies and the governors ensued. Although the royal governors were, in the main, hardly the "men of vicious characters" portrayed by Benjamin Franklin,[22] they were direct agents of the Crown, with commissions and instructions that made them autocrats not beholden to those whom they governed. In England, the prerogative had been bridled by the revolutions overthrowing the Stuarts. In the colonies, the royal prerogative continued, in theory, without diminution. Royal governors were expected to be agents of Whitehall's will. It was inevitable that such agents would be in conflict with the provincial assemblies.

From a constitutional point of view, the colonists remained more Englishmen of the seventeenth century than of the eighteenth century. In England, the seventeenth century was the great age of struggle against government by royal prerogative. That struggle ended with the expulsion of the Stuart kings. Thenceforth, the English Executive was to be subordinate to the representatives of the people. In America, the basic contention between the legislative and executive branches continued, for the blessings 1688 had brought in the mother country (so signally commemorated in Locke's writings) were not extended across the Atlantic. If anything, the establishment of Parliamentary supremacy, with the accession of William and Mary, was to make a sharpening of the constitutional conflict in the colonies inevitable.

Viewed in this manner, it is not hyperbole to characterize the constitutional history of the colonies as a chapter torn from the constitutional history of Stuart England. The earlier battles between Crown and Parliament were again to be fought out, on a smaller scale and at a later time, on the western side of the Atlantic. In America—as it had been in England—the theme would be that of the gradual triumph of the popular assembly. Many of Parliament's hard-won privileges—control over its own procedures, freedom of debate, determination of election disputes, and the qualifications of its members—were fought for and secured by colonial legislatures in the succeeding century. Even more important was the successful assertion by the assemblies of the power that was the very keystone of the Parliamentary arch: the power of the purse. That power, coupled as it was with the failure of the British government to provide a permanent list of those civil servants paid by the British government in each of the colonies [23] (in most colonies, the salary of the governor himself had become dependent upon appropriations by the local legislature), led to the supremacy of the assemblies in most colonial governments by the end of the French and Indian War.

Had the mother country continued to treat the colonies with "a wise and salutary neglect," it is possible that colonial institutions would have taken their own way to the "perfection" of which Burke speaks [24]—thereby anticipating by a century the modern development of the British Commonwealth. Such a peaceful development within the British Empire was made impossible by the assertion of an entirely new theory of imperial power after the successful expulsion of the French from North America. There is constitutional truth in Francis Parkman's well-known statement, "With the fall of Quebec began the history of the United States." [25]

FIRST GUARANTEES OF RIGHTS

Once England recognized representative government in Virginia, subsequent colonial charters contained provisions from the start for self-government through elected legislatures. Thus, the Charter of Massachusetts Bay, 1629,[26] although it took some years before the colonists established fully their right to participate in the Massachusetts legislative process, and the Charter of Maryland, 1632,[27] both granted the right of popular assemblies to the colonists. Those two charters therewith created the second and third self-governing assemblies in America and set a pattern that would prevail until the Revolution—with the brief interruption of the attempt at Stuart autocracy from 1684–88.

Acting through their elected legislatures, the first step taken by the settlers was to give those rights granted them as Englishmen specific content within the colonial context. They did this by the enactment of statutes that more specifically defined the basic rights of the colonists. The most famous of these statutes was the Massachusetts Body of Liberties, 1641. Even before that law was enacted, however, the Maryland General Assembly approved the 1639 Act for the Liberties of the People. Elementary though it was, that document may be considered the first American bill of rights.

The 1639 Maryland Act was another product of the ongoing struggle for greater and greater popular government that characterized political life in all the colonies. The 1632 charter had made Lord Baltimore, the Proprietor of Maryland, a virtual constitutional monarch, with broad authority to govern and dispose of the land.[28] Baltimore intended that the primary role in initiating legislation remain with him, with the popular assembly limited to approving laws he proposed. Assemblies, as Baltimore put it in instructions to his son, Charles, were to be called "for the giving of the advice, assent and approbation by the freemen to such acts as shall be by us at any time ordayned made and enacted." [29] The very first assembly rejected this restricted role and drew up laws of its own to govern the colony. By 1639, Baltimore had acceded to the desires of the colonists. [30] The assembly was thus able to vote the 1639 Act for the Liberties of the People on its own initiative.

Magna Carta was the direct source of the 1639 Maryland statute, [31] which starts by reaffirming the principle that the inhabitants of the colony are entitled to all the rights Englishmen enjoy by virtue of English law. It makes the important point that English common law is part of the legal heritage so carried over. It then goes on to state what is essentially a paraphrase of the most important provision of Magna Carta, providing that no colonist be adversely affected in his person or property except "according to the Laws of this province." This phrase provides an American link between the original language of Magna Carta and the due process clause of the American Federal Constitution.

We should not underestimate the significance of the 1639 Act, particularly in a proprietary colony such as Maryland. Today it may seem to be only a truistic restatement of Chapter 39 of Magna Carta. Yet, at the time of its writing, Charles I was pushing Stuart absolutism to its breaking point, and such a restatement was an act of consequence. Furthermore, a later attempt by the Maryland Assembly to adopt Magna Carta outright, although made *after* the Revolution of 1688, was disallowed by the Crown, on the ground that the liberties of the Great Charter might be inconsistent with the king's use of prerogative. [32]

If the Maryland Act for the Liberties of the People was but a rudimentary reaffirmation of the basic principle of the first Virginia Charter and Chapter 39 of Magna Carta, the same was not true of the second colonial enactment safeguarding individual rights: the 1641 Massachusetts Body of Liberties. This enactment was the first detailed American charter of liberties and, considering its early date, was amazingly detailed in its provisions. It served as the model for future colonial enactments, notably the New York Charter of Liberties, 1683, and the Pennsylvania Charter of Privileges, 1701.[33] Of the documents discussed thus far, there is no doubt that the 1641 Massachusetts Act was the most important forerunner of the Federal Bill of Rights.

Too many Americans today tend to adopt a denigrating attitude toward their Puritan forebears. We forget how much our development was assured by the fact that New England was first settled by a people who, however stiff-necked in their moral attitude, could call on the resources of religious fervor to plant the seeds of colonization in a forbidding environment. It is all too easy to look through twentieth-century spectacles at the harshness of rule and narrow-mindedness of the men who settled Massachusetts. But these people produced a polity in the bleak New England of the seventeenth century that may have been one of the few capable of enduring.

The Mayflower Compact of 1620 itself indicates the intent of the first New England colonists to establish a government that was to be, in their own words, "a civil Body Politick," with "such just and equal Laws, Ordinances, Acts, Constitutions, and Officers, from time to time, as shall be thought most meet and convenient for the general Good of the Colony." [34] In 1629, the Charter of Massachusetts Bay provided for the settlement of the colony by a Company similar to that which had received the Virginia Charter. The patentees were joint proprietors, who were given combined rights of both ownership and government. The Massachusetts Charter repeated the Virginia guaranty of the rights of Englishmen for the colonists and provided for the second self-governing assembly in the colonies.

Most important in the development of government in the colony was the so-called Cambridge Agreement, concluded by the patentees soon after the grant of the charter. By that document, they agreed to transfer control of the government to those who were to emigrate to the colony; local government was thus transferred at the outset "to remain with us and others which shall inhabit upon the said plantation." [35]

In the summer of 1630, a large group of emigrants was transported to Massachusetts Bay, including John Winthrop as governor. Winthrop and the other leaders resisted popular government and a struggle ensued that led to the institution of a system of representative government. The result was stated by Winthrop in a 1634 letter to Sir Nathaniel Rich: "Our Civill Government is mixt: The freemen choose the magistrates everye year . . . and at four Courts in the yeare three out of each towne (there being eight in all) doe assist the magistrates in making of lawes, imposing taxes, and disposing of lands: our Juries are chosen by the freemen of everye towne." [36] As Winthrop stated in his *Journal* in 1646, the colonists possessed "power to make laws, to erect all sorts of magistracy, to correct, punish, pardon, govern and rule." [37]

Enactment of the Body of Liberties was another of the results of the movement to replace the oligarchy established by the Company with a representative system of government. The people, noted Winthrop, "had long desired a body of laws, and thought their condition very unsafe while so much power rested in the discretion of magistrates." [38] This was to be the most common complaint of New World settlers when their legal system was first being formed. The desire for a fixed body of law reduced to writing was very strong, the colonists firm in their desire that the rights of the people not be at the whim of magisterial discretion.

What the Massachusetts colonists called for was a code of law that would guarantee "such liberties Immunities and priveledges as humanitie, Civilitie, and Chrisianitie call for as due to every man in his place and proportion." [39] To give effect to the colonists' desire, a committee consisting of Winthrop and three others was appointed in 1635 to frame "a body of . . . fundamental laws." [40] The committee did not produce the required code, and a year later another committee was appointed "to make a draught of laws . . . which may be the Fundamentals of this Commonwealth." [41] A member of this committee prepared a draft code that Winthrop termed "a model of Moses his judicials." [42] This draft was never voted on, but it led directly to the drafting by Rev. Nathaniel Ward, who had originally been a barrister, of the code that was approved by the General Court in 1641, after it had been fully debated both in the legislature and at the different town meetings of the colony.

The boldness of the Massachusetts men in their pioneering efforts to provide codified statutory protection for individual rights and liberties is striking indeed. "The Body of Liberties marked a notable step not only in the direction of reducing the colony laws to writing, but, more importantly, toward the development of a commonwealth of laws and not of men." [43] That the Massachusetts colonists recognized the fundamental nature of what they were doing is shown by the fact Winthrop noted that they were acting "to frame a body of grounds of laws, in resemblance to a Magna Carta." [44] The document they produced was a blend of Magna Carta itself, the common law, and the principles of Puritan theology—all molded by the experiences and circumstances of the colonists themselves.

Considering the date of its enactment, both the scope and specific provisions of the Body of Liberties are startling. To provide in so early a code for the liberties of women, children, servants, aliens, and dumb animals, as well as those of free men, and to outlaw slavery as well was historically unheard of. In addition, to recognize that individual liberty depended, in the last resort, upon the courts, and to provide in detail for the rights of litigants and accused in judicial proceedings was as perceptive as it was unprecedented at that time. [45]

Many of the fundamental liberties later to be protected in bills of rights were either safeguarded or anticipated in the 1641 Massachusetts statute. These include guarantees covering taking of property without just compensation, freedom of speech and petition at public meetings, right of counsel, trial by jury, double jeopardy, and cruel and inhuman punishments. The Body of Liberties also contained provisions protecting life, liberty, and property in language derived from section 39 of Magna Carta; guaranteeing that every person "shall enjoy the same justice and law" (anticipating by over two centuries the Equal Protection Clause of the Fourteenth Amendment); forbidding monopolies; outlawing imprisonment for debt; prohibiting torture; requiring at least two witnesses for the death penalty; and providing for a right of free access to public records (anticipating the Freedom of Information Act of 1966).

Most important, the Massachusetts Body of Liberties was the first American attempt to give effect to the basic notion that fundamental rights should be contained in a written instrument enacted by the people's representatives—and that at a time when England had only Magna Carta itself and the Petition of Right as legislative foundations of freedom. The 1641 Body of Liberties constituted a quantum leap forward, though it came only two years after the 1639 Maryland Act.

FREEDOM OF RELIGION

Living in a secular century, we tend to minimize the importance of the freedom of religion guaranteed in the very first clause of the Federal Bill of Rights. The framers of the American polity could make no such mistake, for the colonies themselves were, in large part, a product of the religious intolerance of seventeenth-century England. The great constitutional struggles in Stuart days were both political and religious. It was religious strife that aggravated the political controversies of the time and made their resolution possible only by the sword. In the end, during the reign of the last Stuart king, the royal attempt to subvert the Constitution was made chiefly for religious ends.

Although many of the colonists fled to the New World to escape the religious discrimination of the mother country, too few practiced toleration in the new setting. Instead, when some of the very groups most strongly persecuted by the established Church of England found themselves in control of colonial governments, they immediately turned into oppressors. We need submit as evidence only the zeal of the Puritans of New England to enforce adherence to *their* beliefs and to keep their Commonwealth free of anything that smacked of heresy to make our case.

Not all the colonies, however, were dominated by the intolerance of the mother country. Some were specifically founded as refuges of toleration. Notable among these were Maryland and Rhode Island. The first Lord Baltimore may have intended Maryland to serve as a haven for his Catholic coreligionists. Yet he was wise enough to calculate that he could not provide enough settlers unless he attracted immigrants of other religions. As a Catholic proprietor in a Protestant Empire, he knew that he should proceed carefully. The result was a policy of religious toleration that appealed to many of the early settlers. The importance of this policy is shown by a 1678 letter of the third Lord Baltimore, which concedes that, without it, "in all probability this province had never been planted." [46]

The right of toleration was expressly provided for in the 1649 Maryland Act Concerning Religion. This pioneer statute, usually known as the Toleration Act, gives Maryland the distinction of being the first American colony to recognize a measure of freedom of conscience. The Act provided that all professed Christians—Catholics and Protestants alike—should have freedom of conscience and worship, containing in this respect a guaranty similar in terms to the Free Exercise Clause of the First Amendment itself: "noe person . . . professing to believe in Jesus Christ, shall from henceforth bee any waies troubled, Molested or discountenanced for or in respect of his or her religion nor in the free exercise thereof." [47] Although the Toleration Act was limited in its protection to Christians, there is no evidence of persecution of Jews, agnostics, or others in the colony. What the 1649 Act meant in practice is further revealed by events during the Interregnum, when the Puritans obtained control of the colony.

In 1654, the Act of Toleration was repealed and both Catholics and Anglicans were deprived of religious freedom. In 1658, the Lord Proprietor regained his authority and the Act of Toleration was revived. Ultimately, in 1692, Maryland became a royal province, and the Church of England was officially established in 1702.[48] Even so, the religious toleration that had gained a foothold under the Baltimores was continued, ultimately to become one of the cornerstones of the American system.

The American origins of the right to religious liberty are primarily linked to Roger Williams and Rhode Island. It was the 1663 Charter of Rhode Island that first provided for religious liberty in the organic law of a colony. Important though the Maryland Act of Toleration had been, it was only an ordinary statute of the legislature, which could be repealed at will by the colonists themselves. The Rhode Island guaranty was contained in the colony's charter, which was, in the terms used by the Massachusetts General Court in 1661, "the first and maine foundation of our civil politye." [49] That the Rhode Island Charter did in fact have virtually the status of a constitution is shown by the fact that it was kept in force after the Revolution, when other states had drawn up their own constitutions—remaining as the fundamental law of Rhode Island until it was finally replaced by a constitution in 1842 (and it took a mini-revolution, the so-called Dorr Rebellion, to accomplish that).

That Rhode Island was founded upon the doctrine of religious liberty was owing, in large measure, to the character of its founder, Roger Williams. When Williams arrived in Massachusetts in 1631, he proved a sore trial to his Puritan brethren because of his unorthodox ideas. To cleanse the colony of heresy, the Saints banished him at the end of 1635 and he fled to the sanctuary of the Rhode Island Indians, and there founded the settlement of Providence. From the beginning, toleration was the cornerstone of the new colony in accordance with Williams' own tenet that "no person . . . shall be molested or questioned for the matters ·of his conscience." [50] At the very outset, in 1636, the Rhode Island settlers agreed that the authority of government would extend "only in civil things." [51] The plantation agreement of 1640 expressly declared: "Wee agree, as formerly hath bin the liberties of the town, so still, to hould forth liberty of Conscience." [52] Thus, freedom of religion was the basis of the colony even before it was expressly stated in its fundamental law. Even Quakers and Jews were permitted to believe and worship as they chose.

Upon the accession of Charles II, it became necessary for Rhode Island to secure a royal charter to replace the Parliamentary patent obtained during the Interregnum. The charter secured in 1663 guaranteed religious liberty in language broad enough to satisfy even a Roger Williams. It declared that "noe person within the sayd colonye, at any time hereafter, shall bee any wise molested, punished, disquieted, or called in question, for any differences in opinione in matters of religion" so long as he did "not actually disturb the civil peace of our sayd colony." Further, the right thus guaranteed was to prevail, "any laws, statute or clause . . . usage or custome of this realme, to the contrary hereof, in any wise, notwithstanding." [53]

The Rhode Island Charter was the first to contain a grant of religious freedom in the all-inclusive terms that are familiar in American constitutions. For the first time, the present-day observer may find in a historical document an expression of his own belief in the limits to be placed on the governmental power to interfere with individual conscience.

Another early milestone in the history of religious freedom is the document known as the Fundamental Constitutions of Carolina of 1669. [54] In this document, drafted by John Locke, we have the rare example of the platonic ideal in operation with a frame of government actually drawn up by one of the greatest names in political philosophy. Unfortunately, Plato become Solon produced a fundamental law (however attractive it may be to the speculative theorist) that proved itself wholly unworkable as a practical charter of government. It is, indeed, amazing that a mind as acute as Locke's should have produced so clumsy a document, with its reliance upon outmoded feudal conceptions and Graustarkian layers of nobility, with its palatines, signiories, baronies, manors, court-leets, landgraves, and caziques.[55] Certainly, the elaborate structure was completely out of place in a colony like Carolina, a sandy spot ill-fitted as a feudal kingdom in miniature, with moldy institutions that had become anachronisms in the Old World. Locke's plan was never put into full operation and remains of note solely because of the man who drafted it.

The Locke effort to transfer feudal institutions from England, where they may still have had some meaning, to America, where they had none, is, however, less important than the fact that the Carolina Constitutions contains several important provisions protecting individual rights. Best known of these is the provision in Article 109 that "No person whatsoever shall disturb, molest or persecute another for his speculative opinions in religion, or his way of worship." This is an early version of the right to freedom of conscience similar to that found in the Rhode Island Charter. To have freedom of religion stated as a basic right by the political theorist who, more than any other, influenced American constitution-makers was of great significance to the fuller development of that right. Reliance on Locke's ideas during the crisis of 1765 and afterward, in fact, would make him the theoretical godfather of the American Revolution.

LATER COLONIAL GUARANTEES

The colonial antecedents of the Federal Bill of Rights were essentially of three types: 1) guarantees contained in charters granted by the Crown; 2) guarantees contained in instruments issued by colonial proprietors; and 3) guarantees contained in enactments of the colonists themselves. The best known example of the third type was the Massachusetts Body of Liberties. A comparable document was the Charter of Liberties passed by the New York General Assembly in 1683, which guaranteed substantial personal rights to the inhabitants of that colony.

The New York Charter was a direct result of the successful struggle for self-government that had agitated the colony from the beginning of English rule. New York had become the Duke of York's own colony and the future James II was scarcely the ruler to look favorably upon popular government. General assemblies, the heir to the throne wrote to Governor Andros in 1676, "would be of dangerous consequence, nothing being more knowne than the aptness of such bodyes to assume to themselves many priviledges which prove destructive to . . . the peace of ye governmt." [56] Still, even the Duke could not fail to see and so informed the New York governor, that "ye people there seems desirous of [general assemblies] in imitacon of their neighbor Colonies." [57]

Ultimately, the Duke of York gave in to the popular desire for a representative assembly for the same reason other English rulers—notably his father, Charles I—had at earlier times summoned Parliaments, namely, to obtain funds. New York was permitted to elect a general assembly in 1683 on the condition that it vote the funds needed to govern the colony.[58] As had happened so frequently in English history, a legislature called to supply funds used the occasion to redress grievances. The very first law passed by the first General Assembly of New York was the "Charter of Libertyes and Priviledges."

The 1683 charter [59] stated that it was enacted for "The better Establishing the Government of this province of New Yorke and that Justice and Right may be Equally done to all persons within the same"—a very early statement of the notion of equality before the law. Among the substantive provisions were paraphrases of section 39 of Magna Carta, providing that no freeman be deprived of "his ffreehold of Libertye or ffree Customes . . . But by the Lawfull Judgment of his peers and by the Law of this province." and that no one be injured in his person or property "without being brought to Answere by due Course of Law." The latter phrase is another version in the transition between the original language of Magna Carta and the Due Process Clause.

Among other important rights guaranteed by the New York Charter were the right to trial by jury (except in contempt cases), the right to a grand jury (perhaps the earliest version of the right included in the Fifth Amendment), and an absolute right to bail except in treason and felony cases (bearing in mind that felony cases were capital cases at the time). In addition, the Third Amendment was anticipated in a prohibition against the quartering of soldiers and sailors in private homes in peace time, and there was an express prohibition against "proceeding by Marshall Law against any of his Majestyes Subjects" except those in the military—a principle that the United States Supreme Court has had to read into the Federal Constitution in a series of cases from *Ex parte Milligan* [60] to our own day.

The Duke of York was, of course, not the man to acquiesce in a document like the Charter of Liberties; he vetoed that instrument in 1684. Two years later, having become James II, he issued a new commission empowering the governor and council to make laws and directing the Governor "to Declare Our Will and pleasure that ye said Bill or charter of Franchises bee forthwith repealed and disallowed." [61] The New York colonists, however, continued undaunted in their devotion to the 1683 charter. When, after the expulsion of James II they again received the right of self-government, one of the first things the new general assembly, meeting in April, 1691, did was to enact "An Act declareing what are the Rights and Priviledges of their Majesties Subjects inhabiting within their Province of New York." [62] That law repeated the rights guaranteed in the 1683 charter; the one significant change was the inclusion in the 1691 act of a guarantee of liberty of conscience for Christians except for "persons of the Roman religion."

Even more important during the later colonial period was the detailed provision for individual rights contained in organic documents issued by the colonial proprietors in New Jersey and Pennsylvania. New Jersey was set up as a proprietary colony in 1664. To attract settlers, the proprietors (Lord John Berkeley and Sir George Carteret) issued the Concession and Agreement of February, 1664, which provided for freedom of religion in terms similar to those in the Rhode Island Charter, and self-government through an elected legislature. In 1674 Berkeley sold his interest to Edward Byllynge and other Quakers. New Jersey was then divided between Carteret and the Quakers, with the latter occupying the unoccupied western half.

In 1677, the Quaker proprietors issued what Bernard Bailyn has termed a remarkably enlightened document: "The Concessions and Agreements of the Proprietors, Freeholders, and Inhabitants of the Province of West New Jersey." [63] Chapters XIII–XXIII of this document was described in a subtitle as "The Charter or Fundamental Laws of West New Jersey, Agreed Upon."

The basic goal of the concessions was stated by the proprietors in a 1676 letter: "There we lay a foundation for after ages to understand their liberty as men and christians, that they may not be brought in bondage, but by their own consent; for we put the power in the people." [64] They meant Chapters XIII–XXIII to serve as "the common law or fundamental rights and privileges . . . agreed upon . . . to be the foundation of the government." More than that, this fundamental law "is not to be altered by the Legislative authority" and the legislature is "to make such laws as agree with, and maintain the said fundamentals, and to make no laws that in the least contradict, differ or vary from the said fundamentals, under what pretence or allegation soever." [65] Here, for the first time, an express supremacy clause, comparable to that in the Levellers' third draft Agreement of the People,[66] is included in an organic document. With it, we are very close to the notion of a binding written constitution and the doctrine of unconstitutional legislation.

Among the rights guaranteed by the 1677 concessions were religious liberty (in terms even broader than those in the Rhode Island Charter from which it was derived), trial by jury, fair public trials, and freedom from imprisonment for debt. In addition, provision was made for wide dissemination of the concessions, with the order that they "be writ in fair tables, in every common hall of justice within this Province" and be read four times a year to the people. These concessions extended the liberties belonging by right beyond the limits recognized in the England of the day. And they did what English law had not done by providing for the protection of rights through their specification in a written law, binding as "The Charter or Fundamental Laws of West New Jersey." [67]

The colonial experience culminated in the two most influential documents protecting individual rights: the Pennsylvania Frame of Government of 1682 and Charter of Privileges of 1701. Those two basic documents were intimately connected with the personality of William Penn and the persecutions he and his fellow Quakers had suffered in Stuart England. Penn received his charter for Pennsylvania in 1681 and sought to erect there a government in line with his political and religious conceptions. As proprietor, Penn could draw up the fundamental law for what he termed a "holy experiment." [68] In drafting the Frame of Government of 1682, he sought to give effect to the principle that "Any government is free to the people under it . . . where the laws rule." [69]

The Frame of Government was a step closer to the modern constitution than the earlier documents discussed. It was based on a line of distinction between the powers of government and the rights of the individual upon which present-day constitutions turn. The first part of the Penn document—the Frame of Government—was essentially a charter of government setting up the machinery of government and the powers vested in the different officials and institutions (providing in this respect for the first time the fully representative type of government that has come to characterize the American polity). The second part, titled the "Laws Agreed upon in England," was what we should term a bill of rights, containing provisions protecting the essential rights of Pennsylvanians. Equally important was the fact that the frame included another essential element of the modern constitution, an amending clause, the first in any written constitution.

The Frame of Government [70] starts by setting forth Penn's

theory of government. Most interesting is the statement at such an early date of the concept of the rule of law: "Any government is free to the people under it (whatever be the frame) where the laws rule and the people are a party to those laws." The purpose of the frame is to secure the people from the abuse of power and to keep the proper balance between liberty and obedience—itself a good summary of the purpose of any constitution.

The frame declares that it is a "charter of liberties." That it deserves such a characterization is clear when we consider the second part, the "Laws Agreed upon in England," which, like the modern Bill of Rights, is based upon the concept of a government limited in its powers by the rights possessed by the governed. Here Penn was influenced directly by his own experience as a persecuted Quaker. Thus, the frame provided expressly for religious freedom; any person professing a belief in "one Almighty and eternal God" was guaranteed freedom of belief and worship. Though somewhat more restrictive than the already discussed Rhode Island and West New Jersey provisions in the matter, the Penn guaranty also marked a significant break with the authoritarian tradition that still prevailed in England and most of Europe.

The most important guarantees of the Penn document, at least in their influence on later bills of rights, have to do with judicial procedure. They reflect the burdens under which the Quakers themselves had suffered so often in English courts, including Penn himself in his famous prosecution in 1670 for preaching a prohibited sermon to a Quaker meeting. Out of that prosecution had come the Court of Common Pleas decision in *Bushell's Case* [71]—one of the landmarks of Anglo-American liberty, since it settled the jury's right to decide criminal cases according to its own conscience, regardless of contrary direction by the court. His own experience led Penn to provide for public trials and to extend the right of trial by jury to all trials, with the jury to "have the final judgment."

In addition, other basic rights in judicial proceedings were guaranteed. At a time when an accused in English courts did not have the right to testify, all persons were given the right to appear and personally plead their own cause or to plead through their friends—an implied right of counsel. The right of bail was guaranteed in terms that anticipate the language of most present-day state constitutions (the language of the Eighth Amendment is somewhat different). Court proceedings and records were to be "in English and in an ordinary and plain character"; court fees were to be moderate and fixed by a public schedule; fines were also to be moderate and could not reach the defendant's means of livelihood; prisons were to "be free, as to fees, food and lodging."

Most of the rights guaranteed by Penn's frame have become foundations of the American system. In his political philosophy Penn was a Quaker-Whig, although the frame itself may have been influenced—if not written in part—by Penn's republican friend, Algernon Sydney.[72] Yet, whether or not it was solely Penn's Quaker ideology that influenced the philosophy of the frame, the document—written several years before the English Bill of Rights, at a time when the monarchy in England appeared more absolute than it had since before the Long Parliament—owes much to the man. That Penn, vested with all the legal rights of proprietor, could voluntarily limit his own powers by a document so forward-looking, speaks well both of Penn and his political philosophy. Penn no doubt knew that without liberal provisions for individual rights, his colony would find it hard to attract settlers. As he put it in a 1700 letter, "What is the right of the English subject at home should be allowed here, since more and not less seems the Reasons . . . to plant this wilderness." [73]

But at no time did Penn intend the Frame of Government to have anything like the inexorable effect of the fabled laws of the Medes and Persians. On the contrary, he recognized that no constitution could survive for long without changes, and, as already noted, the frame provided expressly for an amending process. "Friends," said Penn in an oft-quoted statement, "if in the Constitution by charter there be anything that jars, alter it." [74]

When Penn himself returned to his colony in 1699, he

found an increasing desire for political changes. Penn settled much of the controversy and, after several months of discussion, the Frame of Government of 1682 was repealed by the necessary six-sevenths vote and the Charter of Privileges of 1701 promulgated in its place. It dealt with the principal cause of popular discontent by providing for a unicameral legislature, and excluding the council (which beginning in 1700 was appointed by the proprietor) from direct participation in legislation.

As had been the case in 1682, one of Penn's principal concerns was to protect the liberties of the colonists, and it is as a fundamental law safeguarding individual rights that the Charter of Privileges [75] is of significance. This time freedom of religion stands first in the rights protected—a position it was to retain in the First Amendment—"Because no People can be truly happy, though under the greatest Enjoyment of Civil Liberties, if abridged of the Freedom of their Consciences." The right to religious freedom is stated in the broadest terms in Article I for all who "acknowledge *One* almighty God"; they are to have freedom of belief and worship and are not to be compelled to attend any established services. In addition, all professed Christians are eligible to hold any office—a significant step forward for the time even though it excluded Jews, Deists, and atheists from office. So fundamental was freedom of religion in the Penn scheme that, although provision was again made for amending the charter, it was expressly provided that attempts to amend Article I would be invalid.

Of the individual rights guaranteed by the Charter of Privileges, three deserve particular notice. Under Article IV, no person was to answer regarding property "but in ordinary Course of Justice," another version of Magna Carta's section 39, which moves us another step closer to the Due Process Clause. Article VIII mitigates the harsh rule of English law by prohibiting forfeiture to the government in cases of suicide. Most forward-looking was the provision in Article V that "all criminals shall have the same Privileges of Witnesses and Council as their Prosecutors." The right to call witnesses was not possessed by all defendants in England until a year after the Pennsylvania Charter was issued.[76] An even greater advance was the express provision for the right of counsel. English law did not fully guarantee that right until the nineteenth century; [77] nor did any other colony in such absolute terms before the Revolution itself. The Pennsylvania Charter was the first to anticipate the Sixth Amendment provision in the matter, and it did so almost a century before the Federal Bill of Rights itself was adopted.

According to Bernard Bailyn, it was the Charter of Privileges "that secured the remarkable rights and privileges of Pennsylvania." [78] It was the last great colonial instrument to lay the foundation for the Revolutionary and post-Revolutionary constitutional protection of individual rights. The 1701 charter continued in force until it was replaced by the Pennsylvania Constitution of 1776. The Liberty Bell, which was to ring out the news of American Independence, was originally cast for the celebration of the fiftieth anniversary of the Charter of Privileges.

COLONIAL PATTERN

Writing in 1764, Thomas Hutchinson, then Lieutenant Governor of Massachusetts, stated that the colonists had "thought themselves at full liberty . . . to establish such sort of government as they thought proper, and to form a new state as full to all intents and purposes as if they had been in a state of nature, and were making their first entrance into civil society." [79]

Hutchinson's comment overstates the case. But there is no doubt that by the end of the colonial period the colonists had gone far toward developing the constitutional polity that is the great American contribution to political science. During the colonial period, the concept of fundamental law to define and limit government and its powers was given its first refinements. That concept had flowed naturally from the establishment of the first colonies under charters granted by the Crown. The next step—colonial creation of their own fundamental laws—was first taken in the Fundamental Orders of Connecticut, 1639. In the Massachusetts Body of Liberties, 1641, protection for individual rights was made a part of the statute book. By the time we get to the Pennsylvania Frame of Government, 1682, we have moved far in the direction of the modern Constitution and Bill of Rights.

The colonial charters and enactments were far more explicit than the comparable documents in English history in their provision of protection for specific individual rights. By the end of the colonial period, many of the rights later guaranteed in the Federal Bill of Rights were already expressly safeguarded in charters and enactments. These include, following the order of the Federal Bill of Rights: freedom of religion (though only insofar as the right to free exercise was concerned—first guaranteed in broad terms in the Rhode Island Charter); freedom of speech and petition at public meetings (guaranteed in the Massachusetts Body of Liberties); the right not to have soldiers quartered in private homes (secured in the New York Charter of Liberties); the right to a grand jury indictment (also first guaranteed in the New York enactment); the right against double jeopardy (first secured in the Massachusetts Body of Liberties); the right to due process (contained, in varying language derived from Magna Carta, in most of the colonial fundamental documents starting with the Maryland Act for the Liberties of the People); the right not to have private property taken without just compensation (guaranteed in the Massachusetts Body of Liberties); the right to a public trial (contained in the West New Jersey Concessions); the right to witnesses and counsel (guaranteed in modern terms in the Pennsylvania Charter of Privileges); the right to trial by jury (guaranteed in virtually all the colonial instruments after the Massachusetts Body of Liberties); the right to bail (first secured in the Massachusetts Body of Liberties); and the right against cruel and unusual punishments (also first provided for in the Massachusetts enactment).

This was an impressive list of guarantees, especially when

we remember that, with the exception of those contained in the Pennsylvania Charter of Privileges, they were all contained in instruments drawn up before the English Bill of Rights. In fact, compared with colonial documents like the Massachusetts Body of Liberties, the English Bill of Rights is clearly a far more primitive document as far as personal rights are concerned.

Nevertheless, recall that both the English Bill of Rights and the colonial documents discussed did not really have the status of constitutions, since they were subject to alteration or repeal at the discretion of the legislature. Even the colonial charters could be changed at will by the Crown or Parliament. To be sure, as the colonial period came toward its end, a sharp conflict developed between the colonies and the mother country on the latter point. "In Britain," wrote Governor Bernard of Massachusetts in 1765, "the American Governments are considered as Corporations empowered to make by-Laws, existing only during the Pleasure of Parliament. . . . In America they claim . . . to be perfect States, no otherwise dependent upon Great Britain than by having the same King." [80]

The constitutional development during the Revolutionary period then may be summarized as a movement from the British to the American conception. In strict law, of course, the British view was correct; while they remained colonies, the American governments were, to quote Lord Mansfield again, "all on the same footing as our great corporations in London." [81] The Revolution would bring about the subsequent triumph of the American view. The governments set up under colonial charters and other organic documents would be replaced, during the Revolution, by governments established under state constitutions adopted by representatives of the people themselves. Those guarantees of individual rights formerly in charters and enactments would be included in constitutions and bills of rights as binding fundamental laws.

three
revolutionary declarations
and constitutions

The American Revolution was the all-important link between colonial liberties and the Federal Bill of Rights. Until Independence, there was no legal authority to draw up constitutions and bills of rights; no instrument drafted by Americans could have other than subordinate status. Once Independence had been declared, the legal picture became different. Now theories developed during the colonial period could be tested in constitutional documents.

The immediate political consequence of Independence was a governing vacuum. Like the Interregnum Levellers, the Americans of this period recognized the opportunity they had been given to break with the past. Following the Leveller theory, they first elected constitutional conventions to draw up constitutions establishing governments in the different states. But the newly independent states also understood that it was not enough to set up political governments and delegate the powers needed to govern effectively. Colonial history had taught them that equally important were the setting out of legal limitations upon the authority of the governing agents and, further, the identifying and protecting of individual rights and liberties as fundamental and beyond attack by the governors.

During the colonial period, the right to self-government had continuously been subjected to challenge by royal authorities. During this century-long period of friction, fundamental law—whether that found in charters or in the principles of the British Constitution—was the major refuge of the colonists. Yet fundamental law was a weak ally at best. "To deduce our rights from the principles of equity, justice and the Constitution, is very well," wrote that important, though little-known, framer of the Pennsylvania constitution, James Cannon, in 1776, "but equity and justice are no defence against power." The slogan, "a government of laws and not of men," was a logical response to the colonial experience, an experience that had prejudiced the colonists toward written law as against unwritten principles.

By 1776 most Americans firmly believed that government should operate only under a system where the status, duties, and powers of the governing were firmly fixed in specific fundamental laws. Constitutional rights, declared Cannon, must be protected and defended "as the apple of your eye;" they must be fixed "on a foundation never more to be shaken"—that is, they must be specified in written documents [1] beyond the reach of those who exercised governmental power. The first state constitutions manifested this requirement with binding written directions that placed certain principles legally beyond the powers of the governing.

The Revolutionary period thus saw the fruition of the colonial development discussed in the last chapter. Now specific guarantees of fundamental personal rights were expressly included in written constitutions vested with the status of supreme law. These were, however, to be the culmination of the Revolutionary period. Before then, the notion of fundamental rights itself had to be further developed in the course of the conflict that arose between the colonies and the mother country.

OTIS AND UNCONSTITUTIONALITY

Despite the fact that England has never had a written constitution, the concept of fundamental law has nevertheless played an important part in English history, particularly during the constitutional disputes of the seventeenth century.[2] The most important expression of the fundamental law notion was by Chief Justice Coke in *Dr. Bonham's Case*. Dr. Bonham had practiced medicine without a certificate from the Royal College of Physicians. The College Censors committed him to prison, and he sued for false imprisonment. The college set forth in defense its statute of incorporation, which authorized it to regulate all physicians and punish with a fine and imprisonment practitioners not admitted by it. The statute, however, gave the college one half of all the fines imposed. This, said Coke, made the college not only judges but parties to cases coming before them, and it is an established maxim of the common law that no man may be judge in his own cause.

But what of the statute which appeared to give the college the power to judge Dr. Bonham? Coke's answer was that the statute could not be interpreted to confer a power so contrary to common right and reason. In his words, "it appears in our books, that in many cases, the common law will controul Acts of Parliament, and sometimes adjudge them to be utterly void: for when an Act of Parliament is against common right and reason, or repugnant, or impossible to be performed, the common law will controul it, and adjudge such Act to be void."[3]

Countless scholars have debated the exact meaning of these words. The modern consensus is that the passage states a canon of construction rather than a constitutional theory: Coke did not mean to assert the theory of a fundamental common law empowering the courts to nullify statutes; he meant only that the basis of statute law, like that of the common law, was reason and justice and that it was the duty of the courts to construe statutes strictly in order to bring them into conformity with accepted legal principles.[4]

If Coke did mean to lay down a doctrine of judicial review, rather than one of statutory interpretation, he was, of course, wrong as a matter of English law. But whether Coke was *right* or not, does not affect the historical impact of his decision.[5]

As Raoul Berger puts it, "The importance of Coke for judicial review does not therefore turn on whether he was 'right' but rather on the fact that . . . Americans believed he was, and proceeded to act on that belief." [6]

During the conflict that led to the Revolution, Americans increasingly took the dictum in *Dr. Bonham's Case* literally, as a statement that there was a fundamental law limiting Parliamentary powers. Had not my Lord Coke concluded, they argued among themselves, that when an Act of Parliament is contrary to such fundamental law, it must be adjudged void? Did this not mean that when the British government acts toward the colonies in a manner contrary to common right and reason, its decrees too must be given no legal force?

From Westminster Hall, where the judgment in *Dr. Bonham's Case* was delivered in 1610, to the Council Chamber of the Boston Town House a century and a half later are not really as far apart as they seem. "That council chamber," wrote John Adams, "was as respectable an apartment as the House of Commons or the House of Lords in Great Britain. . . . In this chamber, round a great fire, were seated five Judges, with Lieutenant-Governor Hutchinson at their head, as Chief Justice, all arrayed in their new, fresh, rich robes of scarlet English broadcloth; in their large cambric bands, and immense judicial wigs." [7] For it was in this chamber, in February, 1761, that James Otis delivered his landmark attack against general writs of assistance.

In his argument in *Lechmere's Case* [8] Otis with "a torrent of impetuous eloquence . . . hurried away every thing before him." He argued the cause, he declared, "with the greater pleasure . . . as it is in opposition to a kind of power, the exercise of which in former periods of English history, cost one King of England his head and another his throne." [9] If Patrick Henry would come close to treason in his 1765 Stamp Act oration, he had before him an excellent model in this Otis speech.

To demonstrate the illegality of the writs of assistance, Otis went straight back to Coke. As Horace Gray (later a Justice of the Supreme Court) put it in an 1865 comment, "His main reliance was the well-known statement of Lord *Coke* in *Dr. Bonham's case.*" [10] This is seen in John Adams' summary of the Otis argument: "As to Acts of Parliament. An Act against the Constitution is void: an Act against natural Equity is void: and if an Act of Parliament should be made, in the very words of this Petition, it would be void. The . . . Courts must pass such Acts into disuse." [11] In this argument, says Justice Gray, Otis "denied that [Parliament] was the final arbiter of the justice and constitutionality of its own acts; and . . . contended that the validity of statutes must be judged by the Courts of Justice; and thus foreshadowed the principle of American Constitutional Law, that it is the duty of the judiciary to declare unconstitutional statutes void." [12]

American constitutional law may have, as the Gray comment indicates, begun with the Otis argument. But Otis himself was by no means as clear in his assertion of the doctrine of unconstitutionality as the Adams summary of his argument implies. As Bernard Bailyn has shown, Otis's views on the matter were a melange of contradictory doctrines, asserting both his version of the *Bonham* dictum and the view that the power of Parliament "is uncontrollable but by themselves, and we must obey." [13] Otis's contemporaries were confused by the contradiction and drew conflicting conclusions. [14] The majority probably still adhered to the Blackstone conception of Parliamentary supremacy summarized eight years after *Lechmere's Case* in Thomas Hutchinson's grand jury charge: "We, Gentlemen, who are to execute the law, are not to inquire into the Reason & Policy of it, or whether it is constitutional or not. . . . If we step over this line, and judge of the Propriety or Impropriety, the Justice or Injustice of the Laws, we introduce the worst sort of Tyranny." [15]

As the struggle with the mother country intensified, however, Americans were increasingly prepared to accept the contrary view articulated in the 1761 Otis argument that there were fundamental legal principles beyond the power of Parliament to disturb and that the courts, not Parliament, might be the branch of government to enforce compliance with them. Otis may not have realized the full import of these ideas, but it was he who put them into play. Starting with the *Lechmere* argument, the dictum in *Dr. Bonham's Case* was put to new use on the western side of the Atlantic. Otis had stated the doctrine that ultimately was to take over in American constitutional law. Others, more aware of political realities, were to carry his ideas to their logical conclusion— the overthrow of Parliamentary authority and the establishment of a new polity in which the legislature was limited by an express fundamental law enforced by the courts.[16]

REVOLUTIONARY DECLARATIONS OF RIGHTS

Eleven years after the event, in 1776, John Adams would declare that the "author of the first Virginia Resolutions against the stamp act . . . will have the glory with posterity, of beginning . . . this great Revolution." [17] His reference, of course, was to Patrick Henry, who arose on May 29, 1765, in the Virginia House of Burgesses while that assembly was considering the newly enacted Stamp Act. It was thought at the time that Mr. Henry was not very learned in the law—he had in fact, been admitted to the Bar after six weeks of study that included Coke and the Virginia Statutes only.[18] Yet from his reading, limited though it was, Henry had come upon *Coke upon Littleton* where Coke argued that an Act of Parliament against the Magna Carta, or common right, or reason was void. And it was on the flyleaf of his old copy of that book that the unlearned young lawyer wrote out a set of resolutions protesting against the Stamp Act. It is these resolutions which Henry presented to the Virginia assembly that day in May, together with the "treasonable" speech with which his name has remained associated. Young Thomas Jefferson, who witnessed the scene, later recalled how "torrents of sublime eloquence from Mr. Henry . . . prevailed" to secure passage of most of the resolutions.[19]

Throughout the colonies, the Stamp Act was opposed on the same ground that Otis had urged in *Lechmere's Case*. John Adams used the Otis argument in presenting a petition to the Governor and Council of Massachusetts, "that the Stamp Act was null because unconstitutional," [20] and a committee of the legislative assembly of that colony resolved that business should be done without stamps. The "prevailing reason" given for their resolve, as well as for the actions of the people in following it, according to Thomas Hutchinson, then lieutenant governor of Massachusetts, was "that the Act of Parliament is against Magna Charta and the natural rights of Englishmen, and therefore, according to Lord *Coke,* null and void." [21]

Colonial judges followed the same approach. Justice William Cushing, a member of the highest Massachusetts bench, in a letter dated "In a hurry Feby. 7, 1766," to Lieutenant Governor Hutchinson (who was then also Chief Justice of Massachusetts), wrote, "Its true It is said an Act of Parliament against natural Equity is void." That being the case, "If we admit evidence unstamped . . . Q. if it can be said we do wrong." Later, his opinion more settled, Cushing could write to John Adams, "I can tell the grand jury the nullity of Acts of Parliament." [22] By then, virtually all the judges in Massachusetts were refusing to apply the Stamp Act and conducting court business without stamps. "I am the only instance of non compliance," plaintively wrote Thomas Hutchinson of his refusal as a probate judge to ignore the Stamp Act. [23]

The judges in Virginia went even further, ruling expressly that the Stamp Act was unconstitutional. Edmund Pendleton, sitting as a County Court judge, declared at the end of 1765 that he, "having taken an oath to decide according to law, shall never consider that act as such for want of power (I mean constitutional authority) in the Parliament to pass it." [24] Other Virginia judges took a similar position. In a noted February, 1766, case, the judges "unanimously declared it to be their opinion," we are told in a contemporary account, "that the said act did not bind, affect, or concern the inhabitants of this colony, in as much as they conceive the same to be unconstitutional." [25]

Men whose education had been, in large part, based upon

Coke naturally gave a legal turn to their disaffection with the Stamp Act. "Our friends to liberty," wrote Thomas Hutchinson during the heat of the Stamp Act controversy, "take advantage of a maxim they find in Lord *Coke* that an Act of Parliament against Magna Charta or the peculiar rights of Englishmen is *ipso facto* void." This, Hutchinson went on, is what "seems to have determined great part of the colonies to oppose the execution of the act with force." [26]

When the time came for the colonists to present a united front in opposition, they convened the Stamp Act Congress. That body, following Coke's example as a leader of the 1628 Parliament, drew up its own Declaration of Rights and Grievances. [27] This document, probably drafted by John Dickinson, starts by affirming the allegiance of the colonists to the Crown and their "due subordination" to Parliament. Moderate though the declaration's tone was, however, it asserted the basic colonial theory that the colonists were entitled to all the rights of Englishmen. It went on to question the constitutionality of the Stamp Act, declaring that such a statute was "unreasonable and inconsistent with the principles and spirit of the British constitution." In addition, it stated flatly that trial by jury was a fundamental right of every colonist and that the colonists had the right to petition the king or Parliament.

As the conflict between the colonies and the mother country grew in intensity during the next decade, the locus of resistance centered in Massachusetts, with Samuel Adams and his Sons of Liberty playing a dominant role in radicalizing that colony. In 1772, the new governor of Massachusetts, Thomas Hutchinson, announced that his salary and those of all Massachusetts judges would thenceforth be paid by the Crown. This change was bitterly opposed by the colonists, for they knew it would render the officials concerned free from local control. At the Boston Town Meeting, the Governor was questioned about the matter and replied in a letter that argued, in effect, that it was none of the colonists' business. Samuel Adams then moved that a Committee of Correspondence be appointed "to State the Rights of the Colonists and of this Province in particular, as Men, as Christians, and as Subjects; and to communicate the same to the several Towns in this Province, and to the World." [28] The committee prepared a report in two parts: the first the Rights of the Colonists, the second a List of Infringements and Violations of Rights. Sam Adams himself played a major role in drafting this document.

The Boston document [29] is noteworthy as an indication of the rights considered fundamental by the colonists on the eve of the Revolution, stated both in affirmative form (in the Rights of the Colonists) and in negative form (in the List of Infringements). Among the rights stated as fundamental are ones that appeared first in earlier colonial documents: freedom of conscience; the right to "all the natural essential, inherent and inseparable Rights Liberties and Privileges of Subjects born in Great Britain"; the right not to have troops quartered without consent; and "their inestimable right to tryals by *Juries*."

Even more significant is the assertion of rights not previously provided for in colonial charters, enactments, and declarations. Foremost among these is the right against unreasonable searches and seizures. This was the first legislative assertion of the right, and its presence is explained by the misfortunes suffered by the colonists from writs of assistance and general warrants, under which "Officers . . . break thro' the sacred rights of the *Domicil*, ransack men's houses, destroy their securities, carry off their property, and . . . commit the most horred murders." In addition, the right of the colonists to life, liberty, and property is declared in ringing terms. Here was the Lockean trilogy later to be protected by the Due Process Clause of the Fifth Amendment. Also stated was a right to be free from the attempts "which have been made and are now making to establish an American Espiscopate"—an assertion for the first time of a right to be free of a particular established Church. This was to develop into the general prohibition against an establishment of religion in the First Amendment.

The Boston Town Meeting sent its statement on the Rights

of the Colonists and a List of Infringements and Violations of Rights, together with a Letter of Correspondence, to the other towns of Massachusetts. The letter, dated November 20, 1772, stated that the Boston meeting had "briefly Recapitulated the sense we have of our invaluable Rights, as Men, as Christians, and as Subjects; and wherein we conceive those Rights to have been violated, which we are desirous may be laid before your Town, that the subject may be weighed as its importance requires and the collected wisdom of the whole People, as far as possible, be obtained. . . . A free communication of your sentiments to this Town, of our common danger, is earnestly solicited and will be gratefully received." [30]

As Samuel Adams and his colleagues had intended, Boston soon received letters of support from many of the Massachusetts towns. Typical of these is an unpublished letter from the Town of Truro which shows that the notion of fundamental rights, upon which the Boston statement was based, was widely supported. When we think of the development of political thought at the time, we tend to confine ourselves to centers like Boston and Philadelphia. We forget that the basic concept upon which later bills of rights were to be constructed was spreading in the hinterland as well. The little town of Truro could solemnly vote endorsement of the Adams inventory, agreeing "that our Rights as Men, as Christians, and as Subjects are therein well stated." It was because of the support of towns such as Truro that the movement to assert the colonists' rights spread. Ultimately, it was such popular recognition of the need to "fix our Just Rights and Liberties on a Solid and Lasting Foundation" [31] that led to the movement to add a Bill of Rights to the Constitution of the new nation.

In the interim, official relations between the colonies and Britain deteriorated rapidly. The American position had been clearly stated by Benjamin Franklin during his questioning in 1766 by a committee of the House of Commons. He was asked whether the repeal of the Stamp Act would induce the American assemblies to acknowledge the right of Parliament to tax them and to erase their resolutions against the Stamp Act. "No, never," was his reply. His questioner went on, "Is there no means of obliging them to erase those resolutions?" "None that I know of," answered the good doctor, "they will never do it unless compelled by force of arms." [32] Within less than a decade precisely that course was chosen by the British Crown. With both sides publicly committed to their constitutional positions, the situation soon became such that in 1774 George III would state: "The die is cast. The colonists must either triumph or submit." [33]

When the Coercive Acts made open rebellion in America all but inevitable, the colonists once again resorted to a congress where a common front could be presented. The First Continental Congress, composed of delegates from all the colonies except Georgia, met early in September, 1774. It was widely believed, as a letter of Samuel Adams put it, that the Congress should "agree in one general Bill of Rights." [34] To give effect to this view, the Congress set up a committee to define the rights of the colonies, as well as the instances in which they had been infringed. The Declaration and Resolves prepared by this committee was adopted on October 14, 1774.

Although the official title of this document is "Declaration and Resolves," the title page of a printing in New York in 1774 calls it "The Bill of Rights." [35] This seems to indicate that the popular conception at the time was, in accordance with Adams's view, that the document was an American equivalent of the Bill of Rights of 1689. This was apparently the first specific use of the term in connection with an American document.

In its declaration, the Continental Congress expressed the prevailing view of the rights possessed by Americans and it did so with substantial accord. The Journal of the Congress tells us that eight of the resolutions were adopted without dissent, *nemine contradicente*, while two encountered some opposition.[36] The declaration, following the theory upon which the colonists' legal case was based, relied upon the basic doctrine of constitutionality, declaring that British acts in violation of the colonists' rights were "unconstitutional," "illegal," "against law," and "infringements."

The 1774 Declaration and Resolves, like the Boston document of two years earlier, starts by asserting the right to life, liberty, and property, as well as the claim "to all the rights, liberties, and immunities" of Englishmen. In addition, the right to trial by jury is reaffirmed—and, more particularly, the right to be tried by a jury "of the vicinage" (perhaps the first express anticipation of the Sixth Amendment guaranty of the right to be tried by a jury "of the . . . district wherein the crime shall have been committed"), as well as the right not to have soldiers quartered and the right "peaceably to assemble, consider of their grievances, and petition the king." Both the English Bill of Rights and the declaration of the Stamp Act Congress had asserted a right to petition the Crown. The 1774 declaration brings us a step closer to the language of the First Amendment by coupling the right to petition with the right to assemble.

The Declaration and Resolves of the First Continental Congress was the direct precursor of the declarations of rights contained in the Revolutionary state constitutions, starting with the Virginia Declaration of Rights of 1776. In the 1774 declaration, the American is emerging from his colonial status, for the rights declared are based upon more than the principles of the English Constitution, colonial charters, and compacts. In declaring that the rights of the colonists are natural rights, the Declaration and Resolves anticipates the more famous statement on this issue in the Declaration of Independence and prepares the way for the elevation of the rights involved to the constitutional plane.

The last of the resolutions of the First Continental Congress described the intention of the assembled to prepare addresses and memorials to the people of Britain, the inhabitants of British America, and the king. Among these was an Address to the Inhabitants of Quebec, approved on October 26, 1774.[37] It contains another expression of the fundamental rights of the colonists, as they were then understood by a representative assembly chosen from all the colonies. This statement is of historical importance in its detailed setting forth of the right to jury trial and its assertion of two rights not previously protected in colonial documents. The first was recognized by both English and colonial law and was later to find specific expression in American constitutions: the right to personal liberty vindicated by the Great Writ of Habeas Corpus (apparently first expressly recognized in the colonies in a 1692 Massachusetts statute modeled upon the English Habeas Corpus Act). The second was the first declaration by an official assembly of the right to freedom of the press, "whereby oppressive officers are ashamed or intimidated, into more honourable and just modes of conducting affairs." This set the pattern for inclusion of freedom of the press in subsequent bills of rights and marked a significant divergence from the practice in Britain, where freedom of the press, although already considered "the great bulwark of Liberty," [38] did not rest upon any general legislative, much less constitutional, provision, but only (as seen at the end of Chapter 1) on the Parliamentary action allowing the Licensing Act to expire in 1695.

INDEPENDENCE AND SELF-GOVERNMENT

"The blessings of society," wrote John Adams in 1776, "depend entirely on the constitutions of government." [39] Hence, it was natural once the conflict with Britain reached the stage where independence was the only real alternative to submission that the men of the Revolution should turn to constitution-making. Full separation from the mother country made necessary a new governmental structure in the colonies, thenceforth to be free states absolved from allegiance to the British Crown.

While British governors fled in the face of popular outcries or were driven from power, civil government had to be carried on; a new legal basis had to be provided to replace that which had been forcibly dissolved. The problem confronting the colonists as a whole simultaneously confronted them as individual states. The experience of New Hampshire, the first colony to draw up its own system of independent self-government, is typical. At the beginning of 1776, the congress of that colony declared:

> The sudden and abrupt departure of . . . our late Governor and several of the Council, leaving us destitute of Legislation; and no Executive Courts being open to punish criminal offenders, whereby the lives and properties of the honest people of the Colony, are liable to the machinations and evil designs of wicked men: Therefore, for the preservation of peace and good order, and for the security of the lives and properties of the inhabitants of this Colony, we conceive ourselves reduced to the necessity of establishing a form of Government.[40]

The governments established to meet the vacuum caused by the departure of the royal governments were treated at first as only temporary expedients, intended, in the words of the New Hampshire congress, "to continue during the present unhappy and unnatural contest." It was soon seen, however, that arrangements more formal and abiding were necessary. "Each colony," John Adams wrote in March, 1776, "should establish its own government and then a league should be formed between them all." [41] Two months later, the Second Continental Congress adopted a resolution calling for the full exercise of local government and the suppression of all royal authority and urging the various colonies to set up governments of their own.[42] Adams termed this "the most important Resolution that ever was taken in America." [43] Although Adams overdid his use of superlatives, this characterization was not too wide of the mark. The May, 1776, resolution signified virtual independence—and that two months before the Declaration of Independence itself.

Effect was given to the May, 1776, resolution by the drawing up of constitutions establishing new state governments. By the end of the Revolution, written constitutions had been adopted in a majority of the states. Eleven of these were wholly new documents, while those of Connecticut and Rhode Island were essentially the old royal charters with only minor modifications.

Most important of all, the May, 1776, resolution and the state constitutions drafted to give effect to it enabled individual rights to be placed for the first time upon a firm constitutional foundation. No longer were those rights contained in charters or concessions granted as a matter of grace and revocable at will by the grantor, or legislative enactments subject to alteration or repeal at the discretion of the legislature, or even declarations and resolutions without binding legal effect. Now the fundamental rights of Americans could be guaranteed in written constitutions, vested with the status of supreme law, and enforceable as such against the American successors of both the Crown and Parliament.

VIRGINIA DECLARATION OF RIGHTS

Virginia was the first state to give effect to the May, 1776, congressional resolution. Even before the Declaration of Independence, it adopted a constitution and declaration of rights. The latter is the first true bill of rights in the modern American sense; it is the first protection of the rights of the individual to be contained in a constitution adopted by the people acting through an elected convention. The Virginia Convention of 1776 was the last of the Virginia colonial conventions that had first been called in 1774 to fill the governmental gap caused by Lord Dunmore's dissolution of the House of Burgesses. On May 15, 1776, the convention adopted Resolutions for Proposing Independence drafted by Edmund Pendleton, the convention president. The first of these resolutions instructed the Virginia delegates in the Continental Congress to propose a declaration of independence—the first formal proposal of the official Declaration. The second resolution provided "that a Committee be appointed to prepare a Declaration of Rights, and such a plan of

Government as will be most likely to maintain peace and order in this Colony and secure substantial and equal liberty to the people." [44]

The committee named on May 15 to prepare a declaration of rights and a constitution, in accordance with Pendleton's second resolution, consisted of 28 members. On May 16, the first day of meeting, and then on May 18, James Madison and George Mason, respectively, were added to the committee. The additions were of critical importance, since Mason would draft virtually the entire Virginia Declaration of Rights and Madison would subsequently be the draftsman of the Federal Bill of Rights. Thus, the 1776 Virginia Convention provided both the first state bill of rights and the training-ground of the man who was to become known as the father of the Federal Constitution and its Bill of Rights. In his brief *Autobiography*, Madison states that he was "initiated into the political career" by his work in the 1776 convention. "Being young," he did not participate in the debates, although he did suggest a key amendment in the guaranty of religious freedom. [45]

On May 27, Archibald Cary, the chairman of the Committee to Prepare a Constitution, reported that the "committee had accordingly prepared a Declaration of Rights; which he read in his place." [46] It was discussed by the convention on June 3–5; on June 11, several amendments were made to it; and on June 12, it passed the convention without opposition. The body of the constitution itself—that providing for the new state government—was adopted on June 29, prefaced by a lengthy preamble written by Thomas Jefferson, which sets forth the grievances of the colonists against George III in language essentially similar to the more famous list of charges in the Declaration of Independence.

The Journal of the Virginia Convention consists only of unrevealing formal entries, making it necessary to use other sources for facts on adoption of the 1776 Declaration of Rights. Of these, the most important is the summary contained in Edmund Randolph's *Essay*, written some thirty-five years after the event. Randolph, who had been the youngest delegate to the convention, tells us that, although "many projects of a bill of rights" were presented to the drafting committee, "that proposed by George Mason swallowed up all the rest." [47] Madison also confirms that "This important and meritorious instrument was drawn by George Mason." [48] Moreover, there is a copy of the first draft of the Virginia Declaration of Rights almost all in Mason's handwriting.[49]

If we compare the first draft with the declaration as adopted, we find only four major additions (Articles 9, 10, 13, and 14). At the end of a copy of the first draft, written in 1778, Mason states that "it received few alterations or additions in the Virginia Convention," saying that only "Two more articles were added, viz., the 10th and 14th in the adopted bill—not of fundamental nature." [50] Mason understates the significance of the changes made. Article 9 concerns excessive bail and unusual punishments, while Article 10 contains the direct antecedent of the Fourth Amendment. Article 13 calls for a militia controlled by civilians; Article 14 deals with a local problem of Virginia's western land holdings. And a change in Article 16, suggested by Madison, contains the term "free exercise of religion" [51]—thus anticipating Madison's use of the term in the First Amendment. Yet, even with this said, it remains true that the declaration was mainly Mason's work. The extent of Mason's contribution is made even clearer when we compare it with the rudimentary provisions protecting personal rights in the draft constitution Jefferson prepared just before the Virginia Convention.[52]

That a planter without formal legal training could draw up a document like the Virginia Declaration of Rights must remain a constant source of wonder. According to the 1855 account by Hugh Grigsby, "when Mason sat down in his room in the Raleigh Tavern to write that paper, it is probable that no copy of the reply to Sir Robert Filmer or of the Essay on Government . . . was within his reach. The diction, the design, the thoughts, are all his own." He goes on to say that "Mason was a planter, untutored in the schools, whose life . . . had been spent in a thinly settled colony." [53] Nonethe-

less, Mason knew Locke, Montesquieu, and Sydney—the trio
that gave the Revolution its theoretical underpinnings.

In a letter written to Richard Henry Lee on the very day he
took his seat in the convention, Mason declared, "We are
now going upon the most important of all Subjects—Government" [54] In settling the constitutional frame of government,
he and his colleagues were at one in the opinion that a declaration of rights had to be an integral part of the new constitution. This explains why so revolutionary an item as the declaration could be drawn up by one man and adopted with few
changes. By 1776, a consensus had clearly developed in the
former colonies on the fundamental rights the law should
protect. In giving specific content to those rights, Mason gave
expression to the shared thoughts of the day on individual
rights; [55] in doing so he was more the codifier than the transforming innovator.

The Virginia Declaration [56] completely omits the references
to English law and colonial charters and grants upon which
the pre-Revolutionary documents already discussed had been
based. Instead—as in the Declaration and Resolves of the
First Continental Congress—it asserts the law of nature as the
source of individual rights and it does so in language remarkably similar to that which Jefferson was shortly to use in
the Declaration of Independence. As in the 1774 Declaration,
the trilogy of life, liberty, and property is stated as the basic
end to be protected.

Of the sixteen articles in the Virginia Declaration, nine
state fundamental general principles of a free republic. Of
these perhaps the most consequential was the statement in
Article 5 of the separation of powers as a rule of positive
law—the first such statement in a constitutional document.
The remaining seven articles safeguard specific individual
rights. Among them, we find those rights emanating from
prior documents, including the right against excessive bail
and fines and cruel and unusual punishment (this time using
the very language of the English Bill of Rights that was to
become the Eighth Amendment); that to trial by jury in both
civil and criminal cases (anticipating the Sixth and Seventh

Amendments in this regard); the right not to be deprived of liberty "except by the law of the land or the judgment of his peers" (still another version of section 39 of Magna Carta on the way to the Due Process Clause of the Fifth Amendment); and the right to freedom of conscience (containing, as already seen, the term "free exercise," which Madison was to use again in the First Amendment).

Article 8 of the Virginia Declaration is of special significance. It directly anticipates the rights guaranteed in the Sixth Amendment: to a speedy trial by a jury of the vicinage, to be informed of the cause and nature of the accusation, to be confronted with the accuser and witnesses, and not to be compelled to give evidence against oneself (the first constitutional statement of what was to become the privilege against self-incrimination of the Fifth Amendment). Leonard Levy has criticized Article 8 as guaranteeing "far less than the ordinary practice of the common law." In particular Levy asserts that the Virginia Declaration's protection against self-incrimination "provided only a stunted version of the common law." [57] The Levy criticism is unfair. Of course the Virginia Declaration was erratic, omitting rights now considered basic (notably, freedom of speech and assembly, the right to counsel, and protection against double jeopardy). But Mason and his colleagues were working hurriedly to assemble the first constitutional charter of individual rights. Their drafting deficiencies (as in the self-incrimination provision) have been corrected by later enactments and decisions. As Levy himself recognizes, the Virginia Declaration was far more comprehensive than the British precedents and covered rights not protected by any other prior document. The most important of these were the guaranty against general warrants (the first constitutional assertion of the right protected by the Fourth Amendment, anticipating the language of the latter on the requirement of particularity in warrants) and that of freedom of the press. The latter was the first enactment, constitutional or statutory, expressly protecting freedom of the press and thus the direct precursor of this freedom as it was guaranteed in the First Amendment.

All in all, the Virginia Declaration was a landmark in the development that was to culminate in the Federal Bill of Rights. The Virginia Declaration was the first document that may truly be called an American bill of rights. Mason and his colleagues recognized this, for they consistently referred to the document in the convention debates as the *Bill of Rights,* just as Randolph was to do in his *Essay* of thirty years later. Technically, of course, the term "bill" was inaccurate—as it is, indeed, in the case of the Federal Bill of Rights. Unlike the English Bill of Rights, neither the Virginia Declaration nor the Federal Bill of Rights had ever been bills enacted as statutes. Both were adopted as constitutional enactments and thus were superior to bills and statutes.

In his *Essay*, Randolph appropriately terms the Virginia Declaration the cornerstone of the constitutional system. He states the two objectives of the document in terms that can be said to describe equally well the generic class of documents and the particular enactment of the Virginia Constitutional Convention: "one, that the legislature should not in their acts violate any of those canons; the other, that in all the revolutions of time, of human opinion, and of government, a perpetual standard should be erected." [58]

OTHER DECLARATIONS OF RIGHTS, 1776–1777

The Virginia Declaration of Rights set the example for seven of the eleven other states that adopted constitutions during the Revolutionary period. Following the example of Virginia, they adopted constitutions that included specific bills of rights. Five of these were adopted during the year following Independence.

The first state to follow Virginia's example was Pennsylvania. That state's Constitutional Convention met in July, 1776, and completed its work the next month. By then, the Virginia Declaration of Rights had been widely distributed. Samuel Adams, writing Richard Henry Lee from Philadelphia on July 15, sent thanks for a copy of "the Form of Govern't agreed upon by your Countrymen. I have not yet had time to peruse it, but dare say it will be a Feast to our little Circle." [59] There is no doubt then that the Pennsylvania constitution-makers had the Virginia Declaration before them as they wrote,[60] and that they were strongly influenced by the Virginia model. Indeed, according to a 1779 statement by John Adams in his *Diary*, "The [Pennsylvania] bill of rights is taken almost verbatim from that of Virginia." [61]

The Adams statement is unfair, although it is repeated by virtually all commentators. It is true that the Pennsylvania Declaration [62] was modeled upon that of Virginia. It is virtually a duplicate of the earlier declaration in its statement of the natural rights of men and the areas of criminal procedure it protects, repeating the right to know the accusation, to confront witnesses, to present one's own evidence, to a speedy public trial by jury, and the privilege against self-incrimination. But even here the Pennsylvania document adds the fundamental right to counsel—the first provision for that right in a bill of rights. In addition, Article X deals with the right against searches and seizures in language somewhat different from that used in the Virginia Declaration.

There are also provisions in the Pennsylvania Declaration that are new in organic documents. Article XIII declares the right of the people to bear arms in language that anticipates the Second Amendment. The provision on religious freedom is somewhat broader than that in the Virginia Declaration, moving in the direction of the future Establishment Clause and forbidding religious tests for official office, as well as exempting conscientious objectors from military service. There is also an express recognition of the right of the people to assemble and petition for redress of grievances, rights later to be included in the First Amendment.

Most important of all is Article XII of the Pennsylvania Declaration. For the first time in any constitutional enactment, guarantees of freedom of speech as well as freedom of the press are included. The inclusion of freedom of speech in the list of fundamental rights guaranteed was a seminal step in the development that led to the Federal Bill of Rights. We do not know how freedom of speech came to be added to the Pennsylvania Declaration, but it may be more than coincidence that Thomas Paine was one of the four principal draftsmen of the Pennsylvania Constitution.

Two further points should be noted about the Pennsylvania Declaration of Rights. The first is that it did not cover the field as far as constitutional protections for individual rights was concerned. The body of the constitution (entitled the Frame of Government, following the Penn 1683 precedent) adopted by the 1776 Pennsylvania convention also contained provisions guaranteeing personal liberties—notably the right to trial by jury "as heretofore," that to bail and against excessive fines—and virtually eliminating imprisonment for debt and most religious tests. There was also an interesting attempt to place fundamental liberties above even the amending process. Section 46 of the constitution provided: "The declaration of rights is hereby declared to be a part of the constitution of this commonwealth, and ought never to be violated on any pretence whatever."

The next states to act were Delaware and Maryland. Delaware's convention met on August 27, 1776; it adopted a Declaration of Rights on September 11 and a constitution on September 20. The Delaware Declaration was plainly drafted with the Pennsylvania and Virginia Declarations of Rights as examples. In addition, the Delaware delegates had available the draft of the Declaration of Rights prepared in August by a committee in the adjoining state of Maryland (though the Maryland Declaration was not formally adopted until almost two months after the Delaware document). According to a September 17, 1776, letter of George Read, Chairman of the committee that drew up the Delaware Declaration, "the Declaration of Rights . . . has been completed somedays past but there being nothing particularly in it—I did not think it an object of much curiosity, it is made out of the Pensilvania & Maryland Draughts." [63]

The Delaware Declaration was, as Read states, based upon the prior work of the Pennsylvania and Virginia conventions, as well as the Maryland draft to which reference has been made. Among the fundamental rights protected by the earlier documents that are also guaranteed in the Delaware Declaration [64] are the rights of petition, to protection for life, liberty, and property, to trial by jury, to be informed of the accusation and confrontation, to counsel, to speedy trial, against self-incrimination, against excessive bail and fines, against cruel and unusual punishments, and against searches and seizures under general warrants, as well as to freedom of the press. But the Delaware Declaration also was the first constitutional document to contain a prohibition against quartering of soldiers, as well as against retrospective legislation. Though a proposal for a similar ex post facto prohibition had been considered by the Virginia convention, it had been defeated largely because of the opposition of Patrick Henry, who, as Edmund Randolph tells us, drew "a terrifying picture of some towering public offender, against whom ordinary laws would be impotent." [65] The Delaware provision was the antecedent of the Ex Post Facto Clauses of Article I, sections 9 and 10, of the Federal Constitution as well as similar prohibitions in later state bills of rights.

As indicated, the Maryland Declaration of Rights was drafted in August, 1776, though it was not approved by the Maryland Convention until November 3, 1776. The Maryland Declaration was drafted by a seven-man committee appointed on motion of Samuel Chase, later a controversial Supreme Court Justice. It included Chase and five other prominent lawyers. The committee reported a draft on August 10, which was debated extensively by the convention in October. The delegates indicated that they well understood, in the words of one of them, that "establishing a Bill of Rights" was a matter "of the utmost importance to the good people of this State, and their posterity." When the debate on the new declaration went slowly, the delegates agreed to remain in session "while that business is transacting, every evening till eight o'clock," and the declaration was finally approved in a Sunday session, on November 3. [66]

The Maryland Declaration of Rights [67] was much more detailed than its predecessors, containing forty-two articles.

Most of them repeat provisions contained in earlier state declarations, though usually with variations in language. These
provisions include guarantees of trial by jury, freedom of
speech (though confined only to legislative proceedings), the
right of petition, that against cruel and unusual punishment,
ex post facto laws (containing the first constitutional use of
the term—the original draft of this provision, Article XV, an-
tedated and probably influenced the Delaware prohibition),
the right to accusation and indictment or charge, counsel,
confrontation, witnesses, and to a speedy trial, protection of
life, liberty, and property (not to be deprived of same "but
by the judgment of his peers, or by the law of the land"), that
against excessive bail and fines, searches on oathless warrants or general warrants, and quartering of soldiers, as well
as for freedom of conscience and freedom of the press.

The most significant innovation made in the Maryland
Declaration was an express prohibition against bills of attainder. This was the first such constitutional prohibition and
was the forerunner of the Bill of Attainder Clauses of Article
I, sections 9 and 10, of the Federal Constitution. The Maryland provision was most liberal for its time. Bills of attainder
were the principal weapons employed against the Tories during the Revolutionary period, and the Maryland convention
deserves all the more credit for outlawing them when it did,
rather than later when there would be, as Charles Carroll of
Carrollton wrote, "greater certainty than we have at present,
of possessing a country & People to govern." [68]

Soon after the Maryland Constitutional Convention adjourned, a similar body convened in North Carolina. The day
after it first met, on November 13, 1776, the North Carolina
delegates selected a committee of eighteen to prepare a Declaration of Rights and a constitution. On December 12, the
committee reported a Declaration of Rights and it was
adopted on December 17. The North Carolina Declaration
was modeled directly upon those already enacted in Virginia,
Pennsylvania, Delaware, and Maryland. The North Carolina
Declaration [69] contains a compendium of most of the fundamental rights that had come to be recognized by American

constitution-makers: trial by jury, right to accusation and confrontation, privilege against self-incrimination, right against excessive bail or fines, cruel and unusual punishment and general warrants, the right not to be deprived of life, liberty, or property "but by the law of the land," freedom of the press, right to bear arms, freedom of conscience, and prohibition of ex post facto laws. Though it is said by commentators that nothing new was added by the North Carolina Declaration, that is not entirely true. Article VIII contains an implied guaranty of the right to an indictment—the first such provision in a state constitution and, as such, the direct precursor of the guaranty in the Fifth Amendment.

A half year later came the Vermont constitution of 1777. It was the first by a political unit that had not been a separate colony before Independence. Though Vermont was not officially admitted as a state until 1791, it set up its own government early in 1777. Later that year, on July 2, a convention met to draw up a constitution. On July 8, both the constitution and the Declaration of Rights by which it is prefaced were adopted. The speed of the convention is explained by the fact that word was received on July 8 that Ticonderoga was being evacuated, and most of the delegates wanted to get home as soon as possible.[70] The declaration [71] repeats the Pennsylvania guarantees of freedom of conscience (though slightly diluted), the right to life, liberty, and property, conscientious objection, criminal procedure, the right against searches and seizures, trial by jury in civil cases, freedom of speech and press, the right to bear arms, and the right of assembly and petition. Each of these provisions is virtually a verbatim repetition of the relevant Pennsylvania articles. At the beginning of the Vermont Declaration, however, there was a new provision—that part of Article I that outlaws slavery and indentured servitude. There was, of course, to be no comparable provision in the Federal Constitution until the ratification of the Thirteenth Amendment. In addition, the Vermont Declaration contains in Article II an express requirement that, where private property is taken for public use, "the owner ought to receive an equivalent in money." This is the forerunner of the just compensation requirement of the Fifth Amendment and is the first constitutional provision containing any such requirement.[72]

A word should also be put in about Connecticut and Rhode Island, the two states that did not frame new constitutions in response to the May, 1776, congressional resolution recommending the establishment of independent state governments. These two states merely enacted as their fundamental laws the rights and restrictions of their colonial charters. The Connecticut enactment to that effect contains a brief Declaration of Rights, containing three guarantees.[73] The first is another version of section 39 of Magna Carta. The second is a forerunner of the Privileges and Immunities Clause of Article IV of the Federal Constitution. The third is a guaranty of the right to bail. The fact that this was the shortest of the Revolutionary bills of rights is to be explained by the fact that it was not drawn up in connection with the framing of a new constitution. Brief though it was, it deserves a place in the catalogue of bills of rights of the period.

GUARANTEES IN CONSTITUTIONS

Four states—New Jersey, Georgia, New York, and South Carolina—did not preface their new constitutions with separate bills of rights. They protected individual rights in the text of their constitutions instead. This was to be the format followed in the drafting of the Federal Constitution, which did not have a separate bill of rights in its original text. Specific guarantees of individual rights were to be included in various provisions of the text itself.

The first state to enact a Revolutionary constitution without a bill of rights was New Jersey. Its convention promulgated a new constitution in July, 1776, a few days after the Virginia convention adjourned. Among the protections for individual rights included in the text of the New Jersey Constitution [74] are trial by jury, which "shall remain confirmed as a part of the law . . . without repeal, forever." In addition, there is an express provision that criminal defendants "shall be admitted to the same privileges of witnesses and counsel, as their prosecutors." This provision is taken verbatim from the Pennsylvania Charter of Privileges, 1701,[75] and is the first expression of the right to counsel in a modern American constitution.

Even more important are the constitutional provisions in the New Jersey document for freedom of religion. These provisions recognize, again apparently for the first time, that this basic right has a two-fold aspect (ultimately manifested in the First Amendment's separate Establishment Clause and Free Exercise Clause). Article XVIII guarantees the right of the individual to worship "in a manner agreeable to the dictates of his own conscience." Article XIX provides, "That there shall be no establishment of any one religious sect." This is the first prohibition against an established Church in an American constitutional provision. It was written almost a decade before Jefferson's famous Bill for Establishing Religious Freedom was enacted in Virginia. Well might Ezra Stiles say that the New Jersey provisions on religion were even superior to those in the Virginia Declaration of Rights, writing that, "The Constitution of New Jersey surpasses it in the Catholic Establishment of Universal, equal religious, protestant Liberty." [76]

When the people of Georgia met in convention in October, 1776, to frame a constitution setting up an independent state government, they followed the example of New Jersey in not prefacing the new organic instrument with any declaration of rights. As was true of the New Jersey Constitution, the Georgia Constitution [77] adopted early in 1777 contained in the body of its text those guarantees for individual liberties more commonly reserved for bills of rights. Included among these guarantees were the rights to be tried in the county where the crime was committed, to free exercise of religion, against excessive fines and bail, to habeas corpus, and to freedom of the press and trial by jury. In addition, Article I provided for the separation of powers in terms that anticipate the famous statement in the Massachusetts Declaration of Rights.[78]

The next state to follow the New Jersey model was New York. As in most other states, the New York lawmakers also began work on a constitution soon after the congressional resolution of May, 1776. The New York convention first met on July 10, 1776. It was not able to finish its work (being continually interrupted by the military operations in the area) until April, 1777, when the constitution was adopted, with only one dissenting vote. The new organic document was drafted by John Jay and contained no separate bill of rights. As in New Jersey, however, the body of the New York Constitution [79] did contain certain guarantees for individual rights. These included a guaranty against deprivation of rights and privileges, "unless by the law of the land, or the judgment of his peers"—still another version of section 39 of Magna Carta: right of counsel; free exercise of religion; trial by jury and prohibition of bills of attainder.

Even before the May, 1776, resolution of the Continental Congress urging the establishment of independent state governments, the Provincial Congress of South Carolina had framed a constitution. That document adopted March 26, 1776, was intended to establish only a temporary form of government and a more permanent constitution was framed by the general assembly in March, 1778. The 1778 constitution,[80] as in the New Jersey, Georgia, and New York constitutions, contains provisions guaranteeing individual rights in the body of its text. Among the rights guaranteed are those to freedom of conscience—though express provision is made for an established religion, a backward step that is fortunately not duplicated in any other Revolutionary constitution—against disproportionate punishments, not to be deprived of life, liberty, or property "but by the judgment of his peers, or by the law of the land," and freedom of the press.

Except for New Jersey, the states that adopted constitutions without bills of rights contributed nothing new to the concept of a bill of rights. The guarantees of individual rights their constitutions contained were all taken from earlier state provisions. In addition, compared to the states that had framed separate bills of rights, their protections were rudimentary, if not skeletal. Most of the protections Americans had come to deem fundamental are omitted from the New Jersey, Georgia, New York, and South Carolina texts.

LATER REVOLUTIONARY BILLS OF RIGHTS

Massachusetts had been the leader in the conflict leading to Independence and New Hampshire the first state to set up its own independent government. But these two states were the last to adopt bills of rights during the Revolutionary period. The first Massachusetts constitution was not adopted until 1780. Government until then was carried on by the General Court [81] acting without a governor. In 1778, the legislature itself drew up a constitution, but it was rejected by an overwhelming majority of the people. One of the more persuasive reasons for its rejection was the absence of a bill of rights in the proposed document. The provisions in the body of the text protecting trial by jury and freedom of religion were not deemed sufficient to ensure personal freedom. The feelings of the people in this respect were amply demonstrated in declarations by the various towns on the 1778 constitution. The best known of these was the declaration prepared by a convention at Ipswich, Essex County, which also published a pamphlet known as the "Essex Result" explaining their position. [82] The Essex theory, which was to play an important part in the subsequent Massachusetts convention that ratified the Federal Constitution, was that a bill of rights was an essential prerequisite to "ratification of any constitution." A bill of rights was "the equivalent every man receives, as a consideration for the rights he has surrendered."

In response to the popular demand, a Constitutional Convention was chosen in 1779. At its first session, on September 2, the delegates voted, "That there be a Declaration of

Rights prepared, previous to the framing a new Constitution of Government." [83] The next day the convention formally "Resolved, that the Convention will prepare a Declaration of Rights of the People of the Massachusetts Bay." [84] The vote on the resolution was 250 to 1. A committee of thirty members was chosen to prepare a draft declaration. It delegated its task to a subcommittee (composed of James Bowdoin, John Adams, and Samuel Adams), which drew up the original draft of both the Declaration of Rights and the constitution itself. John Adams was the principal author of both documents and was, in later life, extremely proud of his accomplishment. As far as the Declaration of Rights is concerned, Adams stated in 1812 that "the Declaration of Rights was drawn by me, who was appointed alone by the Grand Committee to draw it up." [85]

The Adams draft was accepted by the convention with few changes. The most important of these were directed toward Article XXX of the Massachusetts Declaration and included what would subsequently become a celebrated statement on the separation of powers: "to the end it may be a government of laws and not of men." This provision was substituted during the convention debate for the skeleton version contained in Adams's draft—but the convention Journal is silent on who drafted the substitute or what debate it provoked.

To contemporaries, the most significant change was made in Article III of the Adams version. In revised form, this Article turned out to be the most controversial provision of the declaration. [86] It was a backward measure, since its effect was to place the Congregational Church in a favored position, despite a statement at the end of the provision that "no subordination of any one sect or denomination to another shall ever be established by law." Other revisions in the Adams draft were the elimination from Article XVII of "a right to the freedom of speaking," and the addition to Article X of a provision that reasonable compensation must be paid for property taken for public use, the second constitutional forerunner of the Fifth Amendment provision. The just compensation requirement (derived from a provision in the Body of

Liberties, 1641) [87] is, like the rest of the Massachusetts Declaration, marked throughout by the pedantic archaisms of Adams's style, notably in his use of the word "subject" to designate those whose rights are protected.

The Massachusetts Declaration is a compendium of the earlier state declarations of rights. Among the rights protected in terms similar to those in prior declarations are those of criminal accusation, against self-incrimination, to confrontation and counsel, not to be deprived of "life, liberty, or estate, but by the judgment of his peers, or the law of the land," trial by jury, against unreasonable searches and seizures (the language here moves much closer to that in the Fourth Amendment, containing all the essential elements of the later provision), freedom of the press, right to bear arms, freedom of speech (but only in the legislature), right against ex post facto laws, excessive bail or fines, cruel or unusual punishment, quartering of soldiers, and bills of attainder.

There are also provisions that do not appear in earlier constitutional documents. The one commentators have most frequently noted is the statement of the separation of powers. Also worthy of mention are Article IV, providing that the people of the state shall exercise every power not "by them expressly delegated to the United States" (an early statement of the principle to be articulated in the Tenth Amendment that the powers not delegated to the nation are reserved to the states), and the strong provision in Article XXIX for judicial tenure during good behavior and fixed salaries (which has its counterpart in Article III of the Federal Constitution).

The Massachusetts Declaration of Rights is a summary of the fundamental rights of Americans at the end of the Revolutionary period. It gains particular significance from the fact that Massachusetts would be the first state to recommend the addition of a bill of rights to the Federal Constitution in exchange for its vote in favor of ratification.[88] The Massachusetts Declaration of Rights was the precedent for the amendments recommended by the 1788 Massachusetts Ratifying Convention.

New Hampshire was even later than Massachusetts in

adopting a bill of rights. In January, 1776, the New Hampshire Congress had adopted a constitution without any bill of rights. It was intended only as a temporary measure and was incomplete as a frame of government (making no provision, for example, for establishment of the judiciary). As it turned out, the 1776 constitution remained as fundamental law of the state for over seven years. A new constitution was proposed by a convention that met in 1778, but it was rejected by the people. A second convention met in 1781. Its first two drafts, each containing declarations of rights modeled upon that of Massachusetts, were also rejected. A third draft was finally approved in October, 1783, and went into effect the next year.

Few changes of substance were made in the proposed declaration of rights in the successive redrafts. The delegates did, however, change the title in the 1783 draft, calling Part I of the constitution "The Bill of Rights," and that is the title it bears in the document finally approved. Hence the New Hampshire Bill of Rights has the honor of being the first American constitutional document formally to bear the title "Bill of Rights."

In content, the New Hampshire Bill of Rights [89] is basically similar to the Massachusetts Declaration of Rights, even using that document's peculiar reference to "subjects" rather than "persons." It repeats the Massachusetts provisions on protection of life, liberty, and property, criminal procedure and unreasonable searches and seizures, jury trials in civil cases, freedom of the press, quartering of soldiers, freedom of speech (limited to the legislature), assembly and petition, excessive bail and fines, cruel and unusual punishment, as well as judicial independence and separation of powers. The one important Massachusetts provision not repeated was its ban on bills of attainder.

In a few respects, there are important additions made by the New Hampshire document to the Massachusetts model. The New Hampshire provision on religion declares freedom of conscience to be "a natural and unalienable right" (not "the right as well as the duty" of the Massachusetts Declaration); it also forbids subordination of any one sect to another to be established by law. Retrospective laws are expressly outlawed in both civil and criminal matters (earlier declarations had prohibted only retroactive criminal laws, as was to be true of the Ex Post Facto Clauses of the Federal Constitution as they have been interpreted by the Supreme Court).[90] A progressive provision is also contained in Article XVIII of the New Hampshire document, providing that "All penalties ought to be proportioned to the nature of the offence. . . . The true design of all punishments being to reform, not to exterminate, mankind." Though this provision did not lead to a similar Federal Bill of Rights provision, it was the forerunner of modern attempts at penal reform.

Perhaps the most important contribution made by the New Hampshire Bill of Rights was its inclusion in Article XVI of an express prohibition against double jeopardy. This was the first provision in an American bill of rights vesting the common law rule against a second prosecution with constitutional status, and was the immediate precursor of the Fifth Amendment prohibition.

REVOLUTIONARY BILLS OF RIGHTS

In a 1777 article, Thomas Paine defended the Pennsylvania Constitution and Declaration of Rights he had helped to draft. He rejected the claim that "The Bill of Rights should contain the great principles of natural and civil liberty," saying that this confounded rights with principles: "I conceive a Bill of Rights should be a plain positive declaration of the rights themselves." [91] A comparison of the Federal Bill of Rights with the French Declaration of the Rights of Man [92] will demonstrate how right Paine was on this essential point.

At any rate, the Paine position was that upon which Americans acted in drafting the bills of rights of the Revolutionary period. They contain, not so much the broad principles of natural right, which so frequently abound in continental constitutions, as specific guarantees of the individual rights being protected.

By the end of the Revolutionary period, the concept of a bill of rights had been fully developed in the American system. Eleven of the thirteen states (and Vermont as well) had enacted constitutions to fill in the political gap caused by the overthrow of British authority. These were true constitutions in the modern American use of the term, in accordance with Justice Miller's classic definition: "A constitution in the American sense of the word is a written instrument by which the fundamental powers of the government are established, limited, and defined, and by which these powers are distributed among several departments, for their more sage and useful exercise, for the benefit of the body politic." [93] The constitutions drafted during the Revolution were the first documents that may be termed constitutions in this sense.

In the American conception, a constitution both sets forth the frame of government and provides protection for fundamental rights. The latter is the province of a bill of rights. Eight of the Revolutionary constitutions were prefaced by bills of rights, while four contained guarantees of individual rights in the body of their texts. Included in these Revolutionary constitutional provisions were all the rights that were to be protected in the Federal Bill of Rights. By the time of the Treaty of Paris (1783) then, the American inventory of individual rights had been virtually completed and included in the different state constitutions, whether in separate bills of rights or the organic texts themselves.

If we look at the rights protected by the Federal Bill of Rights, we find that virtually all are protected in the state constitutions and bills of rights adopted during the Revolutionary period. The situation in this respect can be seen clearly from the following table.

The table shows that the rights Madison selected for inclusion in the first ten amendments were *all* taken from the first state constitutions and bills of rights (except for the retained rights protected by the Ninth Amendment). Free exercise of

Bill of Rights Guarantees	First Constitutional Guaranty	Other Constitutional Guarantees
Establishment of religion	N.J. Const., Art. XIX	—
Free exercise of religion	Va. Decl. of Rights, S. 16	N.J. Const., Art. XVIII Pa. Dec. of Rights, Art. II Del. Dec. of Rights, s. 2 Md. Dec. of Rights, Art. XXXIII N.C. Dec. of Rights, Art. XIX Ga. Const., Art. LVI N.Y. Const., Art. XXXVIII Vt. Dec. of Rights, Art. III S.C. Const., Art. XXXVIII Mass. Dec. of Rights, Art. II N.H. Bill of Rights, Art. V
Free speech	Pa. Dec. of Rights, Art. XII	Vt. Dec. of Rights, Art. XIV
Free press	Va. Dec. of Rights, s. 12	Pa. Dec. of Rights, Art. XII Del. Dec. of Rights, s. 23 Md. Dec. of Rights, Art. XXXVIII N.C. Dec. of Rights, Art. XV Ga. Const., Art. LXI Vt. Dec. of Rights, Art. XIV S.C. Const., Art. XLIII Mass. Dec. of Rights, Art. XVI N.H. Bill of Rights, Art. XXII
Assembly	Pa. Dec. of Rights, Art. XVI	N.C. Dec. of Rights, Art. XVIII Mass. Dec. of Rights, Art. XIX N.H. Bill of Rights, Art. XXXII
Petition	Pa. Dec. of Rights, Art. XVI	Del. Dec. of Rights, s. 9 Md. Dec. of Rights, Art. XI Mass. Dec. of Rights, Art. XIX N.H. Bill of Rights, Art. XXXII
Right to bear arms	Pa. Dec. of Rights, Art. XIII	N.C. Dec. of Rights, Art. XVII Vt. Dec. of Rights, Art. XV Mass. Dec. of Rights, Art. XVII
Quartering soldiers	Del. Dec. of Rights, s. 21	Md. Dec. of Rights, XXVIII Mass. Dec. of Rights, Art. XXVIII N.H. Bill of Rights, Art. XXVII

Bill of Rights Guarantees	First Constitutional Guaranty	Other Constitutional Guarantees
Searches and seizures	Va. Dec. of Rights, s. 10	Pa. Dec. of Rights, Art. IX Del. Dec. of Rights, s. 17 Md. Dec. of Rights, Art. XXIII N.C. Dec. of Rights, Art. X Vt. Dec. of Rights, Art. X Mass. Dec. of Rights, Art. XIV N.H. Bill of Rights, Art. XIX
Grand jury indictment	N.C. Dec. of Rights, Art. VIII	—
Double jeopardy	N.H. Bill of Rights Art. XVI	—
Self-incrimination	Va. Dec. of Rights, s. 8	Del. Dec. of Rights, s. 15 N.C. Dec. of Rights, Art. VII Vt. Dec. of Rights, Art. X Mass. Dec. of Rights, Art. XII N.H. Dec. of Rights, Art. XV
Due process	Va. Dec. of Rights, s. 8	Pa. Dec. of Rights, Art. IX N.C. Dec. of Rights, Art. XI Conn. Dec. of Rights, s. 2 N.Y. Const., Art. XIII Vt. Dec. of Rights, Art. X S.C. Const., Art. XLI Mass. Dec. of Rights, Art. XII N.H. Bill of Rights, Art. XV
Just compensation	Vt. Dec. of Rights, Art. II	Mass. Dec. of Rights, Art. X
Speedy trial	Va. Dec. of Rights, s. 8	Pa. Dec. of Rights, Art. IX Del. Dec. of Rights, s. 14 Md. Dec. of Rights, Art. XIX Vt. Dec. of Rights, Art. X
Public trial	Pa. Dec. of Rights, Art. IX	Vt. Dec. of Rights, Art. X
Jury trial	Va. Dec. of Rights, s. 8	N.J. Const. Art. XXII Pa. Dec. of Rights, Art. IX Del. Dec. of Rights, s. 14

Bill of Rights Guarantees	First Constitutional Guaranty	Other Constitutional Guarantees
		Md. Dec. of Rights, Art. XIX N.C. Dec. of Rights, Art. IX Ga. Const., Art. LXI N.Y. Const., Art. XLI Vt. Dec. of Rights, Art. X Mass. Dec. of Rights, Art. XII N.H. Bill of Rights, Art. XVI
Accusation	Va. Dec. of Rights, s. 8	Pa. Dec. of Rights, Art. IX Del. Dec. of Rights, s. 14 Md. Dec. of Rights, Art. XIX N.C. Dec. of Rights, Art. VII Vt. Dec. of Rights, Art. X Mass. Dec. of Rights, Art. XII N.H. Bill of Rights, Art. XV
Confrontation	Va. Dec. of Rights, s. 8	Pa. Dec. of Rights, Art. IX Del. Dec. of Rights, s. 14 Md. Dec. of Rights, Art. XIX N.C. Dec. of Rights, Art. VII Vt. Dec. of Rights, Art. X Mass. Dec. of Rights, Art. XII N.H. Bill of Rights, Art. XV
Witnesses	N.J. Const., Art. XVI	Pa. Dec. of Rights, Art. IX Del. Dec. of Rights, s. 14 Md. Dec. of Rights, Art. XIX Mass. Dec. of Rights, Art. XII N.H. Bill of Rights, Art. XV
Counsel	N.J. Const., Art. XVI	Pa. Dec. of Rights, Art. IX Del. Dec. of Rights, s. 14 Md. Dec. of Rights, Art. XIX N.Y. Const., Art. XXXIV Vt. Dec. of Rights, Art. X Mass. Dec. of Rights, Art. XII N.H. Bill of Rights, Art. XV
Jury trial (civil)	Va. Dec. of Rights, s. 11	Pa. Dec. of Rights, Art. XI N.C. Dec. of Rights, Art. XIV Vt. Dec. of Rights, Art. XIII Mass. Dec. of Rights, Art. XV N.H. Bill of Rights, Art. XX

Bill of Rights Guarantees	First Constitutional Guaranty	Other Constitutional Guarantees
Bail	Va. Dec. of Rights, s. 9	Pa. Const., s. 29 Del. Dec. of Rights, s. 16 Md. Dec. of Rights, Art. XXII N.C. Dec. of Rights, Art. X Conn. Dec. of Rights, s. 2 Ga. Const., Art. LIX Mass. Dec. of Rights, Art. XXVI N.H. Bill of Rights, Art. XXXIII
Fines	Va. Dec. of Rights, s. 9	Pa. Const. s. 29 Del. Dec. of Rights, s. 16 Md. Dec. of Rights, Art. XXII N.C. Dec. of Rights, Art. X Ga. Const., Art. LIX Mass. Dec. of Rights, Art. XXVI N.H. Dec. of Rights, Art. XXXIII
Punishment	Va. Dec. of Rights, s. 9	Del. Dec. of Rights, s. 16 Md. Dec. of Rights, Art. XXII N.C. Dec. of Rights, Art. X S.C. Const., Art. XL Mass. Dec. of Rights, Art. XXVI N.H. Bill of Rights, XXXIII
Reserved powers	Mass. Dec. of Rights, Art. IV	—

religion was protected in all of the Revolutionary constitutions and bills of rights (except for the rudimentary Connecticut Declaration of Rights). Trial by jury was guaranteed in eleven of the state organic instruments; freedom of the press in ten; due process and bail in nine. The right against searches and seizures, as well as those of criminal defendants, were also protected in all the state bills of rights.

Other basic rights particularly dear to Madison were not widely protected—notably the prohibition against establishment of religion, freedom of speech, and the right against double jeopardy. Yet they had been elevated to the constitutional plane in one or two states and this paved the way for Madison's inclusion of them in the Federal Bill of Rights.

If we compare the later with the earlier state bills of rights, we do not find real improvement insofar as the rights to be protected are concerned. George Mason was most discerning in his list of fundamental rights. Except for assembly and petition, counsel, and double jeopardy, the Virginia Declaration of Rights includes all the important rights safeguarded in the last of the Revolutionary bills of rights, that of New Hampshire. That a planter without legal training could draw up so complete an inventory of rights as the Virginia Declaration of Rights tells a great deal about the intellectual skills of the Founding Fathers.

In one respect, nevertheless, Mason's lack of legal training was unfortunate. The Virginia Declaration of Rights has the defect of being written in terms of admonition, not legal command. Most of its provisions state the different rights protected and then go on to provide that they "ought not" to be abridged. Not once is there a "shall not"—which, in legal terms, imposes an unmistakable mandatory restriction that the courts can then enforce.[94]

The Mason precedent was followed in the Pennsylvania, Delaware, Maryland, North Carolina, and Vermont Declarations of Rights. Then came the Massachusetts Declaration of Rights, drafted by one of the best lawyers of the day, John Adams. He took the important step of substituting "shall" for "ought" in most of the important provisions—those dealing with free exercise, just compensation, rights of criminal defendants, due process and bail, fines, and punishments. Adams did not eliminate the admonitory aspect entirely; "ought" is retained in several provisions—those dealing with warrants, freedom of the press, and quartering of soldiers. Still, the essential step of substituting imperative for admonitory language had been taken. It only remained for Madison to complete the process by using the imperative "shall" and "shall not" in almost all of the proposed amendments drafted by him.

four
confederation and constitution

JUDICIAL REVIEW

In a 1768 *Dialogue between Europe and America,* published only in 1975, Thomas Hutchinson made the argument that the doctrine of unconstitutionality could not really support the colonists' claims. There was no "umpire or judge" provided under the British Constitution to determine when government had exceeded its authority. The courts had not been given that power; they were part of the law enforcement machinery, not a check upon it. The consequence was that "every man's own conscience must be the judge, and he must follow the evidence of truth in his own mind, and submit or not accordingly." If put into practice, this policy would make of the constitution, he asserted, but "a mere rope of sand." [1]

Bernard Bailyn saw in this argument the intellectual underpinnings of the thought processes by which the American polity would finally come to view judicial review as the ultimate stage in its constitutional evolution. He reasoned that continued colonial opposition based on claims of unconstitutionality against particular governmental acts would lead the colonists to a view of constitutions as fixed, ultimately written documents that would, in turn, lead them to view favorably the empowering of governmental organs with the right to rule on questions of constitutionality. [2] This is, of course, what eventually happened. As seen in the last chapter, the revolutionary period saw the adoption of written constitutions and bills of rights. The next step would be the development of the doctrine of judicial review.

To us today, judicial review is the sine qua non of an effective constitution or bill of rights. Looking back, we tend to think that those who drafted the first American constitutions and bills of rights also felt as we do now about judicial enforcement. From this point of view, judicial review was the inarticulate major premise upon which the Revolutionary constitutional development had been based. Such a view of the Revolutionary period's position on judicial review is, however, unduly simplistic. It is true that the doctrine of unconstitutionality had been asserted by Americans even prior to the first written constitutions; that the inviolability of fundamental law had been at the heart of the argument put forth as the source of colonial rights during the very first stages of the conflict with the mother country. Thus, it was only a small though significant step that the states took when the time came for them to set up their own governments to translate these inviolable precepts of fundamental law into specific provisions written out in constitutions and bills of rights.

But few had carried the problem further, and there was certainly no general consensus of opinion on how the new constitutional provisions were to be enforced and by whom. According to Gordon Wood, the task of the 1780's for the newly organized Americans would be: "To bring their abiding belief in the intrinsic equitableness of all law into harmony with their commitment to legislative supremacy, without doing violence to either." [3] Most Americans at the time of Independence were still adherents of the notion of legislative primacy—with the other branches subordinate to the Jeffersonian concept of "the supreme legislative power." [4] Thus, at the outset, the people were hardly disposed to the idea of empowering the courts with the authority to set aside the law made by the representatives of the people. Madison noted that the investing of the courts with such powers "makes the Judiciary Department paramount in fact to the

Legislature, which was never intended and can never be proper." [5] "If the law is wrong," declared a 1786 newspaper, "the Legislator only can alter it." [6]

But the concept of the constitution as translated precepts of fundamental law was by itself not enough of a check on the legislative will. If the constitution was to be superior in authority to any particular legislature, some other sanction was also needed besides the people's inherent right of resistance. Otherwise, as the radicals in the 1776 convention that drew up the Pennsylvania Constitution put it, "they thereby should have made the legislature their own carvers, and in a convenient time had them as independent, nay indeed, as absolute masters of the lives and fortunes of their constituents in Pennsylvania as they now are in Great-Britain." [7]

The struggle with Britain had demonstrated to the Americans that rights not specified and codified in constitutional documents were hopelessly insecure.[8] But now it came to be recognized that specification of rights in written constitutions brought the nation only part of the way. "The truth is," said John Smilie of Pennsylvania, "that unless some criterion is established by which it could be easily and constitutionally ascertained how far our governors may proceed, and by which it might appear when they transgress their jurisdiction," the principles laid down in constitutions and bills of rights were "mere sound without substance." [9]

The American answer to the question of how constitutional provisions were to be enforced was, of course, ultimately, judicial review. That answer was first given during the period between the Revolution and the ratification of the Federal Constitution. By the end of the period, an increasing number of Americans accepted the view that laws might "be so unconstitutional as to justify the Judges in refusing to give them effect." [10] Oliver Ellsworth, later the third Chief Justice of the United States, was stating far from radical doctrine when he asserted in the 1788 Connecticut ratifying convention, "If the United States go beyond their powers, if they make a law which the Constitution does not authorize, it is void and the judicial power . . . will declare it to be void.[11]

FIRST REVIEW CASES

Between 1780 and 1787 cases in a number of states saw direct assertions of judicial power to rule on constitutionality. There has been some dispute about whether these cases really involved judicial review. Much of the difficulty in assessing their significance arises from the fact that no meaningful reporting of cases in the modern sense existed at the time these cases were heard and decided. Reported opinions were mainly skimpy or nonexistent. For most of these early cases, recourse has to be had to other materials (such as newspapers and pamphlets) rather than to law reports of the modern type.

The first of the pre-Constitution review cases was the 1780 New Jersey case of *Holmes v. Walton.*[12] A 1778 statute, aimed at traffic with the enemy, permitted trial by a six-man jury and provided for punishment by property seizures. The statute was attacked on the ground that it was "contrary to the constitution of New Jersey." The claim was upheld by the court, though the actual decision has been lost. From other materials, it appears that the decision was based on the unconstitutionality of the six-man jury.[13] Some recent commentators have attacked the conclusion that *Holmes v. Walton* set a precedent for judicial review.[14] It was, however, widely thought of as such at the time the Federal Constitution and Bill of Rights were adopted. Soon after the case was decided "a petition from sixty inhabitants of the county of Monmouth" was presented to the New Jersey Assembly. It complained that "the justices of the Supreme Court have set aside some of the laws as unconstitutional." [15] In 1785, Gouverneur Morris sent a message to the Pennsylvania legislature that mentioned that "a law was once passed in New Jersey, which the judges pronounced unconstitutional, and therefore void." [16] In addition, there is an 1802 case that states that in *Holmes v. Walton,* an "act upon solemn argument was adjudged to be unconstitutional and in that case inoperative." [17] At the least, these indicate that contemporaries did regard *Holmes v. Walton* as a precedent for judicial review.

The second case involving judicial review was *Commonwealth v. Caton*,[18] decided in 1782 by the Virginia Court of Appeals. It has been widely assumed, relying on the report of the case in Call's Virginia Reports, that *Caton* was the strongest early precedent for judicial review. The language in Call is, indeed, unequivocally clear: "the judges, were of opinion, that the court had power to declare any resolution or act of the legislature, or of either branch of it to be unconstitutional and void; and, that the resolution of the house of delegates, in this case, was inoperative, as the senate had not concurred in it." [19]

Call's report on *Caton* was not published until 1827; it was based upon the reporter's reconstruction of the case from surviving records, notes, and memoranda. There are significant differences between the Call report and the contemporary notes of Edmund Pendleton, who presided over the *Caton* court. According to Pendleton's account, only one of the eight judges ruled that the statute at issue was unconstitutional, though two others did assert judicial power to declare a law void for repugnancy to the constitution. The two judges in question were Chancellor George Wythe and Pendleton himself. Wythe, perhaps the leading jurist of the day,[20] delivered a ringing affirmation of review authority, declaring that, if a statute conflicted with the Constitution, "I shall not hesitate, sitting in this place, to say, to the general court, Fiat justitia, ruat coelum; and, to the usurping branch of the legislature, you attempt worse than a vain thing." [21] Pendleton also stated that the "awful question" of voiding a statute was one from which "I will not shrink, if ever it shall become my duty to decide it." [22]

The *Caton* Court did not exercise power to hold a law unconstitutional; the majority held "that the Treason Act was not at Variance with the Constitution but a proper exercise of the Power reserved to the Legislature by the latter." [23] Yet three judges did assert power in the courts to void statutes on constitutional grounds, including the two most prestigious members of the court. And it was Wythe's words, in particular, Pendleton's biographer tells us, that were "preserved in the court reports, and they were never forgotten by lawyers and students of government, by whom they were repeated again and again to men who would arrogate to themselves unconstitutional powers or seek to circumvent constitutional limitations." [24]

The most noted [25] of the pre-Constitution review cases was the 1784 New York case of *Rutgers v. Waddington.*[26] It was noted in its day because of Alexander Hamilton's argument for the defendant and because the court's opinion, published at the time, made a considerable stir. It is the best documented of these early cases. Strictly speaking, *Rutgers v. Waddington* did not involve a review of constitutionality, but only judicial power to annul a state statute contrary to a treaty and the law of nations. The statute in question provided for a trespass action against those who had occupied property during the British occupation of New York and barred defendants from any defense based on the following of military orders. Waddington was a British merchant who had occupied Mrs. Rutgers's abandoned property under license of the Commander-in-Chief of the British army of occupation. Hamilton argued that the statutory bar was in conflict both with the law of nations (since defendant had occupied the premises under British authority and thus derived the right of the military occupier over abandoned property sanctioned by the law of war) and the peace treaty with Britain. The court agreed that the statute could not override a treaty or international law and refused to apply it to the extent that there was any conflict. Whether or not *Rutgers v. Waddington* may be regarded as a precedent for judicial review, its lesson was not lost on the Framers' Convention: by the Supremacy Clause state judges were directed to set aside state laws that conflicted with treaties.[27]

The next case involving judicial review was the 1786 Rhode Island case of *Trevett v. Weeden.* That case, too, was unreported, but it was widely known through a 1787 pamphlet published by James M. Varnum (better known as one of Washington's generals), who argued the case against the statute.[28] Varnum's argument received wide dissemination and demonstrated the unconstitutionality of a legislative attempt to deprive Weeden of his right to trial by jury. Weeden, a butcher, was prosecuted under a statute making it an offense to refuse to accept paper money of the state in payment for articles offered for sale, in this case, meats. Appearing for the defense Varnum resorted to the modern distinction between the constitution and ordinary statute law,[29] arguing that the principles of the constitution were superior because they "were ordained by the people anterior to and created the powers of the General Assembly." It was the duty of the courts to measure laws of the legislature against the constitution. The judiciary's task was to "reject all acts of the Legislature that are contrary to the trust reposed in them by the people."[30]

That the Rhode Island judges agreed with Varnum is shown by the following brief newspaper account: "The court adjourned to next morning, upon opening of which, Judge Howell, in a firm, sensible, and judicious speech, assigned the reasons which induced him to be of the opinion that the information was not cognizable by the court, declared himself independent as a judge, the penal law to be repugnant and unconstitutional, and therefore gave it as his opinion that the court could not take cognizance of the information! Judge Devoe was of the same opinion. Judge Tillinghast took notice of the striking repugnancy of the expressions of the act . . . and on that ground gave his judgment the same way. Judge Hazard voted against taking cognizance. The Chief Justice declared the judgment of the court without giving his own opinion."[31]

The clearest pre-Constitution case involving review power was the 1787 North Carolina case of *Bayard v. Singleton*.[32] The contemporary account in the North Carolina Reports shows that the judges there realized the implications of what they were doing when they held that a statute contrary to the guaranty of trial by jury in cases involving property in the North Carolina Declaration of Rights "must of course . . . stand as abrogated and without any effect." No legislative "Act could by any means repeal or alter the Constitution" so long as the constitution remains "standing in full force as the fundamental law of the land." [33]

James Iredell, later a Justice of the Supreme Court, had been attorney for the plaintiff in *Bayard v. Singleton*. While attending the Framers' Convention, Richard Dobbs Spaight wrote Iredell condemning the *Bayard* decision as a "usurpation," which "operated as an absolute negative on the proceedings of the Legislature, which no judiciary ought ever to possess." Iredell replied that "it has ever been my opinion, that an act inconsistent with the Constitution was void; and that the judges, consistently with their duties could not carry it into effect." Far from a "usurpation," the power to declare unconstitutional laws void flowed directly from the judicial duty of applying the law: "either . . . the *fundamental unrepealable* law must be obeyed, by the rejection of an act unwarranted by and inconsistent with it, or you must obey an act founded on authority not given by the people." The exercise of review power, said Iredell was unavoidable. "It is not that the judges are appointed arbiters . . . ; but when an act is necessarily brought in judgment before them, they must, unavoidably, determine one way or another. . . . Must not they say whether they will obey the Constitution or an act inconsistent with it?" [34]

The last review experience prior to ratification of the Federal Constitution did not occur in a litigated case, but on the motion of the court itself, in the 1788 Virginia *Cases of the Judges of the Court of Appeals*.[35] The state legislature had enacted a statute imposing new tasks on the judges of the Court of Appeals without additional compensation. The judges refused to put the statute into operation and prepared a Remonstrance to the legislature, arguing that the law was contrary to the independence of the judiciary provided in the Virginia Constitution. The Remonstrance, "declaring the supremacy of the constitution," asserted that the judges were "obliged to decide, however their delicacy might be wounded, or whatever temporary inconveniences might ensue, and in that decision to declare, that the constitution and the act are in opposition and cannot exist together; and that the former must control the operation of the latter." To the claim that this marked a usurpation of power, the judges answered "that when they decide between an act of the people, and an act of the legislature, they are within the line of their duty, declaring what the law is, and not making a new law" [36]—anticipating the reasoning of Marshall a decade and a half later in *Marbury v. Madison*. [37]

ARTICLES OF CONFEDERATION

The Revolutionary period had witnessed the fruition of the bill of rights concept. By the time Independence was secured, the important rights of the individual were expressly guaranteed in the state constitutions and bills of rights. The first instrument of union for the new nation, on the other hand, was practically bare of protections for individual rights. The Articles of Confederation contain only the provision in Article IV guaranteeing "the free inhabitants of each of these States . . . all privileges and immunities of free citizens in the several states" (the forerunner of the Privileges and Immunities Clause of Article IV of the Federal Constitution), free ingress and egress to and from the states for their citizens, as well as reciprocal privileges of trade and commerce. The Articles are completely silent on the great rights of freedom of religion, freedom of expression, and all the other fundamental rights safeguarded in the different state bills of rights and constitutions.

The omission in the Articles of Confederation of these protections is explained by the limited powers of the new national government. The whole subject of individual rights was left entirely within state competence. This was made categorically clear by Article II of the Articles, which provided, "Each State retains . . . every power, jurisdiction, and right, which is not by this confederation expressly delegated to the United States." This was, of course, the direct precursor of the Tenth Amendment, being closer to that Amendment than the comparable Massachusetts provision mentioned in the last chapter—and earlier than the latter, since the Articles were agreed to by Congress in 1777, though not approved by the states until 1781.

There was to be no need for a national bill of rights until 1789 when the Confederation government was replaced by the federal government. When the Federal Constitution was written, it, like the Articles, did not contain any bill of rights. This time, however, the omission of specific protections for individual liberties did not commend itself to the people. The concentration of power in the new national government led to increasing agitation for express guarantees against infringements upon individual rights. The outcome was the Federal Bill of Rights as an indispensable adjunct of the new fundamental law.

NORTHWEST ORDINANCE

Although the Articles of Confederation did not contain a bill of rights or, indeed, any other provisions guaranteeing fundamental individual rights—except for the minor exceptions already mentioned—the first federal government was not wholly inactive in protecting these liberties. While the Congress had no power in the matter within the several states, the same was not true of the vast territories that came within congressional jurisdiction upon the cession of state claims. The congressional attempt to provide for the government of those territories resulted in the Northwest Ordinance of 1787—the greatest legislative achievement of the Confederation. The Northwest Ordinance contained the first bill of rights enacted by the national government.

The inclusion of broad guarantees of individual rights came comparatively late in the legislative history of the ordinance. The original plan of government for the Northwest Territory, prepared by Jefferson and introduced in 1784, contained no provisions securing personal liberties (though it did abolish slavery after 1800, anticipating the absolute abolition provided in the 1787 ordinance). Jefferson's ordinance was passed, minus its abolition provision, but never went into effect. An ordinance of 1785 called for surveying of the Territory. In the meantime, congressional committees were continuing to consider additional plans for governing the Northwest. In September, 1786, for the first time, a provision was added to the proposed ordinance to protect certain personal rights, providing a guaranty of habeas corpus and trial by jury. The committee's recommendation was embodied in a bill introduced in Congress on May 10, 1787, but the proposed ordinance did not receive the necessary votes.[38]

In the meantime, a committee prepared a new draft ordinance, which was introduced on July 11. This draft [39] marked a substantial step forward from the May 10 version, as far as individual liberties were concerned. It was passed by Congress on July 13, substantially as it was recommended by the committee. There were two changes of importance made during congressional debate. The first was the addition of the most famous provision of the ordinance, that in Article VI prohibiting slavery. The other was the deletion of a phrase "extending *to all parts of the Confederacy* the fundamental principles of civil and religious liberty." [40] We do not have records of the debates that led to the deletion, so we do not know the purposes intended by its supporters. Could it have been intended to make the enactment a true federal bill of rights extending to all parts of the nation? If so, upon what constitutional theory could the provision have been based (bearing in mind the limited powers of the Confederation Congress)?

The Northwest Ordinance as enacted contains a virtual bill of rights "as articles of compact between the original States and the people," which shall "forever remain unalterable, unless by common consent." The rights protected are stated to be "the fundamental principles of civil and religious liberty." The guarantees in this respect were modeled upon the state bills of rights. According to their principal draftsman, Nathan Dane, in an 1830 letter, "The Ordinance of '87 was framed mainly from the laws of Massachusetts." [41] As such the rights guaranteed by the ordinance are the traditional ones covered in the Revolutionary declarations of rights:

freedom of religion, habeas corpus, trial by jury, bail, moderate fines, prohibition of cruel and unusual punishments, deprivation of liberty or property "but by the judgment of his peers, or the law of the land," taking of property without "full compensation," as well as a new prohibition against laws that "interfere with or affect contracts"—the direct precursor of the Contract Clause in Article I, section 10 of the Federal Constitution. In addition, there is a guaranty of republican form of government, which anticipates that in Article IV of the Federal Constitution.

CONSTITUTIONAL CONVENTION

By 1787, the stage was set for a Federal Bill of Rights. By that date, most of the states had adopted bills of rights and their provisions provided a consensus of the fundamental rights to be protected by American constitutions: as already stressed, every one of the important provisions of the Federal Bill of Rights was derived from earlier state declarations of rights. In addition, the decade before the Federal Constitution had seen the first assertions by state courts of judicial review power. Despite these developments, the Federal Constitution in its first public appearance did not contain a bill of rights. How can we explain the Framers' inaction in the matter?

The answer is to be found in the basic goal of the Philadelphia Convention. The convention had been called to remedy the weaknesses of the pre-Constitution government. The Articles of Confederation had provided for a government without power to tax, to raise troops, to regulate commerce, or to execute or enforce its own laws or treaties. The sword and the purse—the two essentials of an effective polity—remained entirely outside the realm of national power. Well might George Washington declare, in 1785, that "the confederation appears to be little more than a shadow without the substance; and congress a nugatory body, their ordinances being little attended to." [42]

The men who came to Philadelphia in the sultry summer of 1787 had the overriding aim of making such alterations in the constitutional structure as would, in the words of the Confederation Congress calling the convention, "render the Federal Constitution adequate to the exigencies of Government." [43] The delegates directed their energies almost entirely to that end: the new Constitution was concerned, not with rights, but with functions and interests.[44] Virtually all the drafting and discussion by the men who burned midnight candles in Philadelphia focused on giving the new federal government the powers it would need to govern effectively.

The proceedings of the Constitutional Convention show that a motion was actually made on September 12 to appoint "a Committee to prepare a Bill of Rights." [45] The stimulus for the motion was provided by George Mason during a debate on trial by jury. The author of the Virginia Declaration of Rights expressed the wish that "the plan had been prefaced with a Bill of Rights and would second a motion made for the purpose." The motion to set up a committee was made by Elbridge Gerry, but with the states voting as units it was defeated unanimously. Mason had asserted that "with the aid of the State declarations, a bill might be prepared in a few hours" [46]—indicating the existence of a contemporary consensus on the fundamental rights that would be protected.

The fact that the Mason proposal for a bill of rights was made so close to the end of the convention (which finally adjourned on September 17) certainly influenced the delegates' almost summary rejection. Having sweltered for months over the difficult issues involved in the new Constitution during Philadelphia's hottest summer within memory, they naturally resented the attempt to bring up an important new subject when they were almost at the end of their endeavors. On the merits, Roger Sherman, the one delegate to speak on the matter, stated the view that was later to be expressed to justify the omission of a bill of rights: that a Federal Bill of Rights was unnecessary: "The State Declarations of Rights are not repealed by this Constitution; and being in force are sufficient" [47] to protect the rights of their citizens. The new federal government was not given any power to infringe upon the rights thus protected.

In addition to Mason's proposal, other attempts were made at the Framers' Convention to protect specific rights later to be included in the Bill of Rights, notably in an August 20 proposal by Charles Pinckney to guarantee liberty of the press and freedom from quartering of troops, as well as supremacy of civil over military power,[48] and a motion on September 14 by Pinckney and Gerry for a declaration "that the liberty of the Press should be inviolably observed," which was defeated after Sherman had repeated the argument that the guaranty was unnecessary, since the "power of Congress does not extend to the Press." [49]

It should, however, be borne in mind that though the Constitution drafted in 1787 did not contain any bill of rights, it did contain provisions protecting individual liberties, which would normally be contained in a bill of rights. These include the guarantees of habeas corpus (the provision authorizing suspension of the writ has uniformly been interpreted as guaranteeing habeas corpus in the absence of suspension), trial by jury in criminal cases, the privileges and immunities of state citizens, and the prohibitions against bills of attainder, ex post facto laws, and religious tests. These guarantees would doubtless have been included in the Federal Bill of Rights, had they not already been contained in the text of the Constitution.

After the Philadelphia Convention, a further attempt to secure a Federal Bill of Rights was made in the Continental Congress. Richard Henry Lee moved that Congress amend the proposed Constitution by adding to it a bill of rights before it was submitted for ratification to the states. Congress rejected Lee's motion and instead passed a resolution approving the ratification procedure recommended by the Philadelphia Convention.[50]

GEORGE MASON'S OBJECTIONS

No sooner had the Confederation Congress submitted the Constitution for ratification than a great debate arose over its failure to contain a bill of rights. Both the Federalists (as the pro-Constitution party came to be called) and the Antifederalists (the popular name for those opposing the Constitution) flooded the public with articles, pamphlets, addresses, and letters explaining the advantages and defects of the new organic law. Much of the writing on the matter focused upon the bill of rights issue. The Antifederalists strongly criticized the absence of a bill of rights, asserting that without one, the Constitution was not an adequate protection of individual rights and liberties. The Federalists, for their part, defensively attempted to shore up with additional arguments their original position that a bill of rights was unnecessary. In fact, the fury of the popular debate was a consequence of its suppression at the convention and thus was first fueled with the arguments of men like George Mason whose *Objections to the Constitution* was written on September 13, or soon thereafter,[51] on the blank pages of his copy of the report of the "Committee on stile and arrangement."

Having been rebuffed by the convention in his attempt to preface the Constitution with a bill of rights, Mason, naturally, begins his *Objections* by the assertion, "There is no Declaration of Rights," and, since federal laws are made supreme, "the Declarations of Rights, in the separate States, are no security." After going over his other objections to the new system, he comes back to the bill of rights issue: "There is no declaration of any kind, for preserving the liberty of the press, or the trial by jury in civil causes; nor against the danger of standing armies in time of peace." [52]

Mason had intended to offer his *Objections* "by Way of Protest" in the Convention itself; consequently, the *Objections* gives every impression of being a first reaction rather than the final comments of a man who had had time to work out his criticisms in detail. Prevented from offering it at the convention "by the precipitate, & intemperate, not to say indecent Manner in which the Business was conducted" at the convention's end,[53] Mason disseminated it publicly.[54] Despite its unpolished nature, it was read widely. The reputation of the author, particularly as the draftsman of the

Virginia Declaration of Rights, ensured a broad popular response to this initial cry for a federal bill of rights.

The Federalists could not leave Mason's attack unanswered. The three best-known answers were written by leading lawyers, who were later to be appointed to the Supreme Court. The first was the *Address* by James Wilson, felt by many to possess perhaps the best legal mind of those at the Constitutional Convention. On October 6, Wilson delivered his speech to a rally in Philadelphia. His talk was hailed by Federalists everywhere, but few recognized it as a refutation of Mason's remarks, since it did not deal specifically with Mason by name.[55] Wilson's address, published in pamphlet form, was widely circulated and set the theme for the principal Federalist defense on the bill of rights issue (later given definitive form by Hamilton in *The Federalist*), namely, that there existed a distinction between delegated and reserved powers. Whatever power is not given to the federal government is reserved: and this "will furnish an answer to those who think the omission of a bill of rights, a defect in the proposed constitution." The Congress has no power to interfere with a liberty like freedom of the press. Hence, explicit protection of such a right is unnecessary; "it would have been superfluous and absurd, to have stipulated with a federal body of our own creation, that we should enjoy those privileges, of which we are not divested either by the intention or the act that has brought that body into existence." [56] Wilson was to repeat this argument in the Pennsylvania Ratifying Convention, and it was to become the standard Federalist answer on the bill of rights issue.

The letters of "A Landholder" were published in a Connecticut newspaper by Oliver Ellsworth. Ellsworth devoted his letter of December 10, 1787, to answering Mason's *Objections*. In the American system, said Ellsworth, bills of rights "are insignificant since . . . all the power government now has is a grant from the people." The Constitution itself limits and defines powers and thus "becomes now to the legislator and magistrate, what originally a bill of rights was to the people." It is not necessary for the Constitution to contain any declaration to preserve liberty of the press, "Nor . . . liberty of conscience, or of matrimony, or of burial of the dead." [57] Congress has no power to prohibit any of these and therefore no provision specifically protecting them is necessary.

The same theme was repeated early in 1788 in a pamphlet by James Iredell, who dealt with the Mason objections *seriatim*, starting with the omission of a bill of rights. Iredell declared that a bill of rights was not necessary in a system where the Constitution delegates only the powers enumerated in it, so that the government may not act beyond those powers: "to say that they shall exercise no other powers . . . would seem to me both nugatory and ridiculous. As well might a Judge when he condemns a man to be hanged, give strong injunctions to the Sheriff that he should not be beheaded." [58]

Wilson, Iredell, and Ellsworth stated what would become the standard Federalist answer to the demand for a bill of rights—to be repeated in classic terms in *The Federalist*—that a bill of rights was unnecessary, since the Constitution did not give the federal government any power over individual rights and liberties. As the debate went on, however, the Federalist answer would become increasingly less persuasive. In the end the Federalists were not merely to yield to popular pressure, but to concede the point itself, joining in the call for these amendments to protect fundamental rights against the powers of the new national government-to-be.

OTHER ANTIFEDERALIST WRITINGS

Aside from Mason's *Objections*, the next most influential of the Antifederalist writings upon the new Constitution were those by Richard Henry Lee and Luther Martin. Because of the arguments of these men, the bill of rights issue soon overtook all others as the leading concern of those opposed to ratification of the proposed Constitution. "No Bill of Rights" became the Antifederalist chant; and so firmly and frequently was it cried that soon the issue would become not one of yes or no but rather when—as a condition of ratification or a later addition to an already functioning Constitution.

Richard Henry Lee's *Letters from the Federal Farmer* was perhaps the most effective of the longer arguments against the Constitution. As a member of the Confederation Congress, Lee had been one of the leaders of the struggle for a bill of rights within that body. He had sought unsuccessfully to have a bill of rights added to the Constitution before it was released to the states for ratification. In his *Farmer* letters, Lee repeated the call for a bill of rights. Letter II deals directly with the bill of rights issue. There are, Lee insists, "certain unalienable and fundamental rights which . . . should be made the basis of every constitution . . . I still believe a complete federal bill of rights to be very practicable." In Letter IV, he rejects the notion that in the absence of express limitations all powers not delegated are reserved in the people. The Constitution does contain a partial bill of rights in Article I, sections 9 and 10. This bill of rights ought to be carried further and other essential rights established as part of the fundamental compact. Then he discusses what would soon become apparent as the core of the controversy between the Federalists and Antifederalists: the question of how to secure the necessary amendments. He characterizes the idea of adopting the Constitution and obtaining later amendments as "a pernicious idea, it argues a servility of character totally unfit for the support of free government." He continues this theme in Letter V, urging the states "to direct their energies to altering and amending the system proposed before they shall adopt it." [59]

Luther Martin was one of the leading lawyers of the day. A dissenting member of the Constitutional Convention, he led the forces in opposition to ratification in his home state of Maryland. Martin's views on the matter were made public in letters published in the *Maryland Journal*. Letter Number II was a reply to one of *The Landholder* letters of Oliver Ellsworth, which had attacked Martin on the bill of rights issue, saying, "You sir, had more candour in the Convention . . .

there you never signified by any motion or expression whatever, that it stood in need of a bill of rights, or in any wise endangered the trial by jury." [60] Martin answers by asserting that his silence did not prove "that I approved the system in those respects." He states that he became convinced of the need for "a complete bill of rights . . . prefixed to the Constitution, to serve as a barrier between the general government and the respective states and their citizens." [61] Martin says he actually drafted a bill of rights before he left the Convention. He did not introduce it because he was persuaded it would be a vain gesture. This was uncharacteristic of Martin, but perhaps true in view of the cold reception of the Mason-Gerry motion for a bill of rights. In Letter Number III, Martin rejects the argument that the Constitution be adopted now, since subsequent amendments could always be secured: "why, I pray you, my fellow citizens, should we not insist upon the necessary amendments being made now . . .?" [62] Thus, Martin, like Lee, joins issue on the soon to be dominant issue—that of previous versus subsequent amendments.

Yet a third influential Antifederalist was James Winthrop. "It is a mere fallacy," declared Winthrop in his *Letters of Agrippa*, "invented by the deceptive powers of Mr. Wilson, that what rights are not given are reserved." [63] This Antifederalist argument was the direct source of the Tenth Amendment—showing that most Americans of that day did not agree with the Supreme Court's later statement that it is "a truism that all is retained which has not been surrendered." [64] On the contrary, as the *Letters of Brutus* in Massachusetts put it, "The powers, rights and authority, granted to the general government by this Constitution, are as complete . . . as that of any State government—it reaches to every thing which concerns human happiness. . . . all the powers which the bills of rights guard against the abuse of, are contained or implied in the general ones granted by this Constitution." [65]

The Antifederalists did not direct their criticisms only to the general need for a federal bill of rights; they discussed the adoption of specific amendments limiting national power and even began the process of proposing their wording. These criticisms, as we shall see in the next chapter, were to culminate in the amendments recommended by the state ratifying conventions. Illustrative of this process were the proposals in Winthrop's *Agrippa Letters.*

Winthrop emphasized the need for amendments and the ones proposed by him bear some resemblance to those conceded by the Federalists and introduced by Hancock in the Massachusetts convention.[66] This tends to bear out what, to the present-day observer, may be Winthrop's most important point, that his amendments "shew how nearly those who are for admitting the system with the necessary alterations, agree with those who are for rejecting this system and amending the confederation." [67] However far apart they might have been at the beginning, as the ratification struggle went on the leading Federalists joined their opponents in recognizing the need for a bill of rights. It was the Federalist concession on this that secured the votes for ratification in doubtful states—even where, as in New York, the Antifederalists had the Convention majority. Only the extremists in the Antifederalist ranks could cry till the end, with Robert Yates in his *Letters of Sydney,* that if the Constitution is "adopted we may (in imitation of the Carthagenians) say, *Delenda vit Americae.*" [68]

LEADING FEDERALIST WRITINGS

Historically, there is nothing as irrelevant as a lost constitutional cause, particularly one that was lost centuries ago. We tend today to ignore those arguments of the Antifederalists against ratification (with or without a bill of rights) and concentrate instead on what we consider the statesmanlike essays of their opponents; it is hard for us to find merit in a political view we consider so plainly wrong as that of opposition to the Constitution. The same should not, however, be true of the controversy over the absence of a bill of rights. Here, the Antifederalists had the stronger case and their opponents were on the defensive from the beginning. It was, indeed, not until the Federalists yielded in their rigid opposition to a bill of rights that ratification of the Constitution was assured.

On the bill of rights issue, it is the Antifederalist writings that are the more interesting and even the more influential. That is why more emphasis has been devoted to the Antifederalist attacks upon the absence of a bill of rights than to the Federalist defenses of the Constitution on that issue. Of the latter the most important was the already-discussed *Address* by James Wilson.[69] Of the other Federalist writers, the ones who had the most popular impact were Roger Sherman and John Dickinson, both leaders in the struggle for Independence, the Confederation Congress, and the Philadelphia Convention. It had been Sherman who alone had expressed opposition to the Mason effort to add a bill of rights to the Constitution and his *Letters of a Countryman*, published in November, 1787, repeated his opposition. Once again, he argued that the federal government was given no power to infringe upon individual rights: "If the members of Congress can take no improper step . . . , we need not apprehend that they will usurp authorities not given them." [70] Dickinson had particular weight as the author of the Revolutionary *Letters of a Pennsylvania Farmer*. His 1788 *Letters of Fabius* emphasized the limited powers delegated by the Constitution: "Our government under the proposed confederation, will be guarded by a repetition of the strongest cautions against excesses." As one trained in English law, Dickinson also stressed that liberty could not really be secured by written guarantees such as those in "a bill of rights, or any characters drawn upon paper or parchment, those frail remembrances." [71]

Other Federalist writers were of importance in the ratification contests in the different states, notably James Sullivan of Massachusetts, Alexander Contee Hanson of Maryland, and Hugh Williamson of North Carolina.[72] They repeated the basic theme that the new government had not been given any authority to tamper with the rights that would be further protected by a bill of rights: "Be pleased to examine the Plan, and you will find that the liberty of the press and the laws of Mahomet are equally affected by it. . . . The citizens of the United States have no more occasion for a second declaration of rights, than they have for a section in favour of the press." [73]

On the whole, however, their stand on the bill of rights issue was the weakest aspect of the Federalist's case. Had the Federalists persisted in their original position, ratification itself might have been defeated. The people simply refused to accept the assurances that a bill of rights was not necessary. In Chief Justice Earl Warren's later estimation, "our people wanted explicit assurances. The Bill of Rights was the result." [74]

The Federalists themselves soon recognized the need for compromise. The focus of the debate then shifted to the question of whether a bill of rights should be secured through prior or subsequent amendments. Here the Federalists were to have the better of the debate, for prior amendments could only be obtained through a second convention. In the later ratification debates, the insistence upon a second convention became the leading Antifederalist threat.

NEW YORK DEBATE

The most famous of the pamphlets and articles written during the ratification debate was, of course, *The Federalist*. Addressed to the people of New York, it contains what has become the best known of all the writings on the bill of rights issue: Alexander Hamilton's essay in No. 84. Here we have the definitive version of the standard Federalist answer to the claim that the new Constitution was defective because it lacked a bill of rights. Hamilton admits that one of the most considerable "objections is that the plan of the convention contains no bill of rights." To this, he answers that a bill of rights is unnecessary under a constitution such as that drafted at Philadelphia: ". . . here, in strictness, the people surrender nothing; and as they retain every thing they have no need of particular reservations." A bill of rights would even be dangerous, since it would contain exceptions to powers not granted and afford a basis for claiming more than was granted. "For why declare that things shall not be done which there is no power to do?"

In No. 85 of *The Federalist,* Hamilton deals with the issue of previous versus subsequent amendments. He takes up the Antifederalist claim that the Constitution should be perfected by amendments before it is irrevocably adopted. "It appears to me susceptible of absolute demonstration that it will be far more easy to obtain subsequent than previous amendments to the Constitution." The argument was aimed directly at the Antifederalists in New York, whose ultimate willingness to settle for a bill of rights through subsequent amendments enabled the New York Federalists to secure the votes needed for ratification.[75] It is probable, however, that *The Federalist* itself contributed little to that result. Nos. 84 and 85 appeared in book form on May 28, 1788, but were not printed in newspapers (except for a small part of 84) until after the New York Ratifying Convention had adjourned.[76] The Hamilton reasoning, though now accepted as the classic state paper on the matter, thus appeared in the popular press too late to influence the Convention for which it was written.

The same is not true of other papers written during the New York ratification debate, particularly those by two of the opposing leaders in the New York contest, John Jay (Federalist) and Melancton Smith (Antifederalist). They both wrote influential *Addresses* on ratification to the people of their state, which point up the arguments used on both sides in what would be the last of the important ratification contests. By this time, the issue was no longer one of whether there should be a bill of rights (though Jay lamely repeated the Federalist theme that a bill of rights was unnecessary) but one of how to accomplish the required guarantees for individual rights. Jay rejected the notion of a second convention to accomplish the needed changes. Let those who urge such a convention "reflect on the delays and risque to which it would expose us." [77] The main thing, said Jay, was to accept the present plan as the best available and work for amendments in the manner specified in the Constitution.

Smith, on the contrary, urged the people to make the prior inclusion of amendments a condition of ratification. He recognized that the Federalists themselves had already come to concede the need for amendments, and so warned the people against accepting their arrangement for amendments afterwards, "provided they will first agree to accept the proferred system as it is." He ridiculed the idea that those in power under the new system would consent to limitations upon their authority: "the idea of receiving a form radically defective, under the notion of making the necessary amendments, is evidently absurd." To the Federalists who now say "adopt it first, and then amend it. I ask, why not amend, and then adopt it?" [78] Smith added a postscript as a direct reply after the Jay *Address* was published. Much of it was devoted to the bill of rights issue and a rejection of the Federalist view that a bill of rights was not necessary. The views stated by Smith were to be repeated by his Antifederalist colleagues in the New York ratification debates, particularly on the need for previous amendments as a condition for ratification. In the end, however, Smith himself was one of the leaders who defected to the Federalists on the issue of previous versus subsequent amendments. [79] That alone, as it turned out, enabled New York to ratify the Constitution.

JEFFERSON-MADISON CORRESPONDENCE

Among the most influential writings in the movement to secure a federal bill of rights were letters written by Thomas Jefferson and James Madison to each other. The Jefferson-Madison correspondence was important for two reasons: 1) each influenced the other's thinking. This was especially true in the evolution of Madison's views on a bill of rights, with Jefferson's unfailing emphasis on the need for one converting Madison's original lukewarm attitude to one of warm support; and 2) the wide publicity given to some of the letters had great impact on the ratification debates. Jefferson's views were extensively used in the debates and his February, 1788, statement that nine states should ratify and four reject, until a bill of rights was added, was strongly relied upon by the Antifederalists who urged ratification conditioned upon previous amendments—even, as we shall see, after Jefferson modified his view in favor of the Massachusetts approach of ratification with recommendatory amendments.[80]

The Jefferson-Madison constitutional correspondence began with Madison's New York letter of October 24, 1787, in which he told Jefferson, then in Paris as Minister to France, about the result of the Philadelphia Convention. The letter started the exchange of views on the Constitution between the two men; it contains a masterful summary both of the work of the Convention and of the new Constitution. At its end Madison summarized the probable reception of the new document, with emphasis on those objecting to the Constitution, particularly George Mason, who "considers the want of a Bill of Rights as a fatal objection." [81]

Jefferson answered in his oft-quoted letter from Paris of December 20, where he stated his general approval of the Constitution, but went on: "I will now add what I do not like. First the omission of a bill of rights providing clearly and without the aid of sophisms" for essential freedoms; he names religion, press, habeas corpus, jury trial, among others. In a famous passage, he asserted "that a bill of rights is what the people are entitled to against every government on earth, general or particular, and what no government should refuse, or rest on inference." Jefferson specifically rejected the argument of James Wilson that a bill of rights was not necessary because the federal government had only the powers delegated to it as "surely gratis dictum, opposed by strong inferences from the body of the instrument, as well as from the omission of the clause of our present confederation which had declared that in express terms." [82]

Then, in his letter to Madison of February 6, 1788, Jefferson made his suggestion, already referred to, that nine states should accept and four reject the Constitution, as "the latter will oblige them to offer a declaration of rights in order to complete the union . . . . and cure its principal defect." [83] In a letter written a day later to Alexander Donald, Jefferson summarized the essentials of a bill of rights: "By a declaration of rights I mean one which shall stipulate freedom of religion, freedom of the press, freedom of commerce against monopolies, trial by juries in all cases, no suspensions of the habeas corpus, no standing armies. These are fetters against doing evil which no honest government should decline." [84]

In a letter of October 17, 1788, Madison indicated a shift toward the Jefferson view on the need for a bill of rights. Madison now stated that he did not fully accept the Wilson argument that all powers not granted were reserved: "My own opinion has always been in favor of a bill of rights," though "I have not viewed it in an important light." He feared that a bill of rights might not be effective; he called it a "parchment barrier." But he conceded that desirable ends might be served by a bill of rights. Should danger of "subversion of liberty . . . exist at all, it is prudent to guard against it, especially when the precaution can do no injury." In this letter, Madison came close to coming out in support of a bill of rights, if not "for any other reason that that it is anxiously desired by others." [85]

With his October 17 letter, Madison enclosed a pamphlet containing the proposed amendments recommended by the state ratifying conventions, starting with those of Massachusetts. This may well have induced Jefferson to come out in favor of the Massachusetts approach as the best practical method of obtaining both the Constitution and a bill of rights. In a March 13, 1789, letter to Francis Hopkinson, Jefferson explained how his first opinion in favor of rejection by four states changed "the moment I saw the much better plan of Massachusetts and which had never occurred to me." He stated firmly that "the majority of the United States are of my opinion," recognizing that after other states had followed the

Massachusetts approach not only the Antifederalists, but also "a very responsible proportion of the federalists think that such a declaration should now be annexed." [86]

On March 15, 1789, Jefferson, still in Paris, replied to Madison's October 17, 1788, assertion that a bill of rights would be ineffective. Jefferson stated that this was not true, for Madison failed to mention, in his arguments, "one which has great weight with me, the legal check which [a bill of rights] puts into the hands of the judiciary." An independent judiciary "merits great confidence," so far as enforcement of a bill of rights is concerned.[87] It may have been the Jefferson assertion on the matter that led Madison to declare, when he later presented his draft of the Bill of Rights to Congress, that the courts would enforce the limitations imposed in his proposed amendments.[88]

five
state ratifying conventions

RATIFICATION AND PROPOSED AMENDMENTS

In 1833, Chief Justice Marshall looked back at the movement to secure a federal bill of rights. Marshall had participated in that movement as a young delegate at the Virginia Ratifying Convention of 1788. Reflecting back to that time he noted: "But it is universally understood, it is a part of the history of the day, that the great revolution which established the Constitution of the United States was not effected without immense opposition. Serious fears were extensively entertained that those powers which the patriot statesmen who then watched over the interests of our country, deemed essential to union, and to the attainment of those invaluable objects for which union was sought, might be exercised in a manner dangerous to liberty. In almost every convention by which the Constitution was adopted, amendments to guard against the abuse of power were recommended. These amendments demanded security against the apprehended encroachments of the general government. . . . In compliance with a sentiment thus generally expressed, to quiet fears thus extensively entertained, amendments were proposed by the required majority in Congress, and adopted by the States." [1]

It was at the state ratifying conventions that the popular demand for a bill of rights found practical expression. In convention after convention, opposition to the new Constitution focused upon its failure to contain any bill of rights. In vain did the Federalist delegates repeat the Wilson-Hamilton theme that a bill of rights was unnecessary—even dangerous. The opposition and (so far as we can tell) the people remained adamant. So strong was the opposition that, for a time, it seemed that ratification might fail in both Virginia and New York, and without those states there could scarcely be an effective Union. At a crucial stage in the two key states, Hamilton could write to Madison, "I am very sorry . . . that your prospects are so critical. Our chance of success here is infinitely slender." The more he thought of it, he noted in yet another letter, "the more I dread the consequences of the non adoption of the Constitution . . . , the more I fear an eventual disunion and civil war." [2]

The gloomy forebodings remained just forebodings because the principal ratifying conventions were able to work out a compromise that secured both ratification and the adoption of a bill of rights in the form of amendments added to the Constitution. The Antifederalists urged that ratification not be voted on until the Constitution was amended to include a bill of rights. The Federalists did not yield on the demand for prior amendments. But they ultimately came to a compromise, first in Massachusetts and then in other states, to accept with the ratification instruments of the states proposed amendments for adoption as part of a federal bill of rights. The ratifying conventions of five states—Massachusetts, South Carolina, New Hampshire, Virginia, and New York—submitted proposed amendments with their instruments of ratification. The Virginia and New York amendments, in particular, contained detailed bills of rights to be added to the Constitution. Taken together, the amendments recommended by the state conventions contained provisions safeguarding all the rights protected by the Federal Bill of Rights (except the right to just compensation guaranteed in the Fifth Amendment).

The action of the ratifying conventions made the movement for a federal bill of rights all but irresistible. Indeed, ratification probably would not have been secured had the

Federalists not agreed to the recommendatory amendments. But it fell to the Federalists to make good on their promises when the first Congress under the Constitution convened. Speedy and calm deliberation and decision-making on this issue was more than a matter of keeping campaign promises. The New York Convention, soon after its instrument of ratification had been sent, sent a circular letter to the other states urging that they call a second constitutional convention to deal with the amendments proposed by the different states. Such a convention presented "The great danger . . . that if another Convention should be soon assembled it would terminate in discord, or in alterations of the federal system." [3] Along with Madison, the Federalists viewed "the prospect of a second Convention . . . as a dark and threatening Cloud hanging over the Constitution just established, and, perhaps over the Union itself." [4] When Madison gave notice in the House of Representatives on May 4, 1789, that he intended to bring up the subject of amendments to the Constitution within a few weeks, he acted to forestall applications from Virginia and New York for the calling of a second convention. Madison's action effectively ended the second convention movement. [5]

PENNSYLVANIA

The first state to ratify the Federal Constitution was Delaware, which acted by a unanimous vote on December 2, 1787. The second state to act was Pennsylvania, where the struggle between supporters and opponents of the Constitution was a closer one. The Antifederalists were claiming (in the words of a Federalist satire):

> That the convention in great fury,
> Hath taken away the trial by jury;
> That liberty of press is gone,
> We shall be hang'd each mothers son;
> Say Lord knows what, as comes in head,
> Pretences for a scare crow made. [6]

The Pennsylvania convention met from November 20 to December 12, 1787. The principal speeches in favor of the motion to ratify were delivered by James Wilson, who sought directly to answer the bill of rights argument of the Antifederalists. Wilson stated that the Framers' Convention had not even considered the addition of a bill of rights until the subject was mentioned a few days before adjournment— "such an idea never entered the mind of many of them" [7]— though he erred in saying no motion was even offered.[8] He repeated the standard argument against a bill of rights: that a bill of rights was both unnecessary, since the federal government was not given authority over individual rights, and dangerous, since it implied possession of such power by the federal government. "A proposition to adopt a measure that would have supposed that we were throwing into the general government every power not expressly reserved by the people, would have been spurned at . . . with the greatest indignation." Wilson turned around a common claim in favor of a bill of rights: What harm could its addition do? "If it can do no good, I think that a sufficient reason to refuse having any thing to do with it." [9]

The Antifederalists sought to answer Wilson on these points, for the lack of a bill of rights was one of their main issues throughout the convention debate. The principal Antifederalist speaker was Robert Whitehill. He emulated Wilson in seeking to turn around his opponents' argument: "Truly, Sir, I will agree that a bill of rights may be a dangerous instrument, but it is to the views and projects of the aspiring ruler, and not the liberties of the citizen." In the Constitution, he asserted, there is no adequate security for the liberties of the people. Since "it is the nature of power to seek its own augmentation, and thus the loss of liberty is the necessary consequence of a loose or extravagant delegation of authority," [10] a bill of rights was vital.

Acute lawyer that he was, Wilson then raised a shrewd legal objection to any action by the Pennsylvania convention on a federal bill of rights. "But to whom are we to report this bill of rights, if we should adopt it? Have we authority from those who sent us here to make one?" [11]

Legally speaking, of course, the Pennsylvania delegates had no authority to adopt any federal bill of rights or to give effect to any adoption by them. But they could recommend amendments containing guarantees for individual rights. Moreover, if their example were followed by the other ratifying states, it would be most difficult for the first Congress under the Constitution, which would have the authority to propose constitutional amendments, to ignore the combined recommendations.

The Antifederalists in the Pennsylvania convention acted on the view just stated. On December 12, 1787, Whitehill introduced fifteen proposed amendments for the convention to recommend as part of its ratification action. The convention rejected the proposed amendments by a vote of 46 to 23 and, later that day, ratified the Constitution itself by the same majority. The minority then issued "The Address and Reasons of Dissent of the Minority of the Convention." This gave wide dissemination to the proposed amendments, which were intended to meet the need for a federal bill of rights, "ascertaining and fundamentally establishing those unalienable and personal rights of men without the full, free and secure enjoyment of which there can be no liberty, and over which it is not necessary for a good government to have the control." [12]

The Pennsylvania-proposed amendments [13] provided that: (1) the right of conscience shall be held inviolable and shall not be infringed by the Federal Government; (2) in federal and state civil cases trial by jury shall remain as heretofore; (3) in criminal prosecutions a man has the right to demand the cause and nature of his accusation, to be heard by himself or counsel, to be confronted with the accusers and witnesses, to call for evidence in his favor, and a speedy trial by an impartial jury of the vicinage, nor can he be compelled to give evidence against himself, and no one can be deprived of liberty except by the law of the land or the judgment of his peers; (4) excessive bail ought not be be required nor excessive fines or cruel and unusual punishments imposed; (5) warrants unsupported by evidence or seizure of persons or property not particularly described shall not be granted; (6) the people have a right to freedom of speech, of writing and publishing their sentiments; therefore, freedom of the press shall not be restrained by any federal law; (7) the people have a right to bear arms, and no law shall be passed for disarming the people, standing armies ought not to be kept up in time of peace, and the military shall be subordinate to the civil power; (8) no federal law shall restrain liberty to fowl and hunt or fish except on private property; (9) no federal law shall restrain the legislatures of the states from imposing taxes, except imposts and duties on goods imported or exported, and no taxes except imposts and duties on goods imported and exported and postage on letters shall be levied by Congress; (10) the House of Representatives shall be increased in number, elections shall remain free, the states shall regulate elections without control by Congress, and the election of representatives shall be annual; (11) the power of organizing, arming and disciplining the militia shall remain with the states, and Congress shall not have authority to call or march the militia out of a state without the state's consent, and for such length of time only as the state shall agree; (12) legislative, executive, and judicial powers shall be kept separate, a constitutional council shall be appointed to advise and assist the President, and the judges be made completely independent; (13) no treaty opposed to existing federal laws shall be valid until such laws shall be repealed or made conformable to the treaty, nor shall treaties in contradiction to the Constitution of the United States or the constitutions of the states be valid; (14) federal judicial power shall be limited by eliminating "diversity of citizenship" jurisdiction, and be limited in criminal cases to such only as are expressly enumerated in the Constitution, and Congress shall not have power to alter the descent and distribution and title of lands or goods or the regulation of contracts in the states; and (15) state sovereignty, freedom and independence shall be retained, as well as every power, jurisdiction and right not expressly delegated to the United States.

The amendments proposed by the Pennsylvania convention minority pointed out a way for those states that desired to ratify the Constitution to express their equally strong interest in a federal bill of rights. Even the Federalist supporters of the Constitution, as we shall see in our discussion of the Massachusetts convention, came to recognize that the Pennsylvania minority had suggested a means of defusing opposition to ratification. The example set by the Pennsylvania minority was soon followed by the Massachusetts Ratifying Convention, and then by the ratifying conventions of four other states: South Carolina, New Hampshire, Virginia, and New York.

The amendments proposed by the Pennsylvania minority bear a direct relation to those ultimately adopted as the Federal Bill of Rights. Eight of the first ten amendments to the Constitution were first suggested as amendments in the proposals of the Pennsylvania minority. These include the following amendments eventually adopted: the First (freedom of conscience, speech, and press—Pennsylvania's proposed amendments 1 and 6); Second (Pennsylvania's proposed amendment 7); Fourth (Pennsylvania's proposed amendment 5); Fifth (privilege against self-incrimination and right not to be deprived of liberty "except by the law of the land or the judgment of his peers"—Pennsylvania's proposed amendment 3); Sixth (right to speedy and public jury trial, to accusation and confrontation, and counsel—Pennsylvania's proposed amendment 3); Seventh (Pennsylvania's proposed amendment 2); Eighth (Pennsylvania's proposed amendment 4); and Tenth (Pennsylvania's proposed amendment 15).

MASSACHUSETTS

New Jersey and Georgia speedily followed Pennsylvania in ratifying the Federal Constitution, each by unanimous votes, on December 18, 1787, and January 2, 1788, respectively. On

January 9, Connecticut ratified by a large majority. In none of the three ratifying conventions, so far as we know from the skimpy records available, was there an express attack upon the absence of a bill of rights. The same was not true in Massachusetts, the next state to ratify. Its convention was sharply divided between the Federalists and Antifederalists. In Madison's summary, "In Massachusetts the conflict was tedious and the event extremely doubtful." [14] It was only after a month of debate, much of it devoted to the bill of rights issue, that Massachusetts was able to vote ratification.

Massachusetts was the first state officially to adopt the method proposed by the Pennsylvania minority but turned down by that state's convention majority; that is, to attach to its ratificatory instrument proposed amendments that would be transmitted to Congress together with the state's ratification. It is not known whether the Massachusetts delegates were directly influenced by the Pennsylvania minority example. There is evidence that the Philadelphia newspapers containing the *Address* of the Pennsylvania minority did not reach Boston until after the Massachusetts Ratifying Convention adjourned. Antifederalists saw this as evidence of a conspiracy among Federalists in the post offices. [15] It is nevertheless all but inconceivable, considering the intense interest in the result of the ratification contest in the crucial states like Pennsylvania, that some news of the Pennsylvania minority proposals did not reach the Massachusetts delegates.

What is particularly noteworthy about the Massachusetts ratificatory amendments is that they were drafted by the Federalist leaders as a convention maneuver. When the delegates convened, on January 9, 1788, it soon became apparent that the convention was closely divided between supporters and opponents of the Constitution. Indeed, as the debate went on, it even seemed that the Antifederalists had a narrow margin. Without some concession to the widespread feeling that a bill of rights was necessary, the Massachusetts ratification itself might be in danger. The Federalist leaders decided upon the introduction of proposed amendments to be sent with the ratification as a compromise. The amendments were

drafted by Theophilus Parsons, who had also written the
Essex Result in 1778, which had led to the Massachusetts Declaration of Rights.[16] The shrewd decision was then made to
allow John Hancock, the convention president, to introduce
them as his own handiwork. Hancock had been reputed an
Antifederalist; thus his sponsorship of the amendments dis-
sipated much of the opposition, particularly since the motion
to consider the Hancock amendments was made by Samuel
Adams who was also supposed an Antifederalist. "We flatter
ourselves," wrote Madison of the Hancock-Adams move,
"that the weight of these two characters will ensure our success." [17] Adams and other Antifederalists joined in praising
the proposed amendments: "they must have a strong tendency to ease the minds of gentlemen, who wish for the immediate operation of some essential parts of the proposed
Constitution, as well as the most speedy and effectual means
of obtaining alterations . . . which they are solicitous should
be made." As Dr. Jarvis summed it up, "The amendments
have a tendency to remove many objections which have been
made to it"—i.e., the Constitution.[18]

Some of the Antifederalists objected that the Hancock
amendments were far from the bill of rights that was necessary. Nor would it be as difficult as the Federalists claimed to
draw up a bill of rights: "any gentlemen in that Convention
could form one in a few hours, as he might take the bill of
rights of Massachusetts for a guide." Parsons made the standard answer, "that no power was given to Congress to infringe on any one of the natural rights of the people." [19] Apparently this was not enough for some delegates, for Adams
introduced amendments to be added to the Hancock proposals. These would have gone far in the direction of a bill of
rights, since they included guarantees of freedom of the press
and conscience, right to bear arms, to petition for redress of
grievances, and against unreasonable searches and seizures.
Lacking any report of the debate on the Adams motion, the
statement in the convention Journal for February 6 must suf-
fice: "the question being put was determined in the negative." [20]

127

Defeat of Adams's additional amendments marked the real end of the ratification debate. Later the same day, the convention voted to ratify the Constitution and, at the same time, to "remove the fears and quiet the apprehensions of many of the good people of this Commonwealth," [21] recommended to Congress the amendments proposed by Hancock. The final vote was close (187 to 168), indicating the wisdom of the Federalists in appropriating the amendment issue for themselves. As a recently published contemporary analysis by a Dutch diplomat put it, "It is all too likely that the same would have been rejected in Massachusetts had not Governor Hancock as President of the Convention proposed some changes whereby the rights of the people are more precisely stipulated and insured." [22]

As a letter from Benjamin Lincoln to Washington points out, after Hancock introduced his proposed amendments, the Antifederalists wanted the ratification to be upon condition that the amendments be adopted.[23] Such a ratification would have been equivalent to none at all, since it would have required a second constitutional convention to make the amendments. At the same time, when Massachusetts and four other states recommended amendments as part of their ratifications, it placed considerable pressure on the first Congress elected under the Constitution to initiate the amending process.

The Massachusetts proposed amendments consisted of nine articles.[24] They provided that: (1) all powers not expressly delegated are reserved to the states; (2) there shall be one representative to every 30,000 persons until House membership amounts to 200; (3) Congress shall not exercise its power over elections except where a state fails to do so or makes regulations "subversive" of the right to free and equal representation; (4) Congress shall not lay direct taxes except where the impost and excise are insufficient, and then only if a requisition upon the states proves unsuccessful; (5) Congress shall erect no company "with exclusive advantages of commerce;" (6) no person shall be tried for an infamous crime without a grand jury indictment; (7) no federal court shall exercise jurisdiction in cases between citizens of different states unless the matter in dispute is of the value of $1500, and the Supreme Court shall have jurisdiction in such cases only if the value is $3,000; (8) every issue of fact in civil actions between citizens of different states shall be tried by jury upon request of any party; (9) Congress shall at no time consent that any person holding an office of trust or profit under the United States shall accept a title of nobility, or any other title or office, from any king, prince, or foreign state.

Four of the Massachusetts proposed amendments were included in the twelve amendments approved by Congress in 1789: the first, that all powers not expressly delegated to the federal government be reserved to the states (later guaranteed in the Tenth Amendment); the second governing representation in the House (a similar provision in the first of the amendments approved by Congress in 1789 was not ratified); the sixth, providing for a right to a grand jury indictment (a direct source of the right later included in the Fifth Amendment); and the eighth, providing for jury trial in civil cases (later guaranteed in the Seventh Amendment).

The Massachusetts-proposed amendments were themselves but a mild version of a bill of rights, since they did not cover the basic rights already guaranteed in the state declarations of rights, such as that in Massachusetts itself. The key rights of freedom of speech, press, and conscience (which had been included, in part, in Sam Adams's abortive amendments) were left unprotected. More important, however, than the details of the Massachusetts-proposed amendments was the fact that they were officially recommended by the state. Madison may have considered the Massachusetts amendments "a blemish." [25] But Jefferson recognized the merits of the Massachusetts plan, which "will I hope be followed by those who are yet to decide." [26] Jefferson's hope was borne out. The other states that followed the Massachusetts example were bolder in protecting individual rights and among them included all the rights later guaranteed in the Federal Bill of Rights.

MARYLAND, SOUTH CAROLINA, AND NEW HAMPSHIRE

Maryland, the seventh state to ratify the Constitution, did so on April 26, 1788. The Maryland Ratifying Convention contained a large Federalist majority. They were determined to ratify and shouted down a motion made by William Paca to adopt proposed amendments to accompany the ratification: "Mr. Paca was not even permitted to read his amendments." Ratification was then voted 63 to 11. Paca renewed his proposition for amendments, saying he had voted for ratification "only . . . under the firm persuasion, and in full confidence that such amendments would be peacably obtained so as to enable the people to live happy under the government." A committee was appointed to draft "such amendments and alterations as may be thought necessary, in the proposed Constitution." [27]

The committee recommended thirteen proposed amendments. Fifteen others were rejected by the committee majority. The minority insisted on their right to present some of their amendments to the convention, but the majority then decided not to consider any amendments and voted not even to record the yeas and nays. The minority, however, appealed to the court of public opinion and issued all twenty-eight proposed amendments in pamphlet form. This minority *Address* was widely distributed; we know, for example, that a copy reached Jefferson in Paris. [28]

The amendments originally recommended by the Maryland committee [29] were that: (1) Congress shall exercise no power not expressly delegated; (2) there shall be trial by jury in all criminal cases, and there shall be no appeal involving questions of fact and no second trial after acquittal; (3) in federal civil actions, trial of the facts shall be by jury; and it shall be expressly declared that state courts have concurrent jurisdiction in such cases with the federal courts, with appeals from either limited to matters of law and to controversies where a minimum amount is involved; (4) inferior federal courts shall not have jurisdiction where less than a minimum amount is involved, in revenue cases appeals shall be on both facts and law and Congress may give the state courts jurisdiction over revenue cases; (5) in trespasses the party injured shall be entitled to trial by jury in the state where the injury was committed; state courts have concurrent jurisdiction with federal courts and there shall be no appeal from either except on matters of law; and no person shall be exempt from such jurisdiction except ambassadors and ministers, (6) no federal jurisdiction shall arise from fictions or collusion; (7) federal judges shall not hold any other office of profit; (8) warrants without oath and general warrants ought not be granted; (9) no soldier shall be enlisted for longer than four years except in time of war, and then only during the war; (10) soldiers shall not be quartered in private houses in time of peace without the consent of the owners; (11) no mutiny bill shall continue in force longer than two years; (12) freedom of the press shall be inviolably preserved; (13) the militia shall not be subject to martial law except in time of war, invasion, or rebellion.

The additional amendments proposed by the minority of the Maryland committee [30] were that: (1) the militia, unless selected by lot or voluntarily enlisted, shall not be marched beyond the limits of an adjoining state without the state's consent; (2) Congress shall have no power to regulate elections unless a state neglects or is prevented by invasion or rebellion from doing so; (3) direct taxes shall not be collected if any state pays the amount imposed; (4) no standing army shall be kept in time of peace without the consent of two thirds of Congress; (5) the President shall not command the army in person without consent of Congress; (6) no treaty shall repeal or abrogate state constitutions or bills of rights; (7) no regulation of commerce or navigation act shall be passed without the consent of two thirds of Congress; (8) no member of Congress shall be eligible to any office of profit during his term; (9) Congress shall have no power to lay a poll tax; (10) no person with conscientious scruples shall be compelled to serve as a soldier; (11) there shall be a responsible council to the President; (12) there shall be no national religion established by law; and all persons shall be equally entitled to protection in their religious liberty; (13) all taxes imposed by Congress shall be credited to the state in which collected and be deducted out of such state's quota of the common expenses of government; (14) every man has a right to petition the legislature for redress of grievances; (15) all persons entrusted with legislative or executive powers are trustees and servants of the people and accountable for their conduct; when the ends of government are perverted and public liberty endangered, the people may of right reform the old or establish a new government; the doctrines of nonresistance against arbitrary power and oppression is absurd, slavish, and destructive of the happiness of mankind.

The proposals of the Maryland committee, as well as those of the minority, were another step in the direction of a federal bill of rights, for they went far beyond the minimal provisions contained in the Massachusetts-proposed amendments. Most important, they directly influenced the proposed amendments later recommended by Virginia, upon which Madison largely drew in writing his draft of the Bill of Rights. The only Maryland proposals that were put forward for the first time (i.e., that were not taken from the Pennsylvania and Massachusetts proposals) not included in those of Virginia were amendments 4, 6, 7, and 11 of the committee, and 1, 5, and 13 of the minority of the committee.

Among the Maryland-proposed amendments are the following guarantees later included in the Federal Bill of Rights: A) Committee amendments: 1) limiting Congress to powers expressly delegated (another version of the Tenth Amendment); 2) providing trial by jury and against double jeopardy (the first protection against double jeopardy in the state-proposed amendments); 8) insuring against oathless warrants and general warrants (parts of the guarantees included in the Fourth Amendment); 10) insuring against quartering of soldiers (the first guaranty in the state-proposed amendments of the right protected by the Third Amendment); 12) providing freedom of the press. B) Minority amendments: 12) prohibiting the establishment of "national religion" and guaranteeing religious liberty (the first attempt to include a prohibition against establishment of religion in the state amendments); 14) insuring the right to petition for redress of grievances (again the first effort to include this right later protected by the First Amendment in a proposed state amendment).

The next state to ratify was South Carolina; it did so on May 23, 1788. The principal speaker for the Constitution in the South Carolina debates was Charles Pinckney, who had attempted to provide specific protections for freedom of the press and from troop quartering in the Framers' Convention.[31] Little was said about the bill of rights issue, aside from some reference to trial by jury, until James Lincoln rose and declared that there was a total silence in the Constitution on fundamental rights, notably liberty of the press. "Why was not this Constitution ushered in with the bill of rights? Are the people to have no rights?" Charles Cotesworth Pinckney answered with the familiar Federalist argument that a bill of rights was unnecessary, since the federal government had no power to infringe upon individual rights. He also made the shrewd argument, in a slaveholding state, that bills of rights "generally begin with declaring that all men are by nature born free. Now, we should make that declaration with a very bad grace, when a large part of our property consists in men who are actually born slaves." [32]

Despite strong opposition, the South Carolina Convention voted for ratification by 149 to 73. As had been true in Massachusetts, the Federalists made the concession of adopting four recommendatory amendments. The only one that bears upon the Federal Bill of Rights is another version of what later became the Tenth Amendment.[33] The importance of the South Carolina proposals is not their substance (which was negligible) but the fact that they gave impetus to the movement to have ratification accompanied by recommendatory amendments.

Further impetus was given when New Hampshire, following the Massachusetts example, ratified the Constitution on June 21, 1788. It was the ninth state to ratify, thus bringing the new Constitution into effect according to its terms. The

Antifederalists had at first appeared so strong in New Hampshire's convention, which met soon after that of Massachusetts had adjourned in February, that the supporters of the Constitution had had to secure a temporary adjournment to ward off defeat. When the convention met again in June, the Antifederalist sentiment was weaker. A committee was appointed to draft recommendatory amendments. Despite strong opposition, the amendments were approved. The effort of the Antifederalists to make ratification conditional until the amendments went into effect was defeated. Ratification was then voted by an eleven-man majority.

The New Hampshire Ratifying Convention recommended twelve proposed amendments.[34] The first nine were taken almost verbatim from those proposed by Massachusetts. The last three were added by the New Hampshire drafting committee: 10) no standing army without a three-fourths vote and a ban on troop quartering (the latter the first official state recommendation of what became the Third Amendment); 11) "Congress shall make no laws touching Religion, or to infringe the rights of Conscience" (the first official state recommendation of the freedom of conscience guaranteed by the First Amendment and, most important, the first use of the prohibitory language with which the First Amendment starts—a vast improvement, from a legal point of view, in the language of the freedom of religion guaranty); 12) right to bear arms (the first official state recommendation to protect the right guaranteed by the Second Amendment).

VIRGINIA

For both supporters and opponents of the Federal Constitution, Virginia was the the crucial state in the ratification contest. The Constitution technically became operational upon ratification by New Hampshire, the ninth state to ratify. But everyone knew that the new Union could scarcely prove effective without Virginia, then the largest and most important state. Moreover, Virginia was closely divided, with its Antifederalist leaders among the best known men in the country: Patrick Henry, George Mason, and Richard Henry Lee. In no state was the opposition to the Constitution led by men of such caliber—but then in no state were the stakes so high or the debate so thorough.

The Virginia Ratifying Convention assembled at Richmond on June 2, 1788. The record we have of its debates is the most complete of any of the state conventions. The bill of rights issue was, even more than in other states, a principal point of difference between the Federalists and Antifederalists. All those who had been responsible for including the pioneer Declaration of Rights in the Virginia Constitution of 1776 were members of the 1788 convention—particularly George Mason. They emphasized the lack of a similar bill of rights in the Federal Constitution and argued against ratification until adequate protections for individual rights were included.

As it turned out, this demand of the Antifederalists became the nub of the bill of rights debate in the Virginia convention, with the issue resolving itself into the question of prior versus subsequent amendments. As Madison foresaw in an April 27, 1788, letter to Jefferson, "The preliminary question will be whether previous alterations shall be insisted on or not?" [35] Federalists like Madison had originally opposed amendments and had characterized the Massachusetts proposed amendments as "a blemish." [36] As had been the case in Massachusetts, however, the closeness of the division in the Richmond convention forced the Virginia Federalists to reconsider. Even Madison, in an April 10 letter to Edmund Randolph, conceded that "Recommendatory alterations" might be necessary.[37] By the time of the convention, the Federalist leaders were willing to concede and follow the example of the Massachusetts-proposed amendments. As Madison put it in a June 22 letter to Hamilton, "The plan meditated by the friends (of) the Constitution is . . . to subjoin a recommendation which may hold up amendments as objects to be pursued in the constitutional mode." [38]

The Federalist concession was not enough for the Antifederalist leaders. They insisted upon prior amendments protecting basic individual rights as a condition for ratification. Their views were expressed again and again by Patrick Henry, the principal speaker against ratification throughout the month-long debate. We tend to think of Henry only as a fiery young orator, with the bloom wearing off in the transition to a mature politician. Reading the reports of the Virginia Ratifying Convention debates makes one realize the shallowness of this conception. Of course, Henry's oratory was delivered in support of what we now consider the *wrong* side, and advocates of lost causes—however close to victory they were at the time—have not fared well at the hands of American historians. But that scarcely dims the brilliance of Henry's performance in 1788. By force of his personality and oratorical ability (and we must remember that the reports we have of his speeches must be only a pale shadow of the reality), he completely dominated a convention composed of some of the greatest men in our political history.

In the Virginia convention itself, the most important early development was Edmund Randolph's open avowal of the Federalist cause. Randolph, then Governor of Virginia, was one of the delegates at Philadelphia who had refused to sign the Constitution, and the Virginia Antifederalists counted upon his leadership. Instead, after Henry opened the case for the opposition on June 4 with his famous attack upon the Constitution: "Who authorized them to speak the language of, *We, the people,* instead of *We, the states?*" [39] Randolph led the answer for the Federalists. Randolph's desertion led the Antifederalists to assert that he deserved comparison with Benedict Arnold.[40]

As already indicated, the chief issue between the Federalists and Antifederalists in the Virginia convention was whether there should be prior or subsequent amendments protecting individual rights: as Madison summarized it in a July 24 letter to Jefferson, "whether previous amendments should be made a condition of ratification." [41] Henry and his followers rejected the notion that the convention "should . . . follow the conduct of Massachusetts," saying, "I can never . . . consent to hazard our most unalienable rights on an absolute uncertainty. . . . Let us not adopt this system till we see them secure"—i.e., by prior amendments.

Madison and the other Federalist leaders strongly challenged "the probability of obtaining previous amendments." To condition ratification on prior amendments would be too great a risk; in Randolph's query, "am I therefore obliged to run the risk of losing the Union, by proposing amendments previously, when amendments without that risk can be obtained afterwards?" Among the most effective Federalist speakers was the young John Marshall. He noted wisely that Henry's argument could be used against him: "for, sir, if subsequent amendments cannot be obtained, shall we get amendments before we ratify?"

Thus the debate went on, with Henry coming back to the bill of rights issue virtually every day—one of his speeches on the matter lasting seven hours. He kept insisting on prior amendments and referred as authority to Jefferson, saying, "His amendments go to that despised thing, called a *bill of rights*, and all the rights which are dear to human nature— trial by jury, the liberty of religion and the press, etc." Jefferson's move in support of the Massachusetts approach [42] was not generally known until later.[43] The Federalists repeated the view asserted in other conventions that a bill of rights was not necessary, and even that it was no security at all. Madison, speaking of freedom of religion, asserted that "a bill of rights would be a poor protection for liberty." Marshall—who was to make judicial review the cornerstone of the constitutional edifice in *Marbury v. Madison* [44]—declared, "The bill of rights is merely recommendatory." These were, however, only statements made in the heat of debate. As previously indicated, the Federalist leaders had already decided upon recommendatory amendments as a concession to the popular sentiment for a bill of rights.

On June 24, George Wythe, one of the judges in the *Caton* case [45] and a leading Federalist, spoke in favor of amendments to be recommended after ratification; he mentioned specifically guarantees of freedom of the press and religion, and trial by jury. Henry remained obdurate and moved for a declaration of rights and other amendments to be referred "to the other states in the confederacy, for their consideration, previous to its ratification" [46] Madison replied that those of Henry's amendments that "are not objectionable, or unsafe . . . may be subsequently recommended—not because they are necessary, but because they can produce no possible danger, and may gratify some gentlemen's wishes. But I never can consent to his previous amendments." The Federalist effort was then devoted to defeating the Henry motion for prior amendments, although only by the narrow vote of 88 to 80. The vote on the motion to ratify quickly followed and carried by 89 to 79. Both votes took place on June 25, 1788.

The next day, a committee was appointed "to prepare and report such amendments as by them shall be deemed necessary, to be recommended." Both Mason and Henry were placed on the drafting committee (along with Madison, Marshall, and Wythe), and these two were able to secure most of the original Henry proposals, though only by way of recommendation for subsequent amendments. On June 27, the committee reported a proposed "declaration or bill of rights asserting, and securing from encroachment, the essential and unalienable rights of the people," in twenty articles to be added to the Constitution, as well as twenty other amendments to the constitutional text. [47] The convention agreed to the committee report, and enjoined "it upon their representatives in Congress to exert all their influence, and use all reasonable and legal methods, to obtain a ratification of the foregoing alterations and provisions."

The Virginia-proposed bill of rights was of decisive significance in the history of the Federal Bill of Rights, both because it was the first state proposal for a detailed bill of rights and because it was recommended by Virginia. Though Madison wrote to Washington in the heat of the convention struggle with regard to the just-adopted recommendatory amendments, "several of them highly objectionable, but which could not be parried," [48] when the time came for him to draft his amendments in the first Congress, he chose as his model the bill of rights recommended by the convention of which he had been an active member.

The Virginia-proposed bill of rights [49] provided that: (1) men possess natural rights to life, liberty, and property, and pursuing and obtaining happiness and safety; (2) all power is derived from the people, and magistrates are their trustees and agents; (3) government ought to be instituted for the benefit, protection, and security of the people, and the doctrine of nonresistance against arbitrary power and oppression is absurd, slavish, and destructive of the happiness of mankind; (4) public offices should not be hereditary; (5) legislative, executive, and judicial powers should be separate, and legislative and executive officials should at fixed periods be reduced to private stations; (6) legislative elections ought to be free and frequent and all men ought to have the right of suffrage, and the people should not be bound by taxes or laws to which they, or their representatives have not consented; (7) no power of suspending laws ought to be exercised; (8) in criminal cases, defendant has the right to the cause and nature of his accusation, to be confronted with accusers and witnesses, to call for evidence and be allowed counsel, to trial by a jury of his vicinage and a unanimous verdict, nor can he be compelled to give evidence against himself; (9) no freeman ought to be deprived of life, liberty, or property but by the law of the land; (10) every freeman restrained of his liberty is entitled to a remedy; (11) trial by jury in civil cases ought to remain sacred and inviolable; (12) every freeman ought to find a remedy for injuries and wrongs without sale, denial or delay; (13) excessive bail ought not to be imposed, nor excessive fines or cruel and unusual punishments imposed; (14) every freeman has a right to be secure against unreasonable searches and seizures and general warrants ought not to be granted; (15) the people have a right to assemble and petition for redress of grievances; (16) the people have a right to freedom of speech, and freedom of the press ought not to be violated; (17) the people have a right to bear arms, a militia is the natural defense of a free state, and standing armies ought to be avoided; (18) no soldier ought to be quartered in any house in peacetime without the owner's consent; (19) conscientious objectors ought to be exempted upon payment of an equivalent; (20) all men have a right to the free exercise of religion and no religious sect ought to be favored or established by law.

The Virginia-proposed additional amendments were that: (1) each state shall retain every power not delegated to the Federal Government; (2) there shall be one representative per 30,000 population until House membership amounts to 200; (3) direct taxes and excises shall not be collected in a state raising its own quota; (4) members of Congress shall be ineligible to hold civil office during their term; (5) the Senate and House Journals shall be published yearly, except parts requiring secrecy; (6) accounts of receipts and expenditures shall be published yearly; (7) ratification of commercial treaties shall require a two-thirds vote of the Senate, and a three-fourths vote of both Houses shall be required for a treaty ceding or limiting territorial rights or claims, or fishing in American seas or navigating American rivers; (8) no navigation laws or law regulating commerce shall be passed without a two-thirds vote of both Houses; (9) no standing army in time of peace shall be kept without a two-thirds vote of both Houses; (10) no soldier shall be enlisted for longer than four years except in time of war; (11) militia shall be subject to state control except in time of war or when in federal service; (12) the power of Congress over the federal district shall be limited to police and government regulation; (13) no one shall be President more than eight out of any sixteen years; (14) federal judicial power shall be limited to the Supreme Court and courts of admiralty, it shall not extend to cases involving diversity jurisdiction and appellate jurisdiction shall not include questions of fact at common law, nor shall it extend to most controversies originating before ratification of the Constitution; (15) the defendant in criminal cases shall have the right to challenge or except to the jury; (16) Congress shall not regulate elections unless a state fails to act;

(17) language that Congress shall not exercise certain powers shall not be interpreted to extend power but as an exception or a precaution; (18) laws fixing Congressional compensation shall become effective only after an intervening Congressional election; (19) some tribunal other than the Senate shall be provided for trying impeachments of Senators; (20) salaries of judges shall not be increased or diminished except by general regulations of salary at not less than seven-year intervals.

The importance of the Virginia Ratifying Convention's proposed bill of rights is shown by the fact that (apart from the political generalities contained in the first seven articles and in the tenth and twelfth) every specific guaranty in the Virginia-proposed bill of rights found a place in the Federal Bill of Rights, except for Article 19, allowing conscientious objectors to hire substitutes—and even that was included in the amendments Madison proposed to Congress.

The following are the guarantees contained in the Virginia-proposed bill of rights that were later included in the Federal Bill of Rights: Article 8: right to nature and cause of accusation, confrontation, evidence, counsel, trial by jury of vicinage (i.e. all of the rights included in the Sixth Amendment), and privilege against self-incrimination (protected by the Fifth Amendment); Article 9: no deprivation of life, liberty, or property "but by the law of the land" (another precursor of the Fifth Amendment's Due Process Clause): Article 11: trial by jury in civil cases (included in the Seventh Amendment); Article 13: prohibition against excessive bail or fines and cruel and unusual punishment (the Eighth Amendment); Article 14: right against unreasonable searches and seizures (the Fourth Amendment); Article 15: right to assemble and petition for redress of grievances (the last right secured by the First Amendment); Article 16: freedom of speech and press (the core rights protected by the First Amendment); Article 17: right to bear arms (guaranteed by the Second Amendment); Article 18: prohibition against quartering of soldiers (the Third Amendment); Article 20: freedom of religion (both guaranteeing free exercise and prohibiting establishment, as was to be done by the First Amendment). In addition, the first of the Virginia-proposed additional amendments anticipated the guaranty of reserved powers contained in the Tenth Amendment.

We can best estimate the importance of the Virginia-proposed bill of rights and amendments by comparing them with the sketchy proposals recommended by Massachusetts, South Carolina, and New Hampshire, the states that had previously adopted recommendatory amendments. In place of the rudimentary protections suggested by the other states, Virginia recommended a complete bill of rights, and one that covered all the essential guarantees later included in the Federal Bill of Rights, except for the rights to just compensation and a grand jury indictment, that against double jeopardy, and the guaranty contained in the Ninth Amendment (and this last was stated, though in different language, in the seventeenth Virginia-proposed additional amendment).

NEW YORK

After the Virginia convention the scene shifted to New York, the next state to act on ratification. Here, too, the ratifying convention was closely divided, if not weighted toward the Antifederalists. A letter from Hamilton to Madison immediately before the convention convened estimated that "the Antifederal party . . . have a majority of two-thirds in the Convention." [50] A letter just after the convention started declared, "Our chance of success here is infinitely slender." [51] In the convention itself, there were leading men of the day on both sides of the debate: John Jay, Alexander Hamilton, and Chancellor Robert Livingston for the Federalists, Governor George Clinton, Melancton Smith, and John Lansing for the Antifederalists. Hamilton was particularly effective in the debate, and some of his speeches deserve comparison with his essays in *The Federalist* [52] or indeed with any other paper on political science ever written.

The New York convention assembled at Poughkeepsie on

June 17, 1788. From then until July 2, the delegates debated the substantive provisions of the Constitution, especially those relating to the powers and composition of Congress, with emphasis on the power of taxation. So far as we can tell from the report of the debates there was no specific reference to protection of individual liberties or to the need for a bill of rights before July 2. Hamilton did, however, deal with the subject by implication, stating that the Constitution provided for both of the objects sought "in forming systems of government—*safety* for the people, and *energy* in the administration." [53] The checks and balances contained in the Constitution furnished ample security for the liberties of the people: "give a perfect proportion and balance to its parts, and the powers you give it will never affect your security." Chancellor Livingston also touched upon the matter indirectly, saying that the opposition "wish for checks against what can do no harm. They contend for a phantom." The Constitution itself rejected the notion "that the powers of Congress would be dangerous."

Finally, on July 2, Antifederalist Thomas Tredwell rose and delivered a long attack upon the Constitution's failure to provide specific protections for personal liberties. He emphasized the failure to provide express guarantees for freedom of the press, trial by jury, and the other basic rights of the people: "in forming the Constitution, we have run into the same error which the lawyers and Pharisees of old were charged with, that is, while we have secured the tithes of mint, anise, and cumin, we have neglected the weightier matters of the law." In the Constitution, "we find no security for the rights of individuals . . .; here is no bill of rights, no proper restriction of power." Government may be likened to a mad horse that may run away with the rider. "Would he not, therefore, justly be deemed a mad man, and deserve to have his neck broken who should trust himself on this horse without any bridle at all?"

Unfortunately, the detailed report of the New York debates, from which most accounts are taken, [54] becomes skimpy for the latter part of the convention, confining itself to a brief account of the motions introduced after Tredwell's speech. Notes were, however, kept by Gilbert Livingston, one of the delegates, [55] and they give us the most complete record we have of the convention between July 14 and final adjournment. The Livingston Notes start on July 14, in the midst of a debate on conditional versus recommendatory ratification. They enable us to follow the debates on that core issue, as well as the adoption of the bill of rights introduced by John Lansing.

After the Tredwell speech, the convention, sitting in Committee of the Whole, dealt with a series of Antifederalist amendments to the body of the Constitution; two of them touched upon personal liberties, since they related to the Habeas Corpus and Ex Post Facto Clauses. Then, on July 7, the bill of rights issue came to the fore, as "Mr. Lansing then read, and presented . . . a bill of rights to be prefixed to the Constitution." A letter from Hamilton to Madison the next day indicates that the Federalists were not certain whether their opponents would insist upon conditional amendments; but that the Federalists themselves were willing to concede the need for "rational" recommendatory amendments. [56]

From a contemporary newspaper we learn that the Federalists agreed on July 10 to join with their opponents on an unofficial committee to consider Lansing's amendments, and to "endeavor to make such an accommodation, and to arrange the amendments as to bring the business to a quick and friendly decision." [57] The newspaper account indicates that the committee proceedings did not go smoothly. But an important step toward accommodation had been taken. Then, on July 11, Jay made a motion to ratify and then recommend "whatever amendments may be deemed useful or expedient." Hamilton delivered a powerful speech the next day supporting the Jay motion and attacking the notion that the convention could ratify on condition: "the present Convention . . . had no possible decisive power, but to accept or reject absolutely: that it had indeed a power to recommend, because this was a natural right of every freeman; but it had none to dictate to or embarrass the union by any restrictions or conditions whatever: . . . conditional adoption included evidently a disagreement to and rejection of a part of the Constitution: that Congress . . . must consider such a partial rejection in the light of a total one." [58] On July 14, Hamilton delivered a second speech attacking the concept of conditional ratification and questioning the power of Congress to call a second convention to add amendments. The opposite position "will lead every man who wishes an adoption into a snare." [59]

Despite Hamilton's argument, Melancton Smith moved for the opposition on July 15 that ratification should be conditional only; the main condition imposed was the calling of a second constitutional convention "for proposing amendments to the said Constitution." In reply, Hamilton expressly stated the Federalist willingness to recommend amendments along with ratification: "they were ready to go as far as they thought safe, in recommendatory & explanatory Amends . . . they will bring forward Amends & will be pledged for to obtain those which they bring forward—as far as they can." Hamilton then "produced the form of a Ratification—and also a number of Amendments which he read—& pledged the Gent of New York to endeavour to obtain them." [60]

Hamilton's amendments were not concerned with protection of individual rights and were consequently far from the bill of rights introduced by Lansing. Nevertheless, they did represent a Federalist concession, which might lead to Antifederalist concessions. "We are endeavouring to agree," declared Jay. "Gent See we have brot forth valuable Amendments." The big question was now that stated by Jay: "Cannot we endeavour further to accommodate?" [61] Ultimately, the accommodation called for took place with the adoption of the substance of the Lansing proposals, but only as recommendatory amendments.

In another speech on July 15, Hamilton attempted further to conciliate Lansing, saying that he "hopes time will be taken to consider of the new propositions—and not pass the rubicon but by hastily taking this questn." [62] Lansing nevertheless went ahead and moved for a conditional ratification, on July 19, with a bill of rights prefixed. At this point the Federalists were hard pressed, a delaying motion by them for adjournment having been defeated decisively. A July 19 letter from Hamilton to Madison shows that the Federalists were even willing to accept ratification with "a right to recede in case our amendments have not been decided upon . . . within a certain number of years." [63] In the meantime, the debate continued on the details of Lansing's proposed bill of rights, with the Federalists led by Hamilton indicating their willingness to accept virtually all the Lansing amendments, provided they were not made conditional. It is of interest that Hamilton was able on July 19 to secure elimination of the word "expressly" in the provision dealing with the reserved powers of the states [64]—anticipating the Hamilton approach to implied powers stated in his famous 1791 opinion on the constitutionality of the United States Bank.[65]

On July 22, Hamilton would write to Madison that there was a great diversity in the views of the Antifederalists. "Upon the whole however our fears diminish." [66] By July 23, a clear split in the Antifederalist ranks became apparent. On that date, the convention took up Lansing's motion that ratification be made conditional upon prior adoption of his bill of rights and other amendments. Samuel Jones, an Antifederalist, now moved that the Lansing motion be expunged and a substitute inserted providing for ratification "in full confidence" that subsequent amendments would be adopted. The Jones amendment carried, after Melancton Smith, the Antifederalist leader who had made the original motion for conditional ratification, rose in support and "gave Reasons—why he will vote for the amendment." [67]

The adoption of the Jones amendment signified that New York would ratify without conditions, though it would recommend amendments. The Jones motion was carried only by a vote of 31 to 29; without Antifederalist votes, especially that of Smith, it could scarcely have prevailed. The Antifederalist split remained in effect on July 26, when "the bill of rights, and form of ratification, with the amendments," were voted on. The affirmative prevailed 30 to 27.

The Antifederalist split needed to obtain unconditional ratification was secured by two principal Federalist concessions. The first was their acceptance of Lansing's bill of rights as a prefix to the instrument of ratification and of a list of proposed amendments to the body of the Constitution. Ratification was declared "in confidence" that the proposals would "receive an early and mature consideration." The second concession was an agreement to send a circular letter to the other states to "earnestly exhort and request . . . that effectual measures be immediately taken for calling" a second constitutional convention to act on the amendments proposed by the different states. The circular letter [68] would be strongly attacked by the Federalists. Madison, in a letter of August 15 to Washington, felt that it "has a most pestilent tendency" [69] and would undermine the Constitution. However, the danger did not materialize; a second convention was never called. The Constitution would go into effect with unconditional state ratifications—which were not weakened, legally speaking, by the fact that five ratifications were accompanied by recommendatory amendments.

As already indicated, the New York ratification was accompanied by a proposed bill of rights and other amendments based upon a draft by John Lansing. The New York proposals are even longer than those of Virginia. The proposed New York bill of rights contains twenty-four unnumbered articles and there are thirty-two other unnumbered proposed amendments. The bill of rights provisions [70] were that: (1) all power is derived from the people) (2) enjoyment of life, liberty, and property and the pursuit of happiness are essential rights which government ought to respect and preserve; (3) every power not delegated remains to the people or their state governments, and language that Congress shall not exercise certain powers does not imply that Congress is entitled to powers not delegated, but shall be construed as an exception or a precaution; (4) the people have a right freely to exercise their religion, and no religious sect shall be favored or established by law; (5) the people have a right to bear arms, and a militia is the proper defense of a free state; (6) the militia should not be subject to martial law except in war; (7) standing armies ought not to be kept except in cases of necessity, and the military should be in strict subordination to the civil power; (8) no soldier ought to be quartered in peacetime in any house without the owner's consent; (9) no person ought to be taken, imprisoned, disseised of his freehold, exiled, or deprived of his privileges, franchises, life, liberty, or property but by due process of law; (10) no person ought to be put twice in jeopardy or punished for the same offense; (11) every person restrained of his liberty is entitled to a prompt remedy, except when on account of public danger Congress shall suspend habeas corpus; (12) excessive bail ought not to be required, nor excessive fines or cruel or unusual punishments imposed; (13) in criminal cases a presentment or indictment ought to be observed, and the trial should be speedy, public, and by a jury of the county, with a unanimous verdict, and the accused ought to be informed of the cause and nature of his accusation, to be confronted with accusers and witnesses, to have means of producing his witnesses and counsel, and should not be compelled to give evidence against himself; (14) trial by jury ought to remain inviolate; (15) every freeman has a right against unreasonable searches and seizures and general warrants ought not to be granted; (16) the people have a right to assemble and petition for redress of grievances, and freedom of the press ought not to be violated or restrained; (17) there should be an election for President and Vice President once in four years, even where Congress appoints in case of removal, death, resignation, or disability of an incumbent; (18) the Constitution shall not limit state power to district and apportion its Representatives; (19) the ex post facto prohibition extends only to laws concerning crimes; (20) all appeals in common law cases ought to be by writ of error and not otherwise; (21) the judicial power in cases in which a state is a party does not extend to criminal prosecutions or authorize suits by any person against a state; (22) the judicial power in cases between citizens of the same state claiming lands under grants of different states is not to extend to any other cases between them; (23) federal court jurisdiction is not to be extended by fiction, collusion, or suggestion; (24) no treaty is to be construed so as to alter any state constitution.

The New York convention proposed additional amendments [71] providing that: (1) there shall be one representative for every 30,000 people until House membership amounts to 200; (2) no excise shall be laid upon articles (except ardent spirits) grown, produced, or manufactured in the United States; (3) no direct taxes shall be imposed unless revenues from the impost and excise are insufficient and then not until after requisitions have proved ineffective; (4) Congress shall not regulate Congressional elections unless the states fail to act; (5) no person shall be President, Vice President, or serve in either House who is not a freeholder and is not a native-born citizen or one naturalized before July 4, 1776, or a person who held a commission during the Revolutionary War and later became a citizen; (6) Congress shall create no monopoly or company with exclusive advantages of commerce; (7) no standing army shall be kept in time of peace without a two-thirds vote of each House; (8) no money shall be borrowed on the credit of the United States without a two-thirds vote of each House; (9) war shall not be declared without a two-thirds vote of each House; (10) habeas corpus shall not be suspended longer than six months or twenty days after the next meeting of Congress; (11) Congress shall not exempt the federal district from taxes imposed in the state in which the district is located, nor exempt those in the district from arrest for crimes committed or debts contracted outside the district; (12) Congress shall not make laws to prevent state laws from extending to places purchased for the use of the United States except as to persons in the service of the United States, nor to them with respect to crimes committed without such places; (13) laws altering Congressional compensation shall not become effective until after an election has intervened; (14) the Journals of Congress, except for parts requiring secrecy, shall be published at least once a year, and the doors of both Houses shall be open except when secrecy is required, and the yeas and nays shall be recorded at the

149

request of two members; (15) no capitation tax shall ever be laid by Congress; (16) no person shall be Senator more than six out of twelve years, and the states may recall a Senator at any time; (17) no Senator or Representative shall hold office under the United States; (18) the authority of the Executives of the states to appoint Senators to fill vacancies shall be given to the legislatures; (19) the bankruptcy power shall be limited to merchants and traders and the states may pass insolvency laws for other debtors; (20) no President shall serve more than two terms; (21) the Executive shall not grant pardons for treason without consent of Congress, but may grant reprieves until the case is laid before Congress; (22) the President shall not command an army in person without the previous desire of Congress; (23) letters patent, commissions, pardons, writs, and process shall run in the name of the people of the United States; (24) no inferior federal courts shall be established except to exercise appellate and admiralty jurisdiction; (25) the court for the trial of impeachments shall be composed of the Senate, the Supreme Court, and the first or senior judge from the highest court of every state; (26) persons aggrieved by Supreme Court decisions in cases of original jurisdiction shall have a right to have the President issue commissions to seven or more men learned in the law to correct errors and do justice to the parties; (27) no judge of the Supreme Court shall hold any other office; (28) the judicial power shall not extend to controversies concerning lands except between states or under grants of different states; (29) the militia of any state shall not be compelled to serve outside the state longer than six months without the consent of its legislature; (30) the words "without the consent of the Congress" shall be deleted from Article I, section 9, clause 7; (31) Members of Congress and all federal officers shall be bound by oath not to infringe or violate the constitutions or rights of the states; (32) state legislatures may provide that electors of election districts shall choose a citizen who has been an inhabitant for one year.

The provisions included in the New York proposals are a motley lot, covering, as they do, both provisions of fundamental importance and some that could serve only to clutter up the Constitution. George Mason, in a letter, declared his belief that the New York amendments were modeled upon those he had helped draft for the Virginia convention.[72] The substance of the New York-proposed bill of rights is, indeed, similar to that recommended by Virginia, even with regard to the language used in many of the provisions, although the New York proposals contain a prohibition against double jeopardy, absent from the Virginia proposals, which is the first official state recommendation for such a prohibition. New York also followed Massachusetts in guaranteeing the right to an indictment.

The differences just referred to are matters of detail. There is, however, another difference between the New York-proposed bill of rights and all the other state-proposed amendments, one so significant that it is surprising that commentators have overlooked it. The difference referred to is in the New York version of section 39 of Magna Carta: "That no Person ought to be taken imprisoned or disseised of his freehold, or to be exiled or deprived of his Privileges, Franchises, Life, Liberty, or Property but by *due process of Law.*"

As early as 1354, it is true, a confirmation of Magna Carta by Edward III replaced section 39's "law of the land" with "due process of the law," [73] and Coke's classic commentary on Magna Carta considered the two phrases as equivalent.[74] But the New York-proposed bill of rights was, as far as can be determined, the first American constitutional provision to use the term "due process of law" in its restatement of section 39, although a 1692 Massachusetts statute did provide for protection of person and property by due process,[75] and the New York Charter of Liberties, 1683, had used the term "due Course of Law." [76]

The New York change in language was no mere matter of style. On the contrary, it constituted a constitutional quantum leap forward. Madison had the New York draft before him, as well as the other state recommendations, when he wrote his draft of what became the Fifth Amendment. Had the Fifth Amendment followed the Virginia "law of the land" rather than the New York "due process" phraseology, the Constitution might have been without its most significant provision. Bearing in mind the extent to which the due process concept, in both the Fifth and Fourteenth Amendments, has served as the basis for the constitutional protection of the rights of Americans, it can scarcely be doubted that a Constitution shorn of the Due Process Clause would have been far less effective in securing such protection.

This is not mere theory. The Constitution of India uses the term "procedure established by law" in place of "due process" and the Supreme Court of that country has interpreted that term to include a law enacted by the Indian Parliament. Hence, property taken by a statute is taken "by law" as the term is used in the Indian Constitution.[77] Similar "law of the land" terminology in the Federal Constitution would, in all probability, have been interpreted the same way.

Since the Due Process Clause in the New York-proposed bill of rights appears in the draft introduced by John Lansing, we can assume it was Lansing himself who made this fundamental contribution to our constitutional development. So far as we know, the New York Convention accepted the due process provision in Lansing's draft without debate. Gilbert Livingston's Notes on the matter state only: "4th article read—agreed."

On January 17, 1787, the New York Legislature had passed "An Act concerning the Rights of the Citizens of this State."[78] That statute contained a provision that no one shall be deprived of any right, but by "due process of law." Lansing undoubtedly took his draft due process clause from this 1787 statute. We do not know who was responsible for the clause there. The 1787 statute was introduced in the New York Assembly by Samuel Jones, who was to move the key amendment that led to New York's ratification, but whether it was he who drafted the "due process" language, or Lansing or Hamilton (also members of the assembly), or perhaps some other member, remains a matter of conjecture. The bill went through both Houses of the New York Legislature without amendment, so that the crucial phrase was in the measure when it was introduced by Jones.[79]

There is a suggestive speech by Hamilton in the New York Assembly on February 6, 1787, which indicates that the term "due process" in the 1787 statute was intended to make it plain that "no man shall be disfranchised or deprived of any right he enjoys under the constitution" by a mere act of the legislature. "Some gentlemen hold that the law of the land will include an act of the legislature. But Lord Coke, that great luminary of the law . . . interprets the law of the land to mean presentment and indictment, and process of outlawry, as contradistinguished from trial by jury." But, Hamilton goes on, "if there were any doubt upon the constitution, the bill of rights enacted in this session [i.e., the January 17, 1787, Act] removes it. It is there declared that, no man shall be disfranchised or deprived of any right, but by due process of law. . . . The words 'due process' have a precise technical import, and are only applicable to the process and proceedings of the courts of justice; they can never be referred to an act of legislature." [80]

The implication is that the words "due process" were inserted into the 1787 statute to ensure that the right of the individual not to be deprived of life, liberty, or property could not be violated by statute alone. Thus, the change from the "law of the land" to the "due process" phraseology was consciously intended to increase the protection given to individual rights—an intent that has clearly been realized by the subsequent development of "due process." We should not, however, assume that the draftsman of the 1787 New York statute used the term "due process" in anything like the broad meaning it has since acquired in our constitutional law. The already quoted Hamilton speech indicates that the contrary was the case. When he said that "due process" was only "applicable to the process and proceedings of the courts of justice," he clearly was thinking only of procedural due process and not of the much broader connotation the due process concept has since acquired.

Without question, Lansing—and later Madison in drafting what became the Fifth Amendment—used "due process" in the same procedural sense. Yet this scarcely affects the crucial significance of what they did. The term "due process" could expand to meet even the substance of legislative power; the same was not true of the "law of the land" phraseology, which probably would have been used in the Fifth Amendment had Lansing and Madison not employed the "due process" language.

NORTH CAROLINA

The last of the state ratifying conventions to take action on the bill of rights issue [81] was the North Carolina convention, which met on July 21, 1788. From the beginning, the convention was dominated by a large Antifederalist majority. They made matters most difficult for those who were supporting ratification. Throughout the debate, the Antifederalists hammered on the bill of rights issue, saying that they would "never swallow the Constitution till it is amended." [82] The Federalists sought to answer their arguments. James Iredell, later a Supreme Court Justice, in particular, argued that there was no need for a bill of rights, except in a system like the British one, where the legislature possessed undefined powers: "Of what use, therefore, can a bill of rights be in this Constitution, where the people expressly declare how much power they do give, and consequently retain all they do not?"

The Antifederalists remained adamant, saying the words spoken by their opponents "have gone in at one ear, and out at the other." Samuel Spencer expressed a widespread view when he declared, "I wish to have a bill of rights, to secure those unalienable rights . . . . though it might not be of any other service, it would at least satisfy the minds of the people."

The Federalists were willing to concede the point in accordance with the Virginia example. But their opponents were unwilling to accept anything less than, to quote their leader, Willie Jones, "amendments to be made previous to adoption by this state." On this issue, the Federalists would not yield, emphasizing that, "In regard to amending before or after the adoption, the difference is very great." They emphasized the danger of proposing amendments and then being "out of the Union till all these be agreed to by the other states." The Federalists knew, however, that they did not have the votes. As Iredell put it, "It is useless to contend any longer against a majority that is irresistible." Nevertheless, Iredell went through the form of moving that amendments "be proposed subsequent to the ratification on the part of this state, and not previous to it." Six proposed amendments to be recommended were added to the motion; [83] only one of them, enunciating the doctrine of reserved powers to be contained in the Tenth Amendment, covered any of the matters dealt with in the Federal Bill of Rights. Iredell's motion was overwhelmingly defeated, 184 to 84.

The majority then voted a resolution that a declaration of rights and other amendments be adopted "previous to the ratification of the Constitution." A declaration of rights and twenty-six proposed additional amendments accompanied the resolution. Before adjourning, the convention adopted "by a large majority" a resolution declaring that "this Convention has thought proper neither to ratify nor reject the Constitution." This left North Carolina outside the new constitutional system, a situation that continued until the first Congress passed the Bill of Rights as amendments to be submitted to the states for ratification. A new North Carolina convention then voted ratification of the Constitution, on November 21, 1789.

The bill of rights and proposed amendments voted by the North Carolina convention are not important for their substantive provisions, since, as Willie Jones expressly conceded, "I have, in my proposition, adopted, word for word, the Virginia amendments, with one or two additional ones." The North Carolina-proposed declaration of rights was a verbatim copy of that recommended by the Virginia Ratifying

Convention. Twenty of the other proposed amendments [84] were also those urged by Virginia, with one copied from Massachusetts, and five new provisions—none of which is relevant to the subject of individual rights. The significance of the North Carolina proposals lies only in the added impetus they gave to the bill of rights movement. North Carolina was the one state to refuse to ratify until a bill of rights was adopted. To gain her adherence to the new Union, and also that of Rhode Island, which failed to call a ratifying convention before 1790, the Federalists knew they would have to propose amendments when the new Congress assembled. Adding to the pressure exerted by the recommendatory amendments proposed by Massachusetts, South Carolina, New Hampshire, Virginia, and New York, the North Carolina failure to ratify the new Constitution gave the bill of rights movement a momentum that was virtually irresistible.

THE FOUNDATION LAID

The state ratifying conventions gave voice to the public sentiment for a Federal Bill of Rights. Their action in ratifying with recommendatory amendments ensured that speedy action would be taken on the matter when the new federal government went into operation. That was so not only because the major states had voted ratification on the Federalist assurance that the Constitution would be amended to provide for a bill of rights but because so much of the difficult part of the job—wording the amendments—had already been done. The state amendments pointed the way to the Bill of Rights' substantive content. Perhaps the situation was not as simple as George Mason had stated when he had raised the bill of rights issue near the end of the Constitutional Convention, saying: "with the aid of the State declarations, a bill might be prepared in a few hours." [85] But when Madison did draw up the amendments he introduced in the first Congress, he had at hand the compendium contained in the state recommendatory amendments.

Critics of the notion of amendments had pointed to the volume and diversity of the state proposals, claiming that it would be impossible to find any common ground among them. From the point of view of numbers alone, there was a basis in the criticism: over two hundred different amendments were proposed by the eight states concerned, and, with duplications omitted, these included nearly one hundred different substantive provisions.[86]

The picture was not, however, as hopeless as it seemed, as far as drawing up a workable Bill of Rights from the plethora of state-recommended amendments was concerned. The state proposals reflected the consensus that had developed among Americans with regard to the fundamental rights that ought to be protected by any Bill of Rights worthy of the name.

The situation in this respect is shown by the following table, which indicates which Federal Bill of Rights guarantees were contained in which state-proposed amendments:

Bill of Rights Guarantees	*Penn.*	*Mass.*	*Maryland Major-ity*	*Maryland Minor-ity*	*S.C.*	*N.H.*	*N.Y.*	*Va.*	*N.C.*	*Total number of states*
Religious freedom	x			x		x	x	x	x	6
Free speech	x						x	x	x	3
Free press	x		x				x	x	x	5
Assembly and petition				x			x	x	x	4
Right to bear arms	x			x		x		x	x	5
Quartering soldiers			x			x	x	x	x	5
Searches and seizures	x		x				x	x	x	5
Grand jury indictment	x		x			x	x			4
Double jeopardy			x				x			2
Self incrimination	x							x	x	3

Bill of Rights Guarantees	Penn.	Mass.	Maryland Major-ity	Maryland Minor-ity	S.C.	N.H.	N.Y.	Va.	N.C.	Total number of states
Due process	x						x	x	x	4
Just compensation										0
Speedy public trial	x						x	x	x	4
Jury trial	x		x				x	x	x	5
Cause and nature of accusation	x							x	x	3
Confrontation	x							x	x	3
Witnesses	x							x	x	3
Counsel	x							x	x	3
Jury trial (civil)	x	x	x			x	x	x	x	7
Bail	x						x	x	x	4
Fines	x						x	x	x	4
Punishment	x						x	x	x	4
Rights retained by people							x	x	x	3
Reserved powers	x	x	x		x	x	x	x	x	8

The table shows that all of the eight states to propose amendments, either officially or otherwise, included as one of their provisions a proposal similar in wording and scope to the Tenth Amendment, reserving to the states powers not delegated to the federal government. Seven states recommended a guaranty of jury trial in civil cases. Six urged protection for religious freedom. Five sought guarantees of freedom of the press (with three adding freedom of speech as well), the right to bear arms, trial by jury of the vicinage, and prohibitions against quartering of troops and unreasonable searches and seizures. Four states asked for protection of the right to "the law of the land" or due process, grand jury indictment, speedy public trial, assembly and petition, and

against excessive bail and fines and cruel and unusual punishments. Of twenty-two amendments supported by four or
more states, fourteen were incorporated by Madison in his
recommendations to Congress.[87]

This does not mean that Madison's job as draftsman of the
Federal Bill of Rights was that of mere compiler. On the contrary, as will be seen, Madison was able to play a most important creative role. He had to choose from the myriad of
state proposals those which were worthy of being raised to
the federal constitutional level. He also had to refine their
language, so that the Federal Bill of Rights would be, at the
same time, both an eloquent inventory of basic rights and a
legally enforceable safeguard of those rights.

Yet, if the ultimate bill of rights edifice was designed by
Madison, it was built from the materials furnished by the
state ratifying conventions. Now it was plain that "this security for liberty seems to be demanded by the general voice of
America." [88] The demand for amendments in the ratification
debates led the Federalists themselves to concede the need
for speedy action. A letter from Jefferson to John Paul Jones,
after referring to the state-recommended amendments, stated
that "the most important of these amendments will be effected by adding a bill of rights; and even the friends of the
Constitution are become sensible of the expediency of such
an addition were it only to conciliate the opposition." [89]

The Jefferson estimate was confirmed by Madison, who
agreed that "The friends of the Constitution . . . are generally agreed that the system should be revised . . . to
supply additional guards for liberty." [90] Looking ahead to
the first Congress under the Constitution, which was soon to
meet, he predicted that, "If the first Congress embrace the
policy which circumstances mark out, they will not fail to
propose of themselves, every desirable safeguard for popular
rights." [91] When the first Congress did meet in New York a
few months later, it was Madison who ensured that his pre-
diction would be borne out by serving as the legislative catalyst for the amendments that were about to become the Federal Bill of Rights.

six

the great rights secured

MADISON AND THE BILL OF RIGHTS

James Madison was originally lukewarm toward the addition of a bill of rights to the Constitution. Yet, when the first Congress under the Constitution assembled in April, 1789, it was nevertheless he who assumed the leadership role in meeting the widespread demand for its creation. Madison's correspondence with Jefferson as well as political realities had caused him to modify his position. On June 8, 1789, he rose in the House of Representatives and moved that the House consider the subject of constitutional amendments: "I shall proceed to bring the amendments before you . . . and advocate them until they shall be finally adopted or rejected by a constitutional majority of this House." Though strongly Federalist, he went on, "this House is bound by every motive of prudence, not to let the first session pass over without proposing to the State Legislatures some things to be incorporated into the constitution, that will render it . . . acceptable to the whole people of the United States." The great mass of the people who opposed the Constitution "disliked it because it did not contain effectual provisions against encroachments on particular rights." Now, he argued, it was for the Congress "to provide those securities for liberty . . . and expressly declare the great rights of mankind secured under this constitution." [1]

The inclusion of a Bill of Rights providing "every desirable safeguard for popular rights," would reconcile at least the more moderate Antifederalists to the new governmental system. This would separate "the well-meaning from the designing opponents, fix on the latter their true character, and give to the Government their due popularity and stability." [2]

In addition, as part of his closely contested campaign for election to Congress, Madison had come out in favor of amendments. The Antifederalists, who ran James Monroe as a strong opponent, had tried to brand Madison as an antiamendment candidate. "It has been very industriously inculcated," wrote Madison to Washington, "that I am dogmatically attached to the Constitution in every clause, syllable & letter, and therefore not a single amendment will be promoted by my vote. . . . This is the report most likely to affect the election, and most difficult to be combated with success." [3] To counter the anti-amendment reports, Madison wrote in a letter to Baptist minister George Eve, who had asked for a statement, "it is my sincere opinion that the Constitution ought to be revised, and that the first Congress meeting under it ought to prepare and recommend to the States for ratification, the most satisfactory provisions for all essential rights, particularly the rights of Conscience in the fullest latitude, the freedom of the press, trials by jury, security against general warrants, &c." [4]

After his election to Congress, Madison acted to make good on his campaign promise by pressing the amendment issue. The remainder of this chapter will trace the legislative history of the Bill of Rights in the first Congress. We are able to follow the proceedings in the House of Representatives both through the report of the debates in the House contained in the *Annals of Congress*—compiled from newspaper accounts and Lloyd's *Congressional Register*—and the *Journal* of the House. It is far from the verbatim transcript contained in the modern *Congressional Record*, though it does give us an adequate picture of what occurred on the floor of the House. For the Senate, the situation is much less satisfactory, for its debates were not reported at that time.

MADISON INTRODUCES HIS AMENDMENTS

When the first Congress convened in the old City Hall on Wall Street in New York, in April, 1789, Madison was at the peak of his powers, both physically and intellectually. He was a slender, short-statured man of thirty-eight, not yet clothed in the habitual black that would later rule his dress. His more likely costume at this earlier period was of ornate blue and buff, with hair powdered and falling behind in the beribboned queue of fashion.[5] "He speaks low," said Fisher Ames, "his person is little and ordinary." [6] In fact, he was so small he could not be seen by all the members and his voice was so weak he could scarcely be heard throughout the hall.[7] Yet it was of Madison that John Marshall once said if eloquence included the art of "persuasion by convincing, Mr. Madison was the most eloquent man I ever heard." [8] Madison may have spoken so softly at times that even the reporter could not catch what he said,[9] but the power of his speeches—in the Philadelphia Convention, in the Virginia Ratifying Convention, and in the first Congress—has, in spite of poor reporting, projected itself through almost two centuries.

It was Madison, acting to fulfill his campaign pledge, who was the prime mover in the congressional chapter of the Bill of Rights. George Washington, now President, had, it is true, noted in his first message to Congress the widespread demand for amendments to the Constitution. He declined, however, to make "particular recommendations on this subject," [10] leaving it to Congress to decide what to do on the matter. The House answered, in an Address to the President drafted by Madison, that the question of amendments "will receive all the attention demanded by its importance." [11]

The new Congress had been scheduled to meet on March 4, but numerous delays had postponed the opening sessions until April 1 in the House and April 6 in the Senate. Both Houses were concerned with other subjects during the first part of the session. The House in particular was involved in a lengthy debate on import and tonnage duties. On May 4, in the midst of the debate, Madison gave notice, in his quiet voice, that he intended "to bring on the subject of amendments to the constitution" on May 25.[12] Madison acted on this date to counter an incipient movement for a second convention to decide on amendments. The very next day, in fact, an application from the Virginia legislature for such a convention was introduced by Congressman Theodorick Bland and a similar application from New York was brought forth on May 6.[13] Madison deftly secured the filing of both applications, instead of having them referred to the Committee of the Whole. When he officially introduced his proposed amendments, on June 8, he effectively ended any chance the applications might otherwise have had for a second convention.

Madison did not bring up the subject of amendments on May 25, as he had announced he would, probably because the House was still in the midst of its debate on import duties. In a May 27 letter to Jefferson, he noted that "The subject of amendments . . . is postponed in order that more urgent business may not be delayed." [14] Apparently it was agreed, though the *Annals* are silent on the point, to postpone the subject for two weeks. On June 8, Madison rose at the beginning of the session and reminded the House that this was the day assigned for considering the subject of constitutional amendments. He said he would bring the amendments forward and hold the House on this issue until a vote was taken to adopt or reject them. He then moved that the House go into Committee of the Whole to consider the matter.

The Madison motion was opposed by those members who objected to the interruption of the revenue business with which the House was engaged. James Jackson of Georgia declared that, "we ought not to be in a hurry with respect to altering the constitution," but even "if gentlemen should think it a subject deserving of attention, they will surely not neglect the more important business which is now unfinished before them . . . without revenue the wheels of Government cannot move." [15] Madison replied that someone like Jackson, who was unfriendly to amendments, was right in opposing his motion; but the same was not true of those who favored amendments: "if we continue to postpone from time to time, ... it may occasion suspicions" and the public "may think we are not sincere in our desire to incorporate such amendments in the constitution as will secure those rights, which they consider as not sufficiently guarded." [16] Madison's statement indicates how widespread was the popular demand for a Bill of Rights, as well as how great was the need for the Federalists, who had a clear Congressional majority, to act speedily as well. Other opponents of the motion then spoke, repeating, in Roger Sherman's words, the argument that it would be "imprudent to neglect much more important concerns for this." [17]

Madison then delivered what is today rightly considered one of the great addresses in our history. [18] In what was, in effect, the sponsor's statement on the legislative measure that was to become the Federal Bill of Rights, he sets out the arguments for adherence to the popular will. He begins by apologizing for being "accessory to the loss of a single moment of time by the House." But, he says, prudence itself requires the House not to let its first session pass "without proposing to the State Legislatures some things to be incorporated into the constitution, that will render it . . . acceptable to the whole people of the United States." It is desirable to quiet the apprehensions felt by many that the Constitution does not adequately protect liberty. "We ought not to disregard their inclination, but, on principles of amity and moderation conform to their wishes" and extinguish "any apprehensions that there are those . . . who wish to deprive them of the liberty for which they valiantly fought and honorably bled." Madison goes on to say that there is everything to gain and nothing to lose if we "provide those securities for liberty which are required by a part of the community." He refers again to the extent of the popular desire for a bill of rights: "the great mass of the people who opposed it, disliked it because it did not contain effectual provisions against encroachments on particular rights, and those safeguards which they have been long accustomed to have interposed between them and the magistrate who exercises the sovereign power." To "obviate the objection, so far as to satisfy the public mind that their liberties will be perpetual," Congress should now declare "the great rights" guaranteed under the Constitution.

Madison then read the list of "amendments which have occurred to me, proper to be recommended by Congress to the State Legislatures." Here we have the crucial first draft of the Federal Bill of Rights. The Madison proposals covered all the articles eventually included in the Bill of Rights, most of them in the language finally adopted. This list was, of course, based directly on the recommended amendments of the various state ratifying conventions, particularly on those submitted by Madison's own state, Virginia. His draft clearly reflected state consensus on those rights to be secured. He purposely avoided controversial provisions, saying, "I shall not propose a single alteration but is likely to meet the concurrence required by the constitution." Or, as he elsewhere put it in contemporary letters, "I need not remark to you the hazard of attempting anything of a controvertible nature which is to depend on the concurrence of ⅔ of both Houses here, and the ratification of ¾ of the State Legislatures." Indeed, "two or three contentious additions would even now prostrate the whole project." [19]

When Madison drafted his amendments, he had available a widely circulated pamphlet printed at Richmond in 1788 containing the text of the amendments recommended by New York, Massachusetts, New Hampshire, South Carolina, Virginia, and North Carolina, as well as those of the committee appointed by the Maryland Convention. [20] The Madison amendments were a distillate of the various proposals emanating from the state conventions. [21] This can be seen clearly by referring again to the table on pages 157–158. Of the Madison provisions ultimately adopted as the first ten amendments, all but the right to just compensation were derived from the state-proposed amendments.

Madison proposed nine amendments for the Bill of Rights. [22] They provided that:

(1) there be prefixed to the Constitution a declaration that all power is derived from the people, who have a right to reform or change their government whenever it is found inadequate;

(2) there shall be one representative for every thirty thousand people;

(3) no law varying Congressional compensation shall become operative before the next ensuing Congressional election;

(4) civil rights shall not be abridged on account of religious belief or worship, nor shall any national religion be established, or the rights of conscience be infringed; the people shall not be deprived of their right to speak, write, or publish their sentiments and freedom of the press shall be inviolable; the right of peaceful assembly and petition for redress of grievances shall not be restrained; the right to bear arms shall not be infringed, but no conscientious objector shall be compelled to render military service in person; no soldiers shall be quartered in peacetime in any house without the consent of the owner; no person shall be subject to more than one punishment for the same offense, nor shall be compelled to be a witness against himself, nor be deprived of life, liberty, or property without due process of law, nor be obliged to relinquish property for public use without just compensation; excessive bail shall not be required, nor excessive fines imposed, nor cruel and unusual punishments inflicted; unreasonable searches and seizures shall be forbidden; in criminal prosecutions the accused shall enjoy the right to a speedy and public trial, to be informed of the cause and nature of the accusation, to be confronted with accusers and witnesses, to have compulsory process for obtaining witnesses, and to have the assistance of counsel; exceptions in the Constitution shall not be construed so as to enlarge delegated powers but as limitations or precautions;

(5) no state shall violate the equal rights of conscience, or freedom of the press, or trial by jury in criminal cases;

(6) no appeal to the Supreme Court shall be allowed where the amount in controversy is less than a minimum value, nor

shall any fact triable by jury be otherwise re-examinable than in accordance with common law principles;

(7) criminal trials shall be by an impartial jury of free-holders of the vicinage, with unanimity required, and other accustomed requisites; presentment or indictment by a grand jury shall be essential in all crimes punishable with loss of life or member; in case of crimes not committed within any county, the trial may be in such county as the laws shall have prescribed; in civil suits at common law trial by jury ought to remain inviolate;

(8) neither the legislative, executive, nor judicial departments shall ever exercise the powers vested in another department; the powers not delegated by the Constitution nor prohibited by it to the states are reserved to the states respectively;

(9) Article VII shall be renumbered as Article VIII.

As a May 27 letter to Jefferson shows,[23] Madison had decided by then to incorporate his bill of rights into the text of the Constitution. The amendments read by him on June 8 were drawn up as insertions into the body of the Constitution, with the exception of his first amendment, which was to be prefixed, as a general declaration before the words "We the People." Madison's second and third amendments were to be inserted in those portions of Article I dealing with the number of representatives and congressional compensation; his fourth amendment to be added to Article I, section 9, which contains restrictions on the powers of Congress; his fifth amendment to be placed in Article I, section 10, which imposes restrictions on state power; his sixth and seventh amendments to be inserted in Article III, which deals with judicial power; his eighth amendment to become a new Article VII; and his ninth amendment renumbered Article VII as Article VIII. As we shall see, the Madison plan in this respect was changed during the debate to the present form of a series of separate amendments to be added at the end of the Constitution.

The remainder of Madison's June 8 speech seeks to explain his amendments and the need for them. There is little new here, though Madison's statement is now considered the classic presentation of the case for a Bill of Rights. Of particular interest is his recognition of the effectiveness of what critics called "paper barriers against the power of the community." To Madison, they "may be one means to control the majority from those acts to which they might otherwise be inclined."

A Bill of Rights will have "a salutary effect against the abuse of power" because "independent tribunals of justice will consider themselves in a peculiar manner the guardians of those rights; they will be an impenetrable bulwark against every assumption of power in the legislative or executive; they will be naturally led to resist every encroachment upon rights expressly stipulated for in the constitution by the declaration of rights." Madison stressed his fifth amendment prohibiting the states from violating the right of conscience, freedom of the press, or jury trial, "because it is proper that every Government should be disarmed of powers which trench upon those particular rights." With acute perception, he urged that "there is more danger of those powers being abused by the State Governments than by the Government of the United States." Madison concluded by withdrawing his earlier motion for consideration of the proposed amendments by the Committee of the Whole (since the other speakers had opposed it) and moved instead that a select committee be now appointed. The other speakers, however, opposed the new motion and a motion to refer Madison's proposals to the House acting as a Committee of the Whole was adopted. This ended the debate of June 8.

MADISON'S CONTRIBUTION

Madison's own notes for his June 8 speech tell us that his amendments "relate 1st to private rights." As such, the Madison proposal "relates to what may be called a bill of rights." The object of it is "To limit and qualify powr. by exceptg. from grant cases in wch. it shall not be exercised or exd. in a particular manner." Its primary purpose is to guard "against the legislative, for it is the most powerful, and most likely to be abused," as well as to guard against abuses by the executive and "the body of the people, operating by the majority against the minority." Thus, it will guard against what he points to "as the greatest danger which in Rep: is Prerogative of majority." [24]

As already stated, the Madison amendments cover every one of the articles that eventually became the Federal Bill of Rights. Four of Madison's amendments were eliminated during the congressional debate: his first amendment containing the general declaration of the theory of popular government; his fifth, prohibiting state violations of freedom of conscience, the press, and trial by jury; his sixth, limiting appeals; and eighth, dealing with the separation of powers. Two failed of ratification: his second and third amendments, dealing with congressional size and compensation. The other Madison amendments survived substantially in their original form as the Federal Bill of Rights itself. Every provision of the Bill of Rights is based directly upon Madison's original draft. Where changes were made during the congressional debate, they related to form rather than substance.

The extent of Madison's achievement is not lessened by the fact that he based his draft upon the state recommendatory amendments, especially those of Virginia. "What a cool & exploring sagacity," wrote St. John Crèvecoeur to Jefferson in October, 1788, "will be wanted in the discussion and acceptation of these numberless amendments, which a few of the States insist upon, in order to please every body, & yet to discriminate the useful from the needless &c." [25] It was Madison who chose which among the pyramid of state proposals should be acted upon by Congress and, with the perspective of two centuries, we can say that he chose remarkably well, including in his list all the great rights appropriate for constitutional protection—except for equal protection, which was not even thought of as a basic right at the time. It was Madison also who tightened the constitutional language, substituting the imperative "shall" for all but one of the flaccid "ought" and "ought nots" of the state proposals,[26] thus virtually completing the process begun by John Adams in the Massachusetts Declaration of Rights.[27] We can see Madison's contribution in this respect in the following sequence:

Bill of Rights, 1689: "That excessive bail *ought not* to be required, nor excessive fines imposed; nor cruel and unusual punishments inflicted."

Virginia Declaration of Rights, 1776: "That excessive bail *ought not* to be required, nor excessive fines imposed, nor cruel and unusual punishments inflicted."

Virginia-Proposed Amendments, 1788: "That excessive bail *ought not* to be required, nor excessive fines imposed, nor cruel and unusual punishments inflicted."

Amendment proposed by Madison, June 8, 1789: "Excessive bail *shall not* be required, nor excessive fines imposed, nor cruel and unusual punishments inflicted." [28]

Madison's amendments were based on the understanding that mere declarations and wishful normatives were not enough, that the situation called for flat commands. In America, as the Virginia-proposed bill of rights had stated expressly, the people were sovereign and officials their mere trustees and agents. "In Europe," wrote Madison, "charters of liberty have been granted by power"; in America, "Charters of power granted by liberty." [29] In Magna Carta, where King John spoke as monarch, "We will not" was deemed proper. In the English Bill of Rights, where William and Mary still spoke as sovereigns, "ought not" was deemed bold enough for the protection of the rights of subjects. Now when the American people prescribed the acts their new federal government were not to do at all or were to do only in a particular manner, it was appropriate to say "shall not"—the language of command. It was Madison who toughened the old flaccid exhortations into imperative law.[30]

In addition, it was Madison who followed the New York rather than the Virginia precedent and drafted his version of section 39 of Magna Carta in terms of "due process of law," instead of "the law of the land." We do not know what led Madison to use the New York due process language. Perhaps it was Hamilton, with whom he was in close contact at the time, who influenced him in this respect. Hamilton was one of the few men at that early date who realized that the phrase "due process" might make a difference. In his already referred to speech in the New York Assembly on February 6, 1787, Hamilton emphasized that the words "due process" in the just enacted "Act concerning the Rights of the Citizens of this State" removed any doubt over whether a person might be disfranchised or deprived of any right by an Act of the legislature. Only "the process and proceedings of the courts of justice" could, consistently with the due process phraseology, disenfranchise or deprive anyone of a right.[31] At any rate, Madison's change from "the law of the land" to "due process of law" was the origin of the Due Process Clause of the Fifth, and later of the Fourteenth Amendment, and was of seminal significance for our subsequent constitutional development—although it may be doubted that Madison (any more than Lansing and Hamilton in New York before him) realized anything like the full import of what he was doing in writing the Due Process Clause into the Constitution.

SELECT COMMITTEE AND COMMITTEE OF THE WHOLE

On July 21, six weeks after he introduced his proposed amendments, Madison again rose and "begged the House to indulge him in the further consideration of amendments." [32] He moved that the House go into Committee of the Whole, in accordance with the motion passed at the end of the June 8 debate. The House instead voted to send Madison's motion, as well as the amendments proposed by the various states, to a select committee, "to consist of a member from each State," with instructions to consider the subject of amendments "and to report thereupon to the House." [33] A Committee of Eleven (North Carolina and Rhode Island had not yet ratified) was appointed, with Madison himself the appointee from Virginia. The only other well-known member was Roger Sherman of Connecticut, who had been a consistent opponent of a bill of rights; in the July 21 debate, he asserted that the House should not "agree to amendments offered on mere speculative points when the constitution has had no kind of trial whatever." [34]

The select committee did its job rapidly and a week later, on July 28, John Vining of Delaware, who acted as chairman, "made a report which was ordered to lie on the table." [35] The amendments as rewritten by the Committee of Eleven made no substantial alteration in the original Madison draft. The committee did, however, make certain stylistic changes that brought the amendments closer to the final bill of rights version. The most important of these were: the direct use of the term "freedom of speech, and of the press"; a change to what was to be the language of the Just Compensation Clause of the Fifth Amendment; the use of almost the exact language ultimately contained in the Ninth Amendment; and the adoption of the substance of what was to be the Seventh Amendment. In addition, Madison's declaratory prefix was shortened to the statement, "Government being intended for the benefit of the people, and the rightful establishment thereof being derived from their authority alone," to be inserted before the words, "We the People," and freedom of speech was added to the proposed prohibition on the states.[36] These changes scarcely alter the fact that the committee version was a virtual restatement of the amendments proposed by Madison. Apparently, an effort had been made in the committee to have it report all the amendments proposed by the states. The reason they did not do so, said Chairman Vining, was that "The committee conceived some of them superfluous or dangerous, and found many of them so contradictory that it was impossible to make any thing of them." [37]

Again Madison had to stir his colleagues to action. On August 3, he moved that the amendments recommended by the Committee of Eleven be made the order of business for August 12. The House agreed, resolving to go into Committee of the Whole on that day to consider the matter. On August 12, the House was busy on other matters and it was not until the next day that the House began in earnest to consider the amendments in Committee of the Whole. The debate lasted until August 24, with the House sitting in Committee of the Whole through August 18 and as the House itself from then on.[38]

The August 13 debate began with a discussion of whether or not time to consider the proposed amendments should be set aside then or at a later session. To the present-day observer, it is amazing that members could believe that "there were several matters before them of more importance than the present" or that "the discussion would take up more time than the House could now spare." [39] To the Federalist majority in the first Congress, the Madison amendments seemed less pressing than the job of ironing out the details of the new governmental system. To carry the motion to consider, Madison had to stress how necessary it was to come to terms with those who had opposed the new system on the bill of rights issue: "Is it desirable to keep up a division among the people of the United States on a point in which they consider their most essential rights are concerned? . . . Already has the subject been delayed much longer than could have been wished."

The motion to consider having carried, the next issue was brought up by Roger Sherman. Sherman argued that the Madison-committee approach of inserting the amendments into the body of the Constitution was not the proper one: "We ought not to interweave our propositions into the work itself, because it will be destructive of the whole fabric. We might as well endeavor to mix brass, iron, and clay, as to incorporate such heterogenous articles." Sherman moved that the amendments be adopted as a series of separate articles to be added at the end of the Constitution. Madison replied that "there is a neatness and propriety in incorporating the amendments into the constitution itself"—an argument that today appears to support the Sherman proposal rather than Madison's. Mr. Vining, the Chairman of the Committee of Eleven, however, agreed with Madison, urging that, "If the mode proposed by the gentleman from Connecticut was adopted, the system would be distorted, and, like a careless written letter, have more attached to it in a postscript than was contained in the original composition." On the other side, it was asserted that, "If the amendments are incorporated in the body of the work, it will appear, unless we refer to the archives . . . , that George Washington, and the other worthy characters who composed the convention, signed an instrument which they never had in contemplation."

At this stage of the debate, a majority supported Madison's position on the form of the amendments and the Sherman motion was defeated, only to be revived on August 19 when it was carried. Probably, at this point, the majority believed with Elbridge Gerry that to spend time on the question of form was "to be trifling about matters of little consequence"—or, as another member put it, "the time of the House was too precious to be squandered away in discussing mere matter of form."

From August 14 to 18, the House considered the amendments reported by the Committee of Eleven in Committee of the Whole. On August 14, members discussed and adopted the general declaration of principles and the provisions on congressional representation and salary increases. On August 15, some of the most important provisions of the proposed amendments were dealt with. First came the discussion of freedom of religion, which was "Madison's first concern, both in drafting his amendments and in the deliberations which now ensued." [40] Members objected to the provision on religious freedom on the ground that it might be "extremely hurtful to the cause of religion." One went so far as to assert that it might "have a tendency to abolish religion altogether."

Madison answered by giving his interpretation of the provision: "that Congress should not establish a religion, and enforce the legal observation of it by law, nor compel men to worship God in any manner contrary to their conscience." The purpose was to prevent Congress from making "laws of such a nature as might infringe the rights of conscience, and establish a national religion." To make this plain, Madison suggested that the word "national" be inserted before "religion." Other members objected, and Madison withdrew his suggestion. Samuel Livermore of New Hampshire then moved that the wording of the provision be changed to that proposed by his state's recommendatory amendment on the matter: "Congress shall make no laws touching religion or infringing the rights of conscience." This change was voted, and the proposed amendments now included, for the first time, the actual introductory language of the First Amendment.

The House then considered the guarantees of freedom of speech and press, and assembly and petition. Theodore Sedgwick of Massachusetts moved to strike out the words "assemble and" saying it was implied and also trifling compared with the other rights covered. If it were covered, why not also the right to wear one's hat as he pleases or to go to bed when one chooses? Other members disagreed, stressing that the right to assemble was important. John Page of Virginia referred to Sedgwick's assertion that the right to assemble was trivial. "He supposes it no more essential than whether a man has a right to wear his hat or not; but let me observe that such rights have been opposed, and a man has been obliged to pull off his hat when he appeared before the face of authority." The reference was to the famous 1670 trial of William Penn, at which the Quaker leader had been fined for contempt for appearing in court with his hat on.[41] Similarly, Page said, "people have also been prevented from assembling together on their lawful occasions, therefore it is well to guard against such stretches of authority." When the question was put, Sedgwick's motion "lost by a considerable majority."

Thomas Tucker of South Carolina then moved to insert expressly the people's right "to instruct their Representatives." The motion was opposed on the ground it would interfere unduly with the discretion and conscience of legislators—"utterly destructive of all ideas of an independent and deliberative body"—though Gerry supported it on the ground that sovereignty was ultimately in the people.

175

Madison now made an important reply to the Tucker motion. He warned against enumerating other than "simple, acknowledged principles" in the provisions to be adopted: "Amendments of a doubtful nature will have a tendency to prejudice the whole system; and the proposition now suggested partakes highly of this nature." With freedom of speech and press protected, the people can freely advise their representatives. To do more would be dangerous. To Gerry's assertion of sovereignty in the people, Madison replied: "My idea of sovereignty of the people is, that the people can change the constitution if they please; but while the constitution exists, they must conform themselves to its dictates."

Madison was making a basic point—that the House should consider the amendments before it and not add others "of a doubtful nature." Gerry chided him: "It is natural, sir, for us to be fond of our own work. We do not like to see it disfigured by other hands." But Madison was not arguing out of mere pride of authorship. Let the proposed bill of rights be opened to all sorts of irrelevant amendments, he noted, and "it obliges us to run the risk of losing the whole system." As Madison put it in a letter to Edmund Randolph, "It has been absolutely necessary in order to effect anything, to abbreviate debate, and exclude every proposition of a doubtful & unimportant nature." [42]

Eventually, Tucker's motion was resoundingly defeated, and the provision on speech, press, assembly, and petition adopted as reported by the Committee of Eleven. By this point, Gerry could refer to the fact that the temper of the debate matched the weather itself: "Gentlemen now feel the weather warm, and the subject is warm; no wonder it produces some degree of heat."

On August 17,[43] the debate began by considering the right to bear arms provisions. There was an attempt to strike out the exemption for conscientious objectors, as well as to require a two-thirds vote for a standing army. Both attempts were defeated, and the provision carried as reported. The same was true of the provision prohibiting the quartering of soldiers. The debate then turned to the provision that was to

become the Fifth Amendment: prohibition of double jeopardy and self-incrimination, and guarantees of due process
and just compensation. John Lawrence of New York moved
to confine the self-incrimination guaranty to criminal cases,
and his motion carried. The provision as reported was then
agreed to unanimously.

The provision governing bail, fines, and punishments was
next agreed to despite earlier objections that it was both in-
definite and too strict. Conceptions of penology strikingly
different from our own manifest themselves in the plaint of
Livermore of New Hampshire that "villains often deserve
whipping, and perhaps having their ears cut off; but are we
in future to be prevented from inflicting these punishments
because they are cruel?" The provision on searches and seizures was considered next. After a mistake in wording was
eliminated by the substitution of new wording provided by
Gerry, the provision was approved speedily.[44] Then the provision that was to become the Ninth Amendment was
quickly approved.

The House next considered the provision prohibiting the
states from infringing on freedom of conscience, speech,
press, and trial by jury in criminal cases. This provision was
approved, as restated in affirmative form by Livermore. The
debate here is important because of Madison's statement that
he "conceived this to be the most valuable amendment in the
whole list. If there was any reason to restrain the Government of the United States from infringing upon these essential rights, it was equally necessary that they should be secured against the State Governments." This provision was to
be eliminated by the Senate. Hence, the Bill of Rights as
adopted imposed restrictions only upon the federal government. Not until ratification of the amendments added in the
post-Civil War period was the Constitution to contain significant limitations upon state power to infringe upon individual liberties.[45]

The only thing of importance considered in the rest of the
August 17 debate was the provision that became the first part
of the Sixth Amendment. Livermore moved that the right to

trial in the state where the offense was committed be added and this was adopted.

When the proposed amendments were considered the next day, August 18, Gerry moved that the House consider all the amendments recommended by the different states, not just those reported by the Committee of Eleven. Both Madison and Vining objected, and Gerry's motion was defeated. The remaining provision on criminal procedure—trial by jury of the vicinage and indictment—was then approved. Thomas Burke of North Carolina moved to change "vicinage" into "district or county in which the offense has been committed." The motion lost, though the Sixth Amendment was ultimately to contain language closer to that proposed by Burke. The provisions on jury trial in civil cases, as well as on separation of powers, were adopted next.

When the provision on reserved powers was taken up, Tucker moved to add the word "expressly," so that "the powers not *expressly* delegated" to the federal government would be reserved to the states. Madison was quick to oppose, arguing that "it was impossible to confine a Government to the exercise of express powers; there must necessarily be admitted powers by implication, unless the constitution descended to recount every minutia." Here we have the first statement of the seminal constitutional doctrine of implied powers—two years before Hamilton would rely on the doctrine in his opinion on the constitutionality of the Bank of the United States [46] and three decades before Marshall would give it constitutional status in *McCulloch v. Maryland*. [47] Had Madison not persuaded his colleagues to defeat Tucker's motion, the landmark *McCulloch* opinion could never have been written.

The amendments of the Committee of Eleven, as changed in Committee of the Whole, were then reported to the House. Tucker moved to refer seventeen additional amendments to the Committee of the Whole. The Tucker motion was defeated and the House could now proceed to final consideration of the amendments.

HOUSE PASSAGE

On August 19, the House began its consideration of the proposed amendments to the Constitution, as reported by the Committee of the Whole. The debate started with a renewal by Sherman of his motion to add the amendments at the end of the Constitution. "Hereupon ensued a debate similar to what took place in the Committee of the Whole" on August 13. This time, the Sherman motion was carried by two-thirds of the House, and this explains why we have the Federal Bill of Rights in its present form, as a series of separate amendments following the original Constitution. This change was of the greatest significance; it may be doubted that the Bill of Rights could have attained its position as the vital center of our constitutional law, had its provisions been dispersed throughout the Constitution. Paradoxically, it is to Sherman—a consistent opponent of a bill of rights—that we owe a debt of thanks for his fight to have a separate bill of rights.

The House also voted on August 19 to reject the proposed addition to the Preamble, containing the general declaration of government as intended for the benefit of the people, from whose authority government alone is derived. This declaration was to be prefixed to the Constitution before the words "We the People." During the discussion in Committee of the Whole, on August 14, Page of Virginia had opposed any addition to the Preamble: "the words 'We the people,' had the neatness and simplicity, while its expression was the most forcible of any he had ever seen prefixed to any constitution." Sherman agreed that "The words 'We the people' in the original constitution are as copious and expressive as possible; any addition will only drag out the sentence." We do not have any report of what was said on the matter on August 19, but objections like those of Page and Sherman probably convinced the House. It is fortunate they did; to have added the general declaration to the Preamble would, despite Madison's disclaimer, involve "loading it with more words [that] may destroy the beauty of the sentence."

On August 20, the House adopted, on motion of Fisher Ames of Massachusetts, the following substitute provision on freedom of religion: "Congress shall make no law establishing religion, or to prevent the free exercise thereof, or to infringe the rights of conscience." Madison's biographer, Irving Brant, claims for his subject authorship of the provision [48] and, if this is so, Madison was able to put his view of religious freedom into the Constitution. The Ames amendment is very close to the actual language of the First Amendment's two-fold prohibition—containing both a provision for free exercise (similar to that which Madison had inserted into the Virginia Declaration of Rights in 1776) [49] and the ban against establishment, which he emphasized in his August 15 speech. The August 20 session ended with some discussion of the exemption from military service of conscientious objectors; the House then approved most of the fourth and the fifth, sixth, and seventh propositions reported.

On August 21, Gerry renewed the motion to add "expressly" to the provision on reserved powers, emphasizing that this was "an amendment of great importance." Again the motion lost. Sherman successfully moved to change the provision's language to that ultimately included in the Tenth Amendment. There was lengthy debate on a Burke motion to add a provision prohibiting Congress from interfering with congressional elections. The Burke amendment was defeated, as were amendments limiting congressional taxing power, and dealing with courts, merchants' companies, and foreign titles of nobility. Fortunately, the House followed Madison's plea not "to delay the amendments now agreed upon, by entering into the consideration" of new and lesser amendments. On August 22, the remaining amendments reported were approved and the amendments were then referred to a three-man committee that included Sherman. The committee was "to prepare and report a proper arrangement of . . . the articles of amendment, as they had been agreed to." The task of this committee was essentially to arrange the House amendments as separate amendments to be added at the end of the Constitution, in accordance with the Sherman motion adopted on August 19. The committee reported on August 24. It had arranged the proposals approved by the House into seventeen amendments to be added "by way of appendix" to the Constitution. One who reads these amendments must conclude, as Madison did in a letter to Alexander White, "The substance of the report of the Committee of eleven has not been much varied." [50] The amendments in the form reported were agreed to by the House on August 24. The House debate concluded on that day when it was ordered that the Clerk of the House carry to the Senate a copy of the House amendments and request their concurrence. [51]

SENATE, CONFERENCE, AND FINAL PASSAGE

The Senate sat behind closed doors until February, 1794, when a resolution directing that future sessions be public was passed. No report of the early Senate debates behind closed doors is therefore available. All that we have are the skeleton-like account of the legislative history in the Senate *Journal* and the even skimpier account in the *Annals of Congress*. They tell us the exact changes made in the House amendments, as well as what further attempted amendments were rejected, but they tell us nothing of the discussion during the Senate debates.

The House amendments were formally read in the Senate on August 25, the day after House approval. At that time, an attempt was made to have Senate consideration postponed until the next session. We know some of the details of this because Senator William Maclay of Pennsylvania kept a diary, which tells us what went on behind the closed doors of the Senate Chamber. Writing of the introduction of the House amendments on August 25, Maclay writes: "They were treated contemptuously by Izard, Langdon, and Mr. Morris. Izard moved that they should be postponed till next session. Langdon seconded, and Mr. Morris got up and spoke angrily but not well. They, however, lost their motion, and Monday was assigned for taking them up. I could not help observing the six-year class [i.e., of Senators] hung together on this business, or the most of them." [52]

Maclay then became ill, and was not present for the actual Senate debates on the Bill of Rights; so we are deprived of further information from his diary accounts. Maclay's diary does, however, tell us the Senate business he discussed with visitors during his illness, and seemingly nothing was mentioned about the proposed constitutional amendments. [53] This tends to confirm the curious point already noted that the Congress was apparently much less concerned with the bill of rights issue than the country at large—if we can judge by the 1787–1788 ratification debates, as well as newspaper and other contemporary writings.

Although Monday, August 31, had been assigned for Senate consideration of the House amendments, the intervention of other business prevented the Senate from taking up the subject until Wednesday, September 2. As already indicated, we do not know what was said during the Senate debates; but we do know what changes the upper House made in the proposed amendments. As a generalization, we can say that the Senate performed the important job of tightening up the language of the House version, striking out surplus wording and provisions.

The most important substantive change made by the Senate was the elimination on September 7 of the amendment Madison considered "the most valuable amendment in the whole list": that prohibiting the states from infringing on freedom of conscience, speech, press, and jury trial. The result, as the Supreme Court was to confirm in the 1833 case of *Barron v. Mayor of Baltimore*, [54] was that the Bill of Rights as adopted could be used to impose limitations upon federal power only. In addition, the Senate made a significant change in form, combining the two House amendments covering freedom of religion and freedom of speech, press, assembly, and petition into one amendment, the form that was to be retained in the First Amendment.

When the Senate began its consideration of the House amendments on September 2 and 3 it made some minor alter-

ations in the first two, relating to representation and congressional pay.[55] The amendment on religious freedom gave
the members some difficulty on September 3. After debate,
in which various alterations were unsuccessfully proposed,
the Senate agreed to the House amendment, with the words
"nor shall the rights of conscience be infringed" eliminated.[56] This was to bring the language closer to that contained in the First Amendment, but a later Senate amendment was to weaken the provision again.

The freedom of speech, press, assembly, and petition
amendment was then discussed. An attempt like that in the
House to insert "to instruct their representatives" was defeated. On September 4, the amendment was approved, to
read "That Congress shall make no law, abridging the freedom of speech, or of the press, or the right of the people
peaceably to assemble and consult for their common good,
and to petition the government for a redress of grievances." [57] The wording was thus brought closer to that ultimately used in the First Amendment. The Senate next
adopted the amendment on the right to bear arms, after eliminating the House provision exempting conscientious objectors from service in person. The House amendments on quartering of soldiers and search and seizure were then agreed to.
Next, the Senate rewrote the provision on double jeopardy
and that on grand jury indictment, in both cases putting in
the language that was to appear in the Fifth Amendment.

The remainder of the Senate debate was concerned with
three things: 1) the rejection of other proposed amendments,
including a whole series based upon the Virginia-recom-
mended amendments that had not been included by Madison in his proposed amendments; 2) the rejection of several
of the House-passed amendments that included the already-
mentioned prohibition upon the states from infringing on
freedom of conscience, speech, press, and jury trial, as well
as the House amendments on appeals to the Supreme Court
and separation of powers; and 3) the strengthening of remaining provisions by changes in language and the combining
of related amendments, particularly in the case of the two

House amendments on freedom of religion and freedom of speech, press, assembly, and petition, which were fused on September 9 into the combined prohibition contained in the First Amendment, though with the religious guaranty considerably weakened—a backward step that was to be corrected in the Conference Committee. The Senate also combined the provisions (after improving their language) relating to indictment, double jeopardy, self-incrimination, due process, and just compensation into one amendment—the form it was to retain in the Fifth Amendment—and did the same for the two House provisions bearing on trial by jury in civil cases, at the same time inserting the twenty dollar limitation that appears in the Seventh Amendment. In the tightening process, the Senate left out the express guaranty of trial by jury in criminal cases. It probably did so because, as Madison indicated to Edmund Pendleton, it felt the limitation to juries "of the vicinage" to be too restrictive.[58] The Senate deletion was later corrected by the Conference Committee. There was also the same attempt as that made in the House to insert "expressly" into what became the Tenth Amendment. Again it failed.[59]

When the Senate finished its debate on the matter, it had reduced the seventeen House amendments to twelve. The first two dealt with the number of representatives and congressional compensation; the remaining ten were (except for the changes to be made in the Conference Committee) the amendments that became the Federal Bill of Rights. Except for the provision on religious freedom, the language of the House amendments had been substantially improved and brought almost to the final language of the Federal Bill of Rights. On September 9, the Senate concurred in the resolution of the House, with the amendments already noted, and ordered communication of this to be made to the House.[60]

The next day the House received the Senate's message that it had agreed to the House amendments, "with several amendments: to which they desire the concurrence of this House." The House considered the subject on September 19 and 21. On the latter date, they voted on the Senate changes, "some of which they agreed to, and disagreed to others." The House then resolved that "a committee of conference was desired with the Senate, on the subject matter of the amendments disagreed to." [61] Madison, Sherman, and Vining—the three members who had played the largest part in the House debate—were appointed managers on the part of the House, and Oliver Ellsworth, Charles Carroll, and William Paterson as Senate conferees. In conference, Madison apparently made an effort to get the Senate conferees "to concur in the limitation on value of appeals to the Supreme Court," but "they say [it is] unnecessary, and might be embarrassing in questions of national or Constitutional importance in their principle, tho' of small pecuniary amount." The Senate conferees "are equally inflexible in opposing a definition of the *locality* of Juries," [62] though they gave way on this, insisting only that the word "vicinage" not be used.

On September 23, Madison made the Conference Report to the House. It recommended that the House accept all the Senate amendments and, in addition, itself called for three further changes. The first was a minor alteration in the wording of the amendment on representation. The third gave the final form to the Sixth Amendment and reinserted the right to a jury trial of the locality (though not restricted to the vicinage), which the Senate had omitted. The second change made by the Conference Committee was of greater importance—replacing the weakened Senate version of the religious freedom guaranty by the simple yet strict prohibitions of what are now the Establishment and Free Exercise Clauses of the First Amendment. Without a doubt, this final version of the first guaranty of the First Amendment was written by Madison; it repeats his earlier House draft, which the Senate had diluted. As Irving Brant puts it, "Of all the versions of the religious guaranty, this most directly covered the thing he was aiming at—absolute separation of church and state and total exclusion of government aid to religion." [63] Madison's success in having the Conference Committee adopt his version of the religious freedom guaranty marked a fitting conclusion of his role in the bill of rights debate.

On September 24, the House voted 37 to 14 to agree to the Conference Report. On the same day, Ellsworth made the Conference Report to the Senate. The next day, the Senate concurred in the amendments as voted by the House. September 25—the day on which the congressional approval was completed—is celebrated as the anniversary of the Bill of Rights. Apart from the first two Articles, which failed of state ratification, the amendments as passed on September 25 (re-numbered to reflect the non-ratification of the first two) now constitute the Federal Bill of Rights.[64]

RATIFICATION

The day after it passed the House-approved amendments, the Senate also agreed to a House resolution "That the President of the United States be requested to transmit to the Executives of the several States . . . copies of the amendments proposed by Congress." [65] On October 2, 1789, President Washington officially transmitted the proposed amendments to the states for ratification. "In pursuance of the enclosed resolution," he wrote to each of the governors, "I have the honor to transmit to your Excellency a copy of the amendments proposed to be added to the constitution of the United States." [66] Thus began the process of ratification of the Bill of Rights by the states. The ratification process ended with the official notice sent by Secretary of State Jefferson on March 1, 1792, to the governors of the several states, announcing that three-fourths of the state legislatures had ratified the first ten amendments.

The Jefferson letter read as follows:

I have the honor to send you herein enclosed, two copies duly authenticated, of an Act concerning certain fisheries of the United States, and for the regulation and government of the fishermen employed therein: also of an Act to establish the post

office and post roads within the United States; also the ratifications by three fourths of the Legislatures of the Several States,
of certain articles in addition and amendment of the Constitution of the United States, proposed by Congress to the said
Legislatures, and of being with sentiments of the most perfect
respect, your Excellency's &.*

It is disappointing considering the crucial significance of
the Federal Bill of Rights, that we know practically nothing
about what went on in the state legislatures during the ratification process. At the time, however, there was nothing in
the states comparable even to the *Annals of Congress*, which
reported, however sketchily, proceedings and debates in the
federal legislature. Even the contemporary newspapers are
virtually silent on the ratification debates in the states. Nor is
this to be explained by the fact that ratification was a mere
perfunctory matter, with virtually no opposition in the state
legislatures. The first two of the amendments proposed by
Congress were never ratified, being rejected or postponed by
five of the states that ratified the Bill of Rights: Delaware,
New Hampshire, New Jersey, New York, and Pennsylvania.
Certainly, there must have been debates in those states on
the matter.

Even in the states that ratified all twelve proposed amendments, there must have been sharp division and debate. We
know this from the facts we have of the Virginia ratification.
The Virginia legislature began its consideration of the
amendments in October, 1789, but it was not until December, 1791, that Virginia could announce its ratification. As a
November 16, 1789, letter from Henry Lee to Hamilton put it,
"The antifederal gentlemen in our assembly do not relish the
amendments." [68]

---

* The author saw the text of this Jefferson letter in *Harper's Magazine,* where,
appropriately enough, it was headed "First Things First." [67] Almost two
centuries later, Jefferson's letter appears a singular way of announcing the
ratification of what many consider the most consequential part of the Constitution itself. Yet it bears out the point already made about the congressional
reluctance to devote the time needed for consideration of the proposed
amendments. In addition, it may help explain the lack of materials on the
ratification debates in the states.

The Virginia House of Delegates gave its overwhelming approval to the amendments in December, 1789. Approval by the state senate was another matter. A letter to Madison describes the situation there: "The amendments . . . are now with the Senate, where from the best information I have been able to collect there is such a division in opinion as not to furnish a ground for probable conjecture as to their decision." [69] The Antifederalists were bolstered by letters to the governor and legislature by Virginia's two Senators, Richard Henry Lee and William Grayson, denouncing the amendments as "inadequate" and "short of the wishes of our Country." [70] A letter to Washington characterized the letter to the legislature as "A very extraordinary letter from our Senators in Congress, complaining of the inefficacy of the proposed amendments, and expressive of their fears, that the State governments would be annihilated." [71] The letter, wrote Madison, "is well calculated to keep alive the disaffection to the Government, and is accordingly applied to that use by the violent partizans." [72] The result on the ratification debate was summarized by Madison for Washington at the beginning of 1790: "the contest . . . on the subject of the amendments ended in the loss of them . . . . the Senate . . . prevented a ratification." [73] By eight to seven, the Virginia Senate voted to strike out the third, eighth, eleventh, and twelfth amendments (ultimately the First, Sixth, Ninth, and Tenth Amendments). The eight man majority then entered in the Virginia Senate Journal a statement of the reasons why they had voted against the amendments. They alleged that the guarantees contained in the rejected amendments were too weak: "they are far short of what the people of Virginia wish, and have asked, and . . . by no means sufficient to secure the rights of the people." In particular, they objected to what was to become the First Amendment, asserting that its prohibition against the passage of any law by Congress infringing upon the rights guaranteed did not adequately "declare and assert the right of the people" or prohibit violations "by the arbitrary decisions of Judges, or by any other means than a legislative act directly to that effect." Thus, despite the bar against "laws establishing any national religion, . . . they might, notwithstanding, levy taxes to any amount, for the support of religion or its preachers." Hence the amendment is "totally inadequate . . . . as it tends to lull the apprehensions of the people on these important points, without affording them security." [74]

The Virginia Senate action meant a two year postponement of the Virginia ratification. As Edmund Randolph wrote to Washington after the senate vote, "It has been thought best by the . . . zealous friends to the constitution to let the whole of them rest." [75] The Virginia legislature delayed final approval until December, 1791. We have no report of the Virginia debates, other than the fragmentary glimpses in the legislative Journals, contemporary newspapers, and letters.

We do not even have such glimpses of the ratification debates in the other states. There are the official notices of ratification, yet we know practically nothing of what went on in the state legislatures during the ratification process. From newspaper accounts, we learn of the messages of the governors of Massachusetts,[76] New York,[77] and New Hampshire [78] submitting the amendments to their legislatures. But all the newspapers give us are the results in several of the legislatures. For example, in a New York newspaper of January 26, 1790, we read that, in the assembly of that state, "The several articles having been read and considered were approved of, excepting the second." [79] Other newspaper accounts tell us only that the amendments were "agreed to" by the legislatures of New Jersey,[80] Pennsylvania ("A variety of opinion prevailing as to [the first and second] articles"),[81] Maryland ("unanimously"),[82] New Hampshire,[83] Delaware,[84] Connecticut ("by large majorities"),[85] and North Carolina.[86]

After Virginia, we know most about what happened in Massachusetts. Our knowledge, however, leaves us with a historical puzzle. Massachusetts was one of the three states that did not send official notice of ratification to the President. Yet the Journals of the Massachusetts legislature indicate that it approved all but three of the proposed amendments. On January 14, 1790, Massachusetts Governor John

Hancock directed the Secretary to lay the amendments before the legislature. A few days later, he delivered a speech to both Houses, in which he stated that "These articles . . . I believe will meet your ready approbation," since they "appear to me as very important to that personal security which is so truly characteristick of a free government." [87]

The Journal of the Massachusetts Senate shows that the senate took up the amendments on January 29, "and the Senate rejected the 1 & 2 and accepted the 3, 4, 5, 6, 7, 8, 9, 10, 11 & 12, and ordered that Mesrs. Bridge & Lyman, with such to be a Com. to bring in a bill or resolve declaring their adoption—Sent down for concurrence. Came up concurred except the 12. which is rejected & Mesrs. Spooner, Jarvis & Bacon joined—Concurred." The Massachusetts House Journal for February 2 states that "The House proceeded . . . to consider the amendments . . . and the question being taken upon each of them the following were accepted viz The third, fourth, fifth, sixth, seventh, eighth, ninth, tenth & eleventh. The first and second were not accepted. . . . The House proceeded to the consideration of the twelfth article . . . and the question being put whether the House would accept the same, it passed in the negative." [88]

The extracts quoted from the Journals of the Massachusetts legislature state that both Houses voted acceptance of all but three of the proposed amendments, the first, second, and twelfth. This would mean that the Massachusetts legislature did adopt what became the first nine amendments. Why then was Massachusetts not included in the states that ratified? The question also puzzled Secretary of State Jefferson, for he wrote Christophor Gore of Boston on August 8, 1791, to inquire what had happened. Gore answered that "I applied to the office of the Secretary of the Commonwelth, for a copy of the supposed act, ratifying the amendments proposed by Congress—The Secretary inform'd me, that no such act ever passed the legislature of Massachusetts." Gore went on to confirm the cryptic account in the legislative Journals: "The Senate agreed to all the amendments except the 1st & 2nd—the House concurr'd except as to the 12th/ The Senate agreed to the alteration of the House, and appointed two of their body, with such as the house should join, to bring in a bill declaratory of their assent—the house joined one of their members to the committee—It does not appear that the Committee ever reported any bill.[89]

Thus, though the two Houses in Massachusetts voted approval of what became the first nine amendments, they failed to vote any bill declaring that they had assented to the amendments; indeed, the committee appointed for that purpose did not report any bill. All this raises a nice legal point. When the Constitution, in Article V, requires an amendment to be ratified by a state legislature, all that appears required is the affirmative vote in favor by the two houses concerned. The further passage of a bill declaring ratification would seem a superfluous formality. If that is the case, Massachusetts did actually ratify the first nine amendments, though official notice was not sent to New York, then the nation's capital.

The state ratifications themselves began with that of Maryland, early in 1790. They ended when Virginia became the tenth state to ratify at the end of 1791.[90] Only ten of the amendments were ratified by the required three-fourths of the states. The first and second of the amendments proposed by Congress, as already stated, were not ratified. The three states that did not officially ratify, Connecticut, Georgia, and Massachusetts, belatedly did so as part of a symbolic gesture in 1939. The Bill of Rights officially became part of the Constitution upon the completion of Virginia's ratification on December 15, 1791.

seven
the bill of rights in operation

ENGLISH LAW COMPARED

In 1970, CBS Television conducted a national poll to determine public reaction now to the Federal Bill of Rights, 180 years after its adoption. Three-fourths of those polled said they would restrict the right of peaceful assembly for protests against government; a majority would abridge the right of free speech and free press for criticisms of government and the right of criminal defendants to confront the witnesses against them, as well as the guaranty against double jeopardy and the privilege against self-incrimination. A third of those questioned would permit the police to search houses for drugs, guns, or other criminal evidence without warrants and a fifth would even permit secret criminal trials.[1]

Chief Justice Earl Warren termed the poll results "disturbing," for they showed how large a segment of the population "believed that the provisions of the Bill of Rights were outdated, and not essential to our way of life." [2] Those of us who nevertheless still recognize in the Bill of Rights essential safeguards for individual liberty have much to thank Madison and his colleagues for. By adding the first ten amendments to the Constitution, they placed these great rights beyond the reach of the ordinary political processes and even beyond that of the angry populace.

The Bill of Rights ensures that the American Constitution will never become, despite Macaulay's famous assertion about it, "all sail and no anchor." [3] Its primary purpose is to place enforceable limitations upon the federal government. Addressing the court in the already-mentioned *Five Knights Case*,[4] Charles I's Attorney-General asked, "Shall any say, The King cannot do this? No, we may only say, He will not do this?" [5] It was precisely to ensure that, in our system, we would be able to say, "The Government *cannot* do this" that the Bill of Rights was added to the Constitution. Its limitations make certain that individual rights are not subject to shifts in public opinion, whether expressed in Gallup-type polls or legislative halls. The Bill of Rights represents a continuing appeal from the people drunk to the people sober in times of tension or hysteria.

Polls such as that taken by CBS make us realize how much was achieved in the framing and voting of the Federal Bill of Rights. The willingness of so many today to give up basic rights gives even sharper focus to the meaning of the bill of rights movement. Were it not for the freedoms guaranteed by the Bill of Rights, says Chief Justice Warren, our Constitution itself could be a sterile document. The rights secured "have become the sacred rights of the American people without which we would have had a form of free government but not the substance of our freedom." [6]

To be sure, the present-day reader tends to look with suspicion on an account that emphasizes anything but the mote in the historical eye. Laudatory history today seems as out of date as the elegant costume of two centuries ago. Yet, if we can no longer in good faith view the past with complete veneration does this mean we must now judge it only with scorn? Twentieth century denigration cannot change the fact that the Federal Bill of Rights was a prodigious accomplishment.

We can best understand the extent of the accomplishment by one last summary comparison of the protections to be found in English law at the time the bills of rights were being drafted in each of the states. Eighteenth-century England was, of course, considered the very home of constitutional liberty. A contemporary observer, the French philosopher

Voltaire, had been sent, in his native country France, to the Bastille for a poem he had not written, whose author he did not know, and with whose views he did not agree. When he came to England, his feeling was one of having left the realm of despotism for a land where, though the laws might sometimes be harsh, men were ruled by law and not by caprice. Here, said Voltaire, the very air one breathes is free, for there is no place for arbitrary power.[7]

Yet even the England of Voltaire's encomium fell short of the standard set by American bills of rights. The rights protected by the Federal Bill of Rights can be grouped into five broad classifications: 1) freedom of religion; 2) the rights of expression and association; 3) the right to privacy; 4) the right to due process; and 5) freedom from arbitrary restraint or trial and from cruel and unusual punishment.[8] By American criteria, these rights were in every case either not protected or inadequately protected in the England of the late eighteenth century.

By the Continental standards with which Voltaire was familiar, England of that day might have looked like the home of free reason.[9] But the consequences of the non-constitutional basis of free expression in England were well illustrated by the libel trial of Thomas Paine, who was prosecuted for publishing the second part of *The Rights of Man*. The trial took place in 1792, the year after the Federal Bill of Rights was ratified. Despite an impassioned defense by Thomas Erskine, Paine was found guilty of sedition for his unfavorable contrast of British monarchism with American republicanism. Erskine's final words at the trial set forth the situation facing his client: "I can reason with the people of England but I cannot fight against the thunder of authority." Without constitutional protection basic rights were always subject to governmental "thunder." So strong was the power of authority that, scarcely had Erskine sat down and the Attorney General risen to reply, when the Paine jury foreman declared, "My lord, I am authorized by the jury to inform the Attorney General that a reply is not necessary. . . . Mr. Attorney General sat down, and the jury gave in their verdict, GUILTY." [10]

The law of seditious libel hung like an albatross on freedom of expression in eighteenth century England. Overt censorship of speech and press had been replaced by the restrictions imposed by power to prosecute under the law of libel. But even a century after Paine's trial, the leading English text could assert "that the legal definition of a seditious libel might easily be so used as to check a great deal of what is ordinarily considered allowable discussion, and would if rigidly enforced be inconsistent with prevailing forms of political agitation." [11] During the eighteenth century, the English law of libel *was* rigorously enforced. "To speak ill of the government was a crime. . . . Every one was a libeller who outraged the sentiments of the dominant party." [12] The crime of seditious libel was used to prohibit criticisms of government. Freedom of expression in England was thus "neither more nor less than this: that a man may publish anything which twelve of his countrymen think is not blamable." [13]

Freedom of association was even more restricted under English law. Until relatively recently, associations we would consider at most venial, including labor unions, benevolent associations, and political clubs, could be condemned as seditious conspiracies. [14] One has only to look at the treatment of the Chartist movement, which sought electoral reforms in nineteenth-century England, to see the reality of English law in this regard.

The situation with regard to freedom of religion was equally unsatisfactory. Freedom of religion in the First Amendment sense was almost totally lacking in England of that day. The established Church of England was the negation of all Madison sought to accomplish by the Establishment Clause, and freedom of conscience meant only the right to free exercise of the established faith, wholly contrary to the Madisonian concept of free exercise without disabilities. [15]

Similarly, due process in the Fifth Amendment sense was unknown in English law. The very notion of due process as a constitutional restraint is inconsistent with the doctrine of Parliamentary supremacy, which has dominated English public law since 1688. English lawyers could scarcely acknowledge a concept like due process, which, as Hamilton noted in his 1787 speech,[16] made clear that fundamental rights could not be taken away even by an Act of the legislature.

But it is when we turn to English criminal law that we understand how forward-looking the Federal Bill of Rights really was. In large part, American bills of rights sought foremost to correct the deficiencies of English criminal law, a legacy of barbarianism that had stretched its long arm across the ocean to touch the colonists time and time again in painful and humiliating ways. In the first place, the right against unreasonable intrusion by governmental agents was made secure. This right had been consistently violated through the general warrants issued toward the end of the Colonial period, and "The Warrant Clause [of the Fourth Amendment] was aimed specifically at the evil of the general warrant, [which was] often regarded as the single immediate cause of the American Revolution." [17] While it is true that the English courts had also started to impose restrictions on the power of the state to obtain evidence of crimes,[18] these restrictions were not anywhere near as strong as those drafted in contemporaneous American bills of rights.

Some of the other rights, those, for instance, safeguarded in the Fifth and Sixth Amendments had, to be sure, also been secured in English criminal law by the end of the eighteenth century, notably the right to jury trial and the privilege against self-incrimination. But other basic rights were still not protected. Not until 1837, for example, was the right to counsel fully recognized in English felony cases and not until 1898 were accused persons given the right to testify in English criminal trials.[19] Without these rights, it is difficult to see how justice could be served. Both were fully guaranteed in the Federal Bill of Rights.

In addition, the Eighth Amendment expressly prohibited cruel and unusual punishments. This provision was derived from a similar clause in the English Bill of Rights, 1689; but a reading of Blackstone tells how barbarous were the punishments still inflicted in English law during the following century.[20] The men who voted for the Eighth Amendment well realized that they were outlawing the cruelties of the eighteenth-century English modes of punishment. We have only to recall the complaint of Samuel Livermore during the House debate that "villains often deserve whipping and perhaps having their ears cut off, but are we in future to be prevented from inflicting these punishments because they are cruel?" [21]

The Eighth Amendment also illustrates the most important difference between the English and American systems of protection of individual rights at the end of the eighteenth century. The Bill of Rights, 1689, spoke only the hortatory words of "ought not" and had only the status of a statute, which could be abrogated by later laws. The Eighth Amendment spoke the imperative of "shall not" and had the status of a constitutional command, which could be enforced by the courts even against the legislature.

The same distinctions applied to the other rights guaranteed by the Federal Bill of Rights as compared with the equivalent rights in the English law of the day. Even where similar rights were recognized in English law, they had nothing like the status they had in the American system. [22] For them to have achieved that status, the English would first have had to do what the Levellers had called for a century and a half earlier: establish a written Constitution as the supreme law of the land and enforceable as such by the courts against abridgement by Parliament, the Crown, and the common law; and the Constitution would have had to have a Bill of Rights with provisions expressly protecting the rights concerned. [23] This was, of course, precisely what was done in the United States through the Federal Constitution and Bill of Rights.

BASIC RIGHTS AND EQUALITY

We come back to the point with which we began this volume: the Bill of Rights concept is almost entirely American in its origins. This can be seen clearly from the following table of the documentary sources of the Federal Bill of Rights:

Bill of Rights Guarantees	*First Document Protecting*	*First American Guaranty*	*First Constitutional Guaranty*
Establishment of religion	Rights of the Colonists (Boston)	Same	N.J. Constitution, Art. XIX
Free exercise of religion	Md. Act Concerning Religion	Same	Va. Declaration of Rights, S. 16
Free speech	Mass. Body of Liberties, S. 12	Same	Pa. Declaration of Rights, Art. XII
Free press	Address to Inhabitants of Quebec	Same	Va. Declaration of Rights, S. 12
Assembly	Declaration and Resolves, Continental Congress	Same	Pa. Declaration of Rights, Art. XVI
Petition	Bill of Rights (1689)	Declaration of Rights and Grievances, (1765). S. XIII	Pa. Declaration of Rights, Art. XVI
Right to bear arms	Bill of Rights (1689)	Pa. Declaration of Rights, Art. XIII	Same
Quartering soldiers	N.Y. Charter of Liberties	Same	Del. Declaration of Rights, S. 21
Searches	Rights of the Colonists (Boston)	Same	Va. Declaration of Rights, S. 10
Seizures	Magna Carta, c. 39	Va. Declaration of Rights, S. 10	Same
Grand jury indictment	N.Y. Charter of Liberties	Same	N.C. Declaration of Rights, Art. VIII
Double jeopardy	Mass. Body of Liberties, S. 42	Same	N.H. Bill of Rights, Art. XVI
Self-incrimination	Va. Declaration of Rights, S. 8	Same	Same
Due process	Magna Carta, c. 39	Md. Act for Liberties of the People	Va. Declaration of Rights, S. 8
Just compensation	Mass. Body of Liberties, S. 8	Same	Vt. Declaration of Rights, Art. II

Bill of Rights Guarantees	First Document Protecting	First American Guaranty	First Constitutional Guaranty
Speedy trial	Va. Declaration of Rights, S. 8	Same	Same
Public trial	West N.J. Concessions, c. XXIII	Same	Pa. Declaration of Rights, Art. IX
Jury trial	Magna Carta, c. 39	Mass. Body of Liberties, S. 29	Va. Declaration of Rights, S. 8
Cause and nature of accusation	Va. Declaration of Rights, S. 8	Same	Same
Witnesses	Pa. Charter of Privileges, Art. V	Same	N.J. Constitution, Art. XVI
Counsel	Mass. Body of Liberties, S. 29	Same	N.J. Constitution, Art. XVI
Jury trial (civil)	Mass. Body of Liberties, S. 29	Same	Va. Declaration of Rights, S. 11
Bail	Mass. Body of Liberties, S. 18	Same	Va. Declaration of Rights, S. 9
Fines	Pa. Frame of Government, S. XVIII	Same	Va. Declaration of Rights, S. 9
Punishment	Mass. Body of Liberties, S. 43, 46	Same	Va. Declaration of Rights, S. 9
Rights retained by people	Va. Convention, proposed amendment 17	Same	Ninth Amendment
Reserved Powers	Mass. Declaration of Rights, Art. IV	Same	Same

The table shows that, except for the right of petition and that to bear arms (which were provided for, albeit only in hortatory form, in the English Bill of Rights, 1689), all the rights safeguarded in the Federal Bill of Rights were first secured in American enactments. It is true that the rights against illegal seizures of the person and to due process and jury trial may be traced to Magna Carta. But its Chapter 39 only sowed the seed; centuries of further development were required before the basic rights concerned could attain the status given them by the Fourth, Fifth, and Sixth Amendments. The rudimentary guarantees in Chapter 39 were first given their modern form in the American constitutions and bills of rights of the Revolutionary period.

Two centuries later, we can see that Madison showed good judgment when he choose from among the plethora of state recommendations the proposed amendments of his first draft. The first Congress also performed a vital role in refining the Madison proposals to the twelve amendments passed and the state legislatures in rejecting the first two, leaving us with the Federal Bill of Rights that was added to the Constitution. The rejected state recommendations were statements of political generalities or matters of unimportant detail that scarcely belong in a charter of rights. The rights safeguarded by the first ten amendments, on the other hand, include the basic rights appropriate for protection by constitutional guaranty, at least as they were understood at the end of the eighteenth century.

The contemporary counterpart of the Federal Bill of Rights was the Declaration of the Rights of Man voted by the National Assembly at the beginning of the French Revolution. The two fundamental documents illustrate the crucial difference between American and French constitutional thinking. The French Declaration lays down not practical rules, but only general principles deemed fundamental to man and hence universally applicable. Madison had also included some general principles in his proposed amendments, but they were eliminated during the congressional debates. What was left in the ten amendments ratified was the appropriate wording to afford specific protection for the basic rights of free expression and association, the rights to privacy and due process, and freedom from arbitrary restraint and trial and cruel and unusual punishments. The provisions protecting them were set forth as legal rules, enforceable as such (as Madison had specifically recognized) by the courts. There is nothing like this in the French Declaration, drafted only in the hortatory terms of the general rights mankind ought to have. The French document does not contain mandatory inhibitions that must be respected by the agents of government; nor does it descend to the level of practical enforcement through specific provision for the basic rights of criminal defendants and others dealing with law enforcement officials.

According to John Rawls, "The basic liberties of citizens are, roughly speaking, political liberty (the right to vote and to be eligible for public office) together with freedom of speech and assembly; liberty of conscience and freedom of thought; freedom of the person along with the right to hold (personal) property; and freedom from arbitrary arrest and seizure." [24] Except for the right to vote and to hold public office (left almost entirely to the states in the original constitutional scheme and hence inappropriate for inclusion in a list of rights that the federal government might not infringe), all the liberties listed by Rawls are safeguarded by the Federal Bill of Rights. Indeed, of the non-political rights that, even today, are deemed suitable for constitutional protection, only one important one is omitted by the Federal Bill of Rights— that to equal protection of the laws.

Two things should be borne in mind about the omission. The first is the restricted notion of equality that prevailed at the end of the eighteenth century. However far-reaching the American conception of equality at the time might have seemed to contemporaries, it was, by present-day standards, rather limited: the American Revolution's emphasis on liberty and equality for all must be sharply distinguished from the twentieth-century meaning of "all." To the Framers, "all" did not include Negroes and women; their concept was basically governed by the Aristotelian notion of the inherent inequality of persons outside the select circle of full citizenship. [25] Even the basic political right of suffrage was restricted by property qualifications in most of the country. Equality before the law in the equal protection sense had not begun to develop. Nowhere in the document drafted in 1787 or in the Federal Bill of Rights was there any guaranty of equality—or even mention of the concept.

Second, and even more important, the Bill of Rights was drafted in language that could include the new right of equal protection as it began to develop. This, in some ways, was Madison's greatest contribution: he wrote in words that enabled later generations to mold the Bill of Rights to accord with changes in the community sense of justice. In particular, as already stressed, he substituted the Due Process Clause for the "law of the land" phraseology, which had been used in the state declarations of rights and recommended amendments.[26] Due process was a plastic conception that could expand to include new rights even a Madison could not foresee. When the right to equal protection was made a constitutional right by the Fourteenth Amendment it was made binding only upon the states. But the due process language proved to be broad enough to include the new right of equality. Hence, the courts subsequently held that a governmental act that violated the Equal Protection Clause of the Fourteenth Amendment if it were taken by a state, violates the Due Process Clause of the Fifth Amendment if it is a federal act.[27]

When Madison wrote "due process" into what became the Fifth Amendment, he ensured that the Bill of Rights could be used to meet future conditions. Due process expresses more than the restricted views of the eighteenth century; it is an enduring reflection of experience with human nature.[28] The due process concept has enabled the Supreme Court to serve as a virtual continuing constitutional convention [29] as it has adapted the black letter text to the needs of later days.

PRE-CIVIL WAR PERIOD

It will be recalled that the proposed amendments introduced by Madison on June 8, 1789, contained a provision prohibiting the states from violating "the equal rights of conscience, or the freedom of the press, or the trial by jury in criminal cases." This provision, which Madison "conceived . . . to be the most valuable amendment in the whole list," was eliminated by the Senate.[30] Consequently, the Federal Bill of Rights, as ratified, contained no restrictions upon state power.

This was confirmed in the last important case decided by the Marshall Court—*Barron v. Mayor of Baltimore.*[31] The plaintiff there had sued the City of Baltimore, claiming a right to compensation because of the city's action in rendering his wharf useless. He relied on the Fifth Amendment prohibition against the taking of private property for public use without just compensation, asserting "that this amendment, being in favor of the liberty of the citizen, ought to be so construed as to restrain the legislative power of a state, as well as that of the United States." Chief Justice Marshall conceded that the issue was of great importance, but, he asserted, "not of much difficulty." He noted that when the Constitution sought to limit state power in Article I, section 10, it did so by providing expressly that "No state shall . . ."—language plainly absent from the Bill of Rights. In addition, he summarized the history of the Bill of Rights, showing how it was enacted to meet the demand for "security against the apprehended encroachments of the general government—not against those of the local governments." The conclusion was that the Fifth Amendment's Just Compensation Clause "is intended solely as a limitation on the exercise of power by the government of the United States, and is not applicable to the . . . states." [32] The same conclusion applies to all other provisions of the Federal Bill of Rights.

The *Barron* decision settled the issue of Bill of Rights application until after the Civil War. The original Federal Constitution therefore was not effective against state infringements upon individual rights, except in those relatively minor limitations upon state power contained in Article I, section 10.

In the early operation of the constitutional system, there were few occasions when the Bill of Rights had to be called upon against the federal government. There was then relatively little interference from Washington. The one great exception was the Sedition Act of 1798.[33] It contained severe restrictions upon the rights secured by the First Amendment. The Sedition Act provided for the punishment of those who uttered or published "false, scandalous, and malicious" writings against the government, the President, or Congress, with the intent to defame or bring them into contempt or disrepute, or to excite the hatred of the people against them, or to stir up sedition, to excite resistance to the law, or to aid the hostile designs of foreign nations against the United States. Persons convicted of violations could be fined up to $2,000 and imprisoned up to two years.[34]

In the year or two after its adoption, the Sedition Act was vigorously enforced in what Jefferson termed a Federalist "reign of witches." [35] The lengths to which enforcement went are shown by some of the extreme cases. Vermont Congressman Matthew Lyon, who wrote a letter to a newspaper complaining of the Executive's "unbounded thirst for ridiculous pomp, foolish adulation, and selfish avarice," was punished by four months in prison and a $1,000 fine.[36] Even more extreme was the case of Luther Baldwin, of New Jersey, who was fined $150 for hoping that a cannon fired in a Presidential salute might hit President Adams on the seat of his pants. This led a Newark reporter to claim that although a British subject might speak of the king's head, Baldwin was punished "for speaking of the president's a--." [37]

The editors of virtually all the leading Republican papers were indicted under the Sedition Act.[38] The statute in operation gave substance to the meaning asserted by a Boston Federalist newspaper: "It is patriotism to write in favor of our government—it is sedition to write against it." [39] A law susceptible to such an interpretation was naturally assailed as an unwarranted invasion of freedom of speech and of the press. Its constitutionality was strongly attacked by Jefferson, who "considered . . . that law to be a nullity as absolute and palpable as if Congress had ordered us to fall down and worship a golden image." [40] When he became President, in 1801, Jefferson pardoned all persons convicted under the law.

Congress eventually ordered all fines to be repaid, and the law itself was permitted to expire in 1801, though, in the words of Justice Story, "it has continued, down to this very day, to be a theme of reproach." [41]

At the present time few would dispute the Story characterization. To us, the Sedition Act was patently unconstitutional. In 1964 (over a century and a half after the ill-starred law itself was enacted), the Supreme Court ruled squarely on the constitutionality of the 1798 statute: "Although the Sedition Act was never tested in this Court, the attack upon its validity has carried the day in the court of history . . . . the Act, because of the restraint it imposed upon criticism of government and public officials, was inconsistent with the First Amendment." [42]

Justice William J. Brennan, speaking for a unanimous Supreme Court, has said that the Sedition Act "first crystallized a national awareness of the central meaning of the First Amendment." [43] In its own day, nevertheless, the 1798 Act was energetically enforced by the lower courts. Historians have condemned the partisan ardor of the Federalist judges, especially Supreme Court Justice Samuel Chase, whose excessive enforcement zeal was one of the factors that led to his later impeachment. Perhaps it is unrealistic to have expected judges who enjoyed using the bench as an anti-Jeffersonian rostrum to consider the constitutional challenge seriously. It must also be remembered that the Sedition Act cases arose in the infancy of our constitutional law. The First Amendment itself had not even begun to receive the broad meaning it has since acquired. In particular, it was not yet settled that the First Amendment was more than a codification of the English law as stated in Blackstone, i.e., as only a prohibition against prior restraints. As James Wilson, perhaps the foremost jurist among the Framers, summarized it at the end of 1787, "what is meant by liberty of the press is, that there should be no antecedent restraint upon it; but that every author is responsible when he attacks the security or welfare of the government, or the safety, character and property of the individual." [44] The Federalists themselves argued that in the

Sedition Act they were merely enacting the common law of seditious libel into the statute book.[45]

However we gloss over it, we must concede that the First Amendment proved ineffective against either the enactment or enforcement of the Sedition Act. Yet the impact on constitutional liberties, though severe, was brief. Popular revulsion against the 1798 legislation was one of the factors that swept the Federalists from power in the 1800 election. During the remainder of the pre-Civil War period, there were no comparable federal restrictions upon freedom of expression or any of the other rights protected by the Bill of Rights.[46] This was true even during the two wars of the period. "There was more genuinely seditious speech and printing to the square foot in the United States during the war of 1812 than to the square mile during the period of the Sedition Act." [47] During the Mexican War, as well, the free expression by anti-war factions of critical comments remained unrestrained.[48] If the Sedition Act of 1798 survives as a horrible example, it is only because it constitutes the extreme transgression of the First Amendment.

While the Sedition Law was in effect, its constitutionality was not expressly considered by any court. The constitutional issue was raised most directly in an 1800 trial before Justice Chase, where the defense attorneys sought to address the jury on the matter. Chase refused to allow them to do so, ruling that the question of constitutionality was to be considered by the judge alone. He read an opinion justifying the judges' sole power to rule on constitutionality.[49] In his opinion, Chase stated the substance of the doctrine of judicial review laid down three years later in *Marbury v. Madison;* [50] the Chase opinion anticipates the classic Marshall presentation in that case.

Marbury v. Madison itself definitely elevated judicial review to the constitutional plane. Since the Court's decision there, the right of the Court to review the constitutionality of all governmental acts has been established doctrine. This has meant that violations of the Bill of Rights, like other constitutional violations, present judicial questions. Any one aggrieved by an infringement upon a right secured by the Bill of Rights has available a judicial remedy by which the right can be vindicated. Without such a remedy, the Bill of Rights would have proved no more effective than the Declaration of the Rights of Man or the host of similar hortatory documents issued during the past two centuries.

FOURTEENTH AMENDMENT

One of the principal purposes of the Fourteenth Amendment was to overrule the decision in *Barron v. Mayor of Baltimore*.[51] This was made plain by Representative John A. Bingham, who has been characterized as "the Madison of the first section of the Fourteenth Amendment." [52] Bingham states that in drafting the language of section 1 of the amendment, which prohibits the states from abridging privileges and immunities or denying due process or equal protection, he relied specifically on Marshall's statement in *Barron* that, had the Framers of the Bill of Rights intended to limit the states, "they would have imitated the framers of the original constitution." Bingham tells us that he did imitate the original Framers in their drafting of Article I, section 10, which contained express limitations upon state power. Imitating their example "to the letter," he drafted his proposed section 1 so that it began, "No State shall . . ." [53]

The result was the imposition of substantial restrictions upon state power by the Federal Constitution. The states were now prohibited from violating the basic rights of conscience, freedom of the press, and trial by jury as fully as if Madison's original amendment restricting state power had not been rejected by the Senate.[54] But the Fourteenth Amendment was, in time, to do more than revive Madison's amendment. Before the Civil War, the states were the primary guardians of their citizens' rights and liberties, and they alone could determine the character and extent of such rights. With the Fourteenth Amendment, this situation would eventually be dramatically altered. This new addition would be read as protecting the citizens of the states against the states themselves. The Fourteenth Amendment therefore was to make the federal government responsible for the great guarantees of life, liberty, and property, no matter which government—federal or state—sought to abridge them. The consequence would be a subsequent national-ization of the Bill of Rights, which, in turn, would affect the entire constitutional system of the nation.

Despite the intent of the Framers that it do so immediately, the Fourteenth Amendment did not have this effect for the better part of a century. During the years following its ratifi-cation, both this amendment and the Bill of Rights were con-strued narrowly by the Congress and the courts. The Recon-struction era emphasis upon protection of individual rights soon gave way to protections of purely economic concerns. Commerce became the great power,[55] with the Constitution increasingly construed to serve its ends. The Fourteenth Amendment, particularly its Due Process Clause, became the Great Charter for the protection of the corporate enterprise, which was in the process of transforming the society.

Thus before the effects of this nationalization could be felt the constitutional emphasis had to shift from property to per-sonal rights. Such a shift could scarcely occur in a society set in the stamp of Mark Twain's *Gilded Age*, with its grandiose material dreams, its flexible ethics, and all its energies oriented in one direction—the making of money.[56] It was not until half a century later that the change in emphasis could occur, bringing with it a renewed stress upon the Bill of Rights as the central feature of the constitutional document.

BILL OF RIGHTS INCORPORATION

During the Gilded Age itself, Sir Henry Maine, the famous legal historian, characterized the Federal Bill of Rights as "a certain number of amendments on comparatively unimpor-tant points." [57] Such a statement reflected the society's con-cern with property rights and their protection as the be-all-

and-end-all of the legal order. It was during this period that a federal judge could declare "that of the three fundamental principles which underlie government, and for which government exists, the protection of life, liberty, and property, the chief of these is property." [58]

The judicial attitude inevitably led to a restrictive interpretation of the Bill of Rights and its protections for personal rights. In practical terms, the problem was that of the extent to which the Fourteenth Amendment made the Bill of Rights binding upon the states, since most violations of individual rights have historically occurred at the state, rather than the federal, level.

The Fourteenth Amendment plainly placed limitations upon state power. Though it did not impose specific restraints similar to those that the Bill of Rights had imposed on the federal government, its first section did provide that no state could "abridge the privileges or immunities of citizens of the United States; nor . . . deprive any person of life, liberty, or property, without due process of law; nor deny to any person . . . the equal protection of the laws." This provision furnished federal constitutional protection against state deprivation of individual rights: the difficult question was that of the relationship of the new protection to the Bill of Rights. More specifically, which of the rights guaranteed by the first amendments were now made binding upon the states?

According to Justice Hugo L. Black's famous 1947 dissent in *Adamson v. California*,[59] "one of the chief objects that the provisions of the [Fourteenth] Amendment's first section . . . were intended to accomplish was to make the Bill of Rights, applicable to the states." The purpose of the Fourteenth Amendment was "to overturn the constitutional rule that case [i.e., *Barron v. Mayor of Baltimore*] had announced." [60] But the Black view on the matter has never commanded a majority of the Supreme Court. The first cases to arise were heard not long after the Fourteenth Amendment itself had been ratified. In the 1873 *Slaughter-House Cases*,[61] the Court ruled that the Privileges and Immunities Clause of the amendment protected only the privileges and immunities of United States citizens, not those of state citizens. The Court found crucial decisional significance in the difference in language between the Fourteenth Amendment's Citizenship Clause and its Privileges and Immunities Clause. The opinion stressed the fact that while the first sentence of the amendment makes all persons born or naturalized in this country both "citizens of the United States and of the State wherein they reside," the next sentence protects only "the privileges or immunities of citizens of the United States" from state abridgement.

The Privileges and Immunities Clause did not transform the rights of citizens of each state into rights of national citizenship enforceable as such in the federal courts. It only protected against state encroachment on those rights "which owe their existence to the Federal Government, its national character, its Constitution, or its laws." [62] The rights protected are solely those that would not have existed but for the presence of the federal government. Rights that antedate and thus do not owe their existence to that government are privileges and immunities of state citizenship alone. The result was virtually to read the Privileges and Immunities Clause out of the Fourteenth Amendment. [63] The fundamental rights of life, liberty, and property, which existed prior to the creation of the federal government, were untouched by the clause and they remained, as always, with the states.

But what of the Fourteenth Amendment's Due Process Clause? In *Hurtado v. California*, [64] in 1884, the Supreme Court refused to hold that due process required a grand jury indictment in a felony prosecution, even though the Fifth Amendment expressly requires a grand jury indictment in federal prosecutions. Due process, said the Court, is not synonymous with the process prescribed by the Bill of Rights. Over two decades later, in the 1908 case of *Twining v. New Jersey*, [65] the Court ruled that exemption from self-incrimination, though specifically secured by the Fifth Amendment, was not safeguarded against state action by the Fourteenth Amendment's Due Process Clause. The Bill of Rights may not be relied on to determine what rights are protected by due process. Some of the rights safeguarded by the first amendments against national action may also be safeguarded against state action because a denial of them would be a denial of due process of law. Yet that is not because those rights are enumerated in the Bill of Rights, but because they are of such a nature that they are included in the conception of due process.

What rights are so included? Only those rights that are "so fundamental that there could be no due process without it. . . . Is it a fundamental principle of liberty and justice which inheres in the very idea of free government and is the inalienable right of a citizen of such a government?" [66] A negative answer had to be given, according to the Court, with regard to the privilege against self-incrimination. The Court emphasized the fact that only four of the original thirteen states included protection against self-incrimination in the proposed amendments they submitted with their ratifications of the Constitution.[67] This showed that it was not then the general belief in this country that the privilege ranked with the fundamental rights of mankind.

One may question the *Twining* conclusion that the privilege against self-incrimination was not considered fundamental in the original thirteen states. As Justice Harlan put it in his *Twining* dissent, "the wise men who laid the foundations of our constitutional government would have stood aghast at the suggestion that immunity from self-incrimination was not among the essential, fundamental principles of English law." [68] The privilege against self-incrimination was recognized as a right enforceable at common law in all the states when the Constitution was drafted; six had included guarantees of the privilege in the constitutions adopted after Independence. By the time of *Twining* itself, every state except New Jersey had given the privilege constitutional status.[69] In these circumstances, it is difficult to see how the *Twining* Court could rank the guaranty against self-incrimination as anything less than fundamental.

The *Twining* approach is open to an even more fundamen-

tal criticism: that it ties due process requirements to the notions that prevailed at the time the Constitution and Bill of
Rights were adopted. The great advantage of the due process
concept has always been its eminently flexible character. That
is one of the favorable aspects of such a plastic concept: it can
expand or contract to meet changing conceptions of justice.
Due process thus becomes a concept that has its roots in
Magna Carta and contemplates advances in both justice and
liberty by a progressive society.[70]

Despite the strong attack of Justice Black, the Supreme
Court has never departed from the *Twining* refusal to incorporate the Bill of Rights as such into the Due Process Clause
of the Fourteenth Amendment. As Justice Douglas, who has
been a stalwart backer of the Black view, has conceded, "To
date the Court has never accepted the view that all of the
guarantees of the Bill of Rights are applicable to the States as
a result of the Fourteenth Amendment." [71]

The Supreme Court's refusal to hold that the Bill of Rights
as such is incorporated into the Fourteenth Amendment may
be supported by analysis of the relevant constitutional provisions. The life of the law may not, as the famous Holmes
statement has it, be logic but experience.[72] Logic must, nevertheless, remain a prime desideratum of any system of legal
interpretation. To read a portion of a legal document—be it a
constitution, a statute, a contract, or a will—in a manner that
is not logically consistent with other portions of the document is, to say the least, to violate sound canons of construction. Yet that is precisely what the Black interpretation of the
Due Process Clause in the Fourteenth Amendment does.
Even Justice Douglas, the strongest supporter on the recent
Court (next to Black himself) of the view that the Fourteenth
Amendment made the entire Bill of Rights applicable to the
states, has acknowledged the strong logic of the contrary position: "The Fifth Amendment, like the Fourteenth Amendment, banned the deprivation of a person's 'life, liberty, or
property without due process of law.' That clause must,
therefore, mean less in the Fifth Amendment than it does in

the Fourteenth, if in the latter it is given a scope so broad as to include all of the Bill of Rights." [73]

To follow the Black view is to charge the Framers of the Bill of Rights with writing into it a meaningless clause: "The Fifth Amendment specifically prohibits prosecution of an 'infamous crime' except by indictment; it forbids double jeopardy and self-incrimination, as well as deprivation of 'life, liberty, or property, without due process of law.' Not to attribute to due process of law an independent function but to consider it a shorthand statement of other specific clauses in the same Amendment is to charge those who secured the adoption of this Amendment with meretricious redundancy by indifference to a phrase—'due process of law'—which was one of the great instruments in the very arsenal of constitutional freedom which the Bill of Rights was to protect and strengthen. Of course the Due Process Clause of the Fourteenth Amendment has the same meaning. To suppose that 'due process of law' meant one thing in the Fifth Amendment and another in the Fourteenth is too frivolous to require elaborate rejection." [74] The short answer to the view that the Due Process Clause of the Fourteenth Amendment was a way of saying that every state is now bound by the entire Bill of Rights is that it is a singularly strange way of saying it. [75]

SELECTIVE INCORPORATION

We have just seen that the Supreme Court has refused to follow the view that the Due Process Clause of the Fourteenth Amendment requires the states to comply with all the demands of the Bill of Rights. Upon what basis then does the highest tribunal act in reviewing the constitutionality of state violations of the rights guaranteed in the Bill of Rights? More specifically, what rights of the individual are included in the concept of due process contained in the Fourteenth Amendment?

The answer the Supreme Court gives to this question still

depends upon its answer to the query posed in *Twining:* Is the right the state has violated "a fundamental principle of liberty and justice which inheres in the very idea of a free government and is the inalienable right of a citizen of such a government?" [76] If the answer is in the affirmative, then the right in question is included in due process; otherwise, it is not, and the state violation of it does not call for Supreme Court correction, even if a similar federal violation would contravene a specific provision of the Bill of Rights.

More recently, the *Twining* test has been more precisely stated. According to Justice Benjamin N. Cardozo, the line of division depends upon whether the particular right is one that has "been found to be implicit in the concept of ordered liberty"; is it one that is "of the very essence of a scheme of ordered liberty"? [77] If it is, the Fourteenth Amendment has absorbed it, in the belief that neither liberty nor justice would exist if such a right were sacrificed.

The Supreme Court has proceeded on a basis of ad hoc selective incorporation [78] in determining which of the rights guaranteed in the Bill of Rights are included "by a process of absorption" [79] within due process. Some Bill of Rights provisions protect petty preferences, not basic principles—for example, the Seventh Amendment right to jury trial in cases where the amount in controversy exceeds twenty dollars. We recognize today that justice is possible without jury trial in civil cases. The same is true of the Fifth Amendment's provision requiring prosecutions to be initiated via the grand-jury route. This, too, might be lost, and justice still be done.[80] Rights of this type, which reflect temporary preferences of the Framers, are not the kind protected by due process.

What the Fourteenth Amendment protects are rights "so fundamental to the protection of justice and liberty that 'due process of law' cannot be accorded without [them]." [81] These are the rights the Fourteenth Amendment has absorbed—the rights "necessary to an Anglo-American regime of ordered liberty." [82] It is not enough that there has been a violation of a specific Bill of Rights provision: the right at issue must be included among "those fundamental principles of liberty and justice which lie at the base of all our civil and political institutions." [83]

Justice Hugo L. Black has characterized this selective incorporation approach as a revival of adjudication under "natural law." "This decision," he asserted in his *Adamson* dissent, "reasserts a constitutional theory . . . that this Court is endowed by the Constitution with boundless power under 'natural law' periodically to expand and contract constitutional standards to conform to the Court's conception of what at a particular time constitutes 'civilized decency' and 'fundamental liberty and justice.' " [84] In the Black view, the Court is "substituting natural law concepts for the Bill of Rights." [85]

The Black characterization of selective incorporation as a natural-law notion is a serious charge. Under it, the judge himself must determine whether a particular state act violates a right that is of the very essence of ordered liberty, or only some lesser part. Is there not in such a subjective approach an element of serious uncertainty and a temptation to judicial arbitrariness? Declaring himself the servant of the natural-law principle, the judge may, in fact, be its creator. Such a philosophy must inevitably have "accordion-like qualities," [86] expanding and contracting according to the personal notions of the judge.

Must we then echo in our day, against the Supreme Court's application of due process, the complaint of the seventeenth-century common lawyers against the Court of Chancery—that the justice dispensed by it is so uncontrolled by fixed principles that it might just as well depend on the size of the particular justice's foot?

The Black criticism proves too much, for it might with equal validity be directed against a large part of the law. What the Supreme Court is applying in these cases is a broad standard, rather than a closely defined precept. But the same thing is done in most important areas of modern law. Indeed, it is in its application of such standards instead of only mechanical rules that a developed legal system differs most from a primitive one.

FROM PROPERTY TO PERSONAL RIGHTS

As already stressed, infringement of individual rights has taken place more often at the state than the federal level. Thus, the critical issue has been the extent to which the Federal Bill of Rights can be made applicable to the states. *Barron v. Mayor* [87] *of Baltimore* brought forth from the Court a categorical negative. But the issue was revived after the Civil War with new challenges brought under the Fourteenth Amendment. In *Hurtado* [88] and *Twining*,[89] the Court refused to incorporate the Bill of Rights as such into the amendment's Due Process Clause. The *Twining* opinion did, however, furnish the tool of selective incorporation through which at least the fundamental guarantees of the first amendments might be held binding upon the states.

Twining was decided in an age that emphasized property more than personal rights. A paper read at a 1900 American Bar Association meeting referred to "the foundations on which [our law] is bottomed—individual ownership, free contract and free competition." [90] In such an era, the Fourteenth Amendment expanded individual freedom almost entirely in the economic sphere. When, toward the end of the century, the Supreme Court finally adopted the view that the Due Process Clause of the Fourteenth Amendment was intended to work a fundamental change, its decisions were all but limited to property. For a generation thereafter, property rights remained the main concern of the courts. Louis D. Brandeis gave contemporaneous expression to this development: "Property is only a means. It has been a frequent error of our courts that they have made the means an end." [91]

The judicial emphasis began to change during the second quarter of this century. The change brought about a reorienting of the constitutional center of the Fourteenth Amendment from property to personal rights that has resulted in a new place for the Bill of Rights in the constitutional scheme; the first amendments were finally to be given real meaning at the level of government where danger of abridgement existed in practice. The Supreme Court held for the first time in 1925 that the states were also bound by specific guarantees of the Bill of Rights and then gave substantive content to the guarantees themselves.

The *Twining* case had laid down the "fundamental right" test to determine whether a particular right guaranteed in the Bill of Rights was to be included in the Fourteenth Amendment. While the emphasis remained on property rights, none of the personal liberties protected by the Bill of Rights was ruled "fundamental" enough to meet the test—not even the privilege against self-incrimination at issue in *Twining* itself. It was not until constitutional concern started its shift to personal rights, that this situation could be altered. Now the "fundamental right" test could serve as the vehicle for including an increasing number of Bill of Rights guarantees in the Fourteenth Amendment.

During the 1920's, the Supreme Court began to hold that specific guarantees of the Bill of Rights were so fundamental as to be included in due process. Two 1925 decisions held that the rights protected by the First Amendment "are among the fundamental personal rights and 'liberties' protected by the due process clause of the Fourteenth Amendment from impairment by the States." [92] The domain of "liberty," withdrawn by the Fourteenth Amendment from encroachment by the states, was thus enlarged to include liberty of mind and beliefs as well as of action. [93]

In 1923, the Supreme Court for the first time reversed a state conviction on the ground that the trial had departed from due process. [94] In the next two and a half decades, the Court held an increasing number of the rights guaranteed by the Bill of Rights binding on the states. These included the Fourth Amendment's right against illegal searches and seizures, [95] the Fifth Amendment's right against coerced confessions, [96] the Sixth Amendment's right to a public trial, [97] impartial jury, [98] and counsel (at least in capital cases and where a "fair trial" could not be obtained), [99] and the Eighth Amendment's right against cruel and unusual punishments. [100]

True, the Court did not go far enough for dissenting justices. Left out of the due process catalogue—and consequently, not yet binding on the states—were many rights that today are clearly considered fundamental: the rights against use of illegally seized evidence,[101] double jeopardy,[102] self-incrimination,[103] that to a jury trial,[104] and to counsel as a general proposition.[105] But the Court by midcentury had only begun the process of absorbing the Bill of Rights. Most important, it had developed the tool by which an ever-increasing inventory of rights could be held binding on the states.

PREFERRED POSITION AND INCORPORATION

The widest application of due process and the Bill of Rights' provisions for individual liberties has thus far been given by the Warren Court. "When the generation of 1980 receives from us the Bill of Rights," Chief Justice Warren once declared, "the document will not have exactly the same meaning it had when we received it from our fathers." [106] The Bill of Rights as interpreted by the Warren Court has been used to defend far greater freedoms than those it supported during earlier Courts.

Even before midcentury, we saw, the constitutional emphasis started to shift from the safeguarding of property rights to the protection of personal rights. Since that time, solicitude for individual rights has become ever more apparent. Freedom of speech, press, religion, the rights of minorities and those accused of crime, those of individuals subjected to legislative and administrative inquisitions—have all come under the Supreme Court's fostering guardianship.

There were two important developments during the Warren years regarding the protection of the personal rights guaranteed by the Bill of Rights: (1) acceptance of the preferred position theory and (2) extension of the trend toward holding Bill of Rights guarantees binding on the states.

The preferred position theory was first stated by Justice Harlan F. Stone in 1938.[107] Under Chief Justice Warren it became accepted doctrine. The theory is based on the view that the Constitution gives a preferred status to personal, as opposed to property, rights. The result is a double standard in the exercise by the courts of their review function. The tenet of judicial self-restraint does not rigidly bind the judge in cases involving civil liberties and other personal rights.[108] The presumption of validity gives way far more readily in cases where life and liberty are restrained. In those cases, the legislative judgment must be scrutinized with much greater care.

Critics say that the preferred position approach, with its elevation of personal rights, creates a hierarchy of rights not provided for in the Constitution.[109] It should, however, be recognized that each generation must necessarily have its own scale of values. In nineteenth-century America, concerned as it was with the economic conquest of a continent, property rights occupied the dominant place. A century later, in a world in which individuality was being dwarfed by concentrations of power, concern with the maintenance of personal rights had become more important. With the focus of concern on the need to preserve an area for the development of individuality, judges were more ready to find legislative invasion when personal rights were involved than in the sphere of economics.[110]

The Supreme Court, as already seen, has not adopted the thesis that the entire Bill of Rights is incorporated in the Fourteenth Amendment's Due Process Clause, adopting instead a selective approach under which only those rights deemed "fundamental" are included in due process. The Warren Court did not formally abandon the selective incorporation approach. But it made the Due Process Clause increasingly inclusive, enfolding within its provisions more and more rights that had come to be considered fundamental.[111] Selective incorporation has absorbed one by one most of the individual guarantees of the Bill of Rights into due process.[112]

The key decisions in this regard are those in *Mapp v. Ohio* [113] and *Gideon v. Wainwright*.[114] Both overruled earlier

Supreme Court decisions. In the first, earlier decision, the right against illegally secured evidence and in the second, the right to counsel were deemed not sufficiently fundamental as to be included in due process. In overruling these two decisions, the Court spoke in broad terms of the need to protect individual rights; *Mapp* and *Gideon* signaled a trend to include ever more of the Bill of Rights guarantees in the Fourteenth Amendment. In the decade that followed, the courts held the following rights fundamental and hence binding upon the states: rights against double jeopardy [115] and self-incrimination,[116] that to jury trial in criminal cases,[117] to a speedy trial,[118] to confrontation,[119] and to bail.[120]

Add to these rights those that had been held binding on the states before midcentury,[121] and they include all the rights guaranteed by the Bill of Rights except for the right to a grand jury indictment and that to a jury in civil cases involving over twenty dollars. The two exclusions hardly alter the overriding tendency to make the Due Process Clause ever more inclusive. As a result, the Fourteenth Amendment now includes well-nigh all the rights safeguarded by the Bill of Rights.

INCORPORATION TODAY

The development just described may appear to render academic the century-long controversy between those who urged that due process incorporates the entire Bill of Rights as such and those who took the contrary view. From this point of view, even if Justice Black seemingly lost the Bill of Rights incorporation battle, did he not really win the due process war? What difference does it make that the Supreme Court has not formally adopted the Black position when, as just seen, it has held practically all the Bill of Rights guarantees to be incorporated into due process?

Johnson v. Louisiana [122] shows that the division over incorporation is still of practical significance to enforcement of the Bill of Rights guarantees. At issue were state criminal convictions by non-unanimous juries. The Court held that the requirement of jury unanimity was not included in due process. In *Duncan v. Louisiana*,[123] the Court had previously ruled that the right to jury trial is so basic in our system that it is incorporated in due process. Thus, the Fourteenth Amendment guarantees a right of jury trial in all state criminal cases that, were they to be tried in a federal court, would come within the Sixth Amendment's guaranty.[124]

While the right to jury is fundamental, the same is not necessarily the case with regard to all the details of common-law jury machinery. The Sixth Amendment was written with the common-law system in mind; it may well be construed as codifying its essentials. Hence a federal conviction must be based upon a unanimous verdict: "unanimity is one of the essential features of *federal* jury trial." [125] The same is not true of the states, governed not by the Sixth Amendment but by the Due Process Clause of the Fourteenth Amendment. The latter does not incorporate "jot-for-jot and case-for-case" [126] every element of the Sixth Amendment. Jury unanimity is not fundamental and is not obligatory upon the states. Provided that the essentials of jury trial in serious criminal cases are maintained, the mechanics of the jury system are left to the state concerned.[127]

Johnson v. Louisiana shows that due process still has a role to play apart from the specifics of the Bill of Rights guarantees. Even where the particular right protected by the Bill of Rights is fundamental and hence incorporated in due process, the states may have leeway with regard to its detailed implementation. The flexibility of due process may enable state implementation of constitutional rights to differ from federal implementation, provided that the fundamentals of the particular right are maintained. Such an interpretation of due process enables practical meaning to be given to Louis D. Brandeis's famous concept of the states as laboratories that may try legal experiments without risk to the rest of the country.[128] It is preferable to "a course of constitutional construction which deprives the States of freedom to experiment with . . . processes different from the federal model." [129]

PERSONAL RIGHTS AND COMPELLING INTEREST

More recently, the Supreme Court has developed a doctrine even further restricting governmental power to infringe on Bill of Rights guarantees. This is the so-called "compelling interest" doctrine, which was first stated in *Shapiro v. Thompson.* [130] The decision there struck down state laws requiring a year's residence for welfare applicants. The states had urged that the requirement bore a rational relationship to legitimate governmental objectives connected with fiscal management and administration of welfare programs. The Court held that the normal rational-basis test for reviewing constitutionality did not apply. Since the residence requirement restricted the fundamental right of interstate movement, its constitutionality must be judged by the stricter standard of whether it promoted a *compelling* state interest. Under that standard, the waiting-period requirement for new residents had to fall.

The implication is that whenever a "fundamental" right is involved, governmental restrictions must be justified by a compelling governmental interest. This implication was confirmed in *Roe v. Wade,* [131] which invalidated state abortion laws as violative of the right of privacy guaranteed by "the Fourteenth Amendment's concept of personal liberty and restrictions upon state action." [132] The Court stated the compelling-interest doctrine in broad terms: "Where certain 'fundamental rights' are involved, . . . regulation limiting these rights may be justified only by a 'compelling state interest.' " [133] In this case, the state failed to meet the burden of demonstrating that restriction on the performance of abortions during the first trimester of pregnancy was necessary to support a compelling state interest.

The compelling-interest doctrine is of great potential significance to enforcement of the Bill of Rights. As already seen, virtually all the rights guaranteed by the Bill of Rights have now been ruled "fundamental" for purposes of inclusion in the Due Process Clause of the Fourteenth Amendment. It is difficult to see why the same would not be true for purposes of the "compelling-interest" doctrine; it would be most anomalous for a right to be considered "fundamental" for one constitutional purpose, but not for another. The result will be for the compelling-interest doctrine ultimately to swallow the preferred position doctrine, since almost all the personal rights protected by the Bill of Rights are now deemed "fundamental." [134] Extending the compelling-interest rule to all cases involving these rights would mean a substantial broadening of judicial review under the Bill of Rights and Fourteenth Amendment. The judges would not only scrutinize restrictions upon personal rights more closely than those upon property rights, they would strike down such restrictions even when they have a rational relation to a valid state objective, where the states fail to meet the burden of showing that they are supported by a compelling state interest—a burden that has not been met thus far in any of the cases in which the compelling-interest doctrine has been used.

The compelling-interest doctrine may be a natural development from the preferred position doctrine. If the personal rights protected by the Bill of Rights are in a preferred position in the constitutional scheme, it follows that restrictions upon them must undergo more careful scrutiny than that permitted under the rational-basis test Justice Holmes had urged and the Supreme Court adopted during the "constitutional revolution" of the 1930's. [135] The logical next step is a test like that of "compelling interest" that restrictions on personal rights must pass.

It may, however, be questioned whether the distinction between personal and property rights—with the latter placed upon a lower constitutional plane—is itself justified. During the present century the Court has shifted away from property rights in contrast to the original emphasis of American law. "An accurate view of the matter," it was declared during the Philadelphia Convention, "would . . . prove that property was the main object of Society." [136] Without property rights,

223

the Framers believed, all other rights would be without practical value. "Property must be secured," affirmed John Adams, "or liberty cannot exist." [137]

Such an emphasis on property now seems misplaced. In the twentieth century hierarchy of legal values, property rights have been relegated to a lesser level. Yet one should not lose sight of the fact that the ultimate social interest is in the individual life, nor that the fulfillment of that interest is impossible without protection of private property. But if the individual is deprived of hope to acquire property, asks Pius XII, what other natural stimulus can be offered him? [138] The very maintenance of individuality is entwined with the property rights of the individual: [139] "you take my life When you do take the means whereby I live." [140]

The emphasis in recent law on the conflict between individual and social interests may be unduly simplistic. If balance we must, should we not place on the individual's side the importance of the institution of property in the free society? [141] The vindication of property rights themselves may be stated in terms of social interest. "Both human rights and property rights are foundations of our society." [142] Individual property rights should be secured because and to the extent that they coincide with social interests. [143]

The Supreme Court has recently indicated agreement with this view. In a 1972 opinion, the Court declared that "the dichotomy between personal liberties and property rights is a false one. Property does not have rights. People have rights. The right to enjoy property without unlawful deprivation, no less than the right to speak or the right to travel, is, in truth, a 'personal' right, whether the 'property' in question be a welfare check, a home, or a savings account. In fact, a fundamental interdependence exists between the personal right to liberty and the personal right in property. Neither could have meaning without the other." [144]

Does this statement, buttressed by citations to John Adams and other eighteenth-century writers, foreshadow a narrowing of the gap between personal and property rights that has dominated our constitutional law for a generation? If so, does this mean that strict scrutiny will increasingly take over from the hands-off type of review that has been afforded in cases involving only economic issues? [145]

The ultimate result may be to have all the rights guaranteed by the Bill of Rights, at least to the extent that they are considered "fundamental" enough to be incorporated in the Fourteenth Amendment, protected by the compelling-interest doctrine. This will place the rights safeguarded by the first amendments upon a higher plane than they have heretofore reached in the constitutional scheme, virtually rendering them immune from governmental restriction. But it may also revive in our system the danger of "government by judiciary," [146] which, not too long ago, "constitute[d] this court a perpetual censor upon all legislation of the States." [147] What was it that the Supreme Court had done in the first part of this century to which much of the country objected so strongly? It was the erection of the Justices' personal predilections into due process dogmas that could not be touched by the legislature. Now the compelling-interest doctrine may lead the Court once again to assume the role of a super-legislature in exercising its review power. "As in *Lochner* [148] and similar cases applying substantive due process standards to economic and social welfare legislation, the adoption of the compelling state interest standard will inevitably require this Court to examine the legislative policies and pass on the wisdom of these policies in the very process of deciding whether a particular state interest put forward may or may not be 'compelling.' " [149]

BEYOND THE BILL OF RIGHTS?

The need to broaden the constitutional protection of individual rights has received added emphasis from the growth and misuse of governmental power in the twentieth-century world. Totalitarian systems have shown dramatically what it means for the individual to live in a society in which Leviathan has become a reality. The "Blessings of Liberty," which the Framers took such pains to safeguard, have been placed in even sharper relief in a world that has seen so clearly the consequences of their denial.

When the Constitution and the Bill of Rights were written, government was only an arbiter, allowing the individual to go unrestrained except at extreme limits of conduct. In the almost two centuries that followed, the system gradually shifted to one in which government had a positive duty to promote the welfare of the community, even at the cost of individual rights. From a constitutional, as well as from a political point of view, the welfare state has become an established fact.

But the problem has ceased to be one of the exertion of governmental authority over property rights to further the public welfare. In the words of Justice Douglas, "the welfare state is a side issue. The central problem of the age is the scientific revolution and all the wonders and the damage it brings." [150] The "Machine, the genie that man has thoughtlessly let out of its bottle and cannot put back again," [151] has created new concentrations of power, particularly in government, which dwarf the individual and threaten individuality as never before. "Where in this tightly knit regime," asks Douglas, "is man to find liberty?" [152]

In the welfare state, however, the emphasis inevitably shifts from liberty to equality. John Stuart Mill gives way to John Maynard Keynes and the primary function of the legal as of the social order becomes distributive. With the acceptance of those views that hold forth that the economic burdens incident to life must increasingly be borne by the society to ensure the individual at least the minimum requirements of a decent human life, the society assumes a new distributive role. Its laws must likewise follow in this new path. Constitutional justifications for the assumption or this new task depend primarily upon the Equal Protection Clause of the Fourteenth Amendment. As already seen, when Madison wrote the Bill of Rights, the one right he omitted was the right to equal protection of the laws. At that time, the right to equality in the twentieth-century sense had not yet

begun to be developed. It was not until 1868, when the Fourteenth Amendment with its Equal Protection Clause was ratified, that equality was raised to the constitutional plane.
For the better part of a century, it was construed narrowly to
mean equality of opportunity in the marketplace. The security of acquired interests was emphasized, even, if need be,
at the expense of the interests of the community. It was not
until well into this century that this situation was called into
question.

The constitutional right of equality was almost a century
old before our law, in W. H. Auden's phrase, really "found
the notion of equality." During the second half of this century, the courts began vigorously to enforce the equal protection guaranty. Racial equality, sexual equality, political
equality, equality in criminal justice—in all these areas the
law has been moving to give practical meaning to equal protection. Equality has, indeed, been the great theme in our
recent public law: equality as between races, between sexes,
between citizens, between citizens and aliens, between rich
and poor, between prosecutor and defendant. The result has
been called "the most profound and pervasive revolution
ever achieved by substantially peaceful means." [153] More, it
has been that rarest of all political animals: a judicially in-
spired and led revolution. Without the Supreme Court decisions giving ever-wider effect to the right to equality, most of
the movements for equality that permeate the society might
never have gotten started.

Nor may we assume that egalitarian development has
reached its peak. On the contrary, as Tocqueville noted, "the
desire of equality always becomes more insatiable in proportion as equality is more complete." [154] The contemporary
movement for equality is starting to transform the very pos-
tulates underlying the legal order.

In fact, a view of equality is emerging that goes far beyond
any previous notion of equality before the law. The classical
distinction used to be between *égalité de droit* and *égalité de
fait*—between formal or legal equality and practical or factual
equality. Until the present day, the primary aim of reformers

was the achievement of the first, since once that was established, the second (insofar as was desirable) would, it was thought, establish itself.[155] Now the law is starting to consider this approach too narrow. The end of law is seen to be provision in fact of equality with regard to more and more of the elements that make life meaningful in the contemporary community. The law is beginning to recognize as a claim the right in fact to conditions comparable to those enjoyed by the majority.[156] The postulate that men might assume that a standard human life be assured them may give way to a broader assumption that they are entitled to equal conditions of life as compared with their fellows.

Daniel Bell has described the contemporary thrust for equality as one from the long-standing tenet of *equality of opportunity* to the new demand for *equality of result:* "What is at stake today is the redefinition of equality. . . . the principle of equality of opportunity, is now seen as leading to a new hierarchy, and the current demand is that the 'just precedence' of society, in Locke's phrase, requires the reduction of all inequality, or the creation of *equality of result* . . . for all men in society." [157] This issue has become a central value problem of the present-day society.

"Equality of result" has received its philosophical foundation in John Rawls's *A Theory of Justice.* For Rawls, justice demands the priority of equality in a distributive sense. The social system should be set up "so that no one gains or loses from his arbitrary place in the distribution of natural assets or his initial position in society without giving or receiving compensating advantages in return." This leads Rawls to his basic principle of social justice: "All social primary goods— liberty and opportunity, income and wealth, and the bases of self-respect—are to be distributed equally unless an unequal distribution of any or all of these goods is to the advantage of the least favored." [158]

One of the basic elements in the Rawls conception of justice is what he calls the *principle of redress.* "This is the principle that undeserved inequalities call for redress; and since inequalities of birth and natural endowment are undeserved, these inequalities are to be somehow compensated for." [159] Under the redress principle, society must treat more favorably those with fewer native assets and those born into less favorable social positions. The example given by Rawls is the spending of greater resources on the education of those less intelligent rather than, as has been the case, on those more so.

The Rawls approach rejects the adequacy of traditional equality before the law. Equality of opportunity and treatment fail to take account of undeserved inequalities in natural endowment. Hence the claim with which the society and the legal order are being presented is that there is a societal duty to make "redress" for the inequalities under which less favored members of the community otherwise have to live—a claim that the law is being urged to recognize and further.

Rawls may be the most important non-lawyer to have a seminal influence on the law since the days when the legal system sat at the feet of Herbert Spencer. In a famous dissent Justice Holmes protested that "The Fourteenth Amendment does not enact Mr. Herbert Spencer's Social Statics." [160] But the reality was quite the opposite. Spencer's application of the theory of evolution to society became the dominant legal philosophy. Despite the Holmes stricture the Constitution itself was read through Spencerean spectacles: the Fourteenth Amendment was treated as a legal sanction to the Survival of the Fittest. [161]

To American jurists Spencer may have appeared as Saturn returned, who brought back the Golden Age of Justice. But it did not turn out that way. The result in practice, was, Louis D. Brandeis was later to say, that the law of the day was based upon "the sacredness of private property. Early nineteenth century scientific half-truths, like 'The survivial of the fittest,' which translated into practice meant 'The devil take the hindmost,' were erected by judicial sanction into a moral law." [162] Unlimited laissez faire had turned Spencer's Golden Age into one of brass.

The Spencer example should caution us today against blind acceptance of the Rawls conception of equality of result. One may go further and question whether the liberal bases of the Bill of Rights are compatible with the Rawls notion. That notion tends toward a bloc view of life rather than an individual one; it reverses the historic movement toward respect for the individual and substitutes virtual proportionate representation of groups in all aspects of society.[163] The price of equality of result is a merging of individual rights into group rights.[164] Alexander Bickel summed it up just before his death: " 'all men have equal rights but not to equal things,' since a levelling egalitarianism which does not reward merit and ability is harmful to all and is unjust as well." [165]

Will the Bill of Rights and its enforcement machinery prove adequate in a society in which the new equality is pressed to the extreme? It is still too soon to answer with assurance. The second half of this century appears to be a period of transition for the society and the law. We seem to be moving from an ideal of individual rights to one of individual entitlements in societal distributive processes. Equality of result may not be possible without eclipse of the self in the community and the largess dispensed by it.

The Bill of Rights as a document contains the same words Madison and his colleagues put down in 1789. But that is far from true of the meaning the law now reads into those words. We live in the midst of a dynamic, even explosive, change in the interpretation of constitutional rights—a change catalyzed by the contemporary thrust for equality. The Bill of Rights as living law is plainly in a state of flux. Concepts and principles that not too long ago appeared unduly radical have become accepted rules of constitutional law. All that can be stated with assurance is that we are going through a tremendous evolutionary development, destined still to produce changes in vindication of constitutional rights as profound as those it will bring about in the society at large.

appendix a

First. That there be prefixed to the Constitution a declaration, that all power is originally vested in, and consequently derived from, the people.

That Government is instituted and ought to be exercised for the benefit of the people; which consists in the enjoyment of life and liberty, with the right of acquiring and using property, and generally of pursuing and obtaining happiness and safety.

That the people have an indubitable, unalienable, and indefeasible right to reform or change their Government, whenever it be found adverse or inadequate to the purposes of its institution.

Secondly. That in article 1st, section 2, clause 3, these words be struck out, to wit: "The number of Representatives shall not exceed one for every thirty thousand, but each State shall have at least one Representative, and until such enumeration shall be made;" and that in place thereof be inserted these words, to wit: "After the first actual enumeration, there shall be one Representative for every thirty thousand, until the number amounts to ———, after which the proportion shall be so regulated by Congress, that the number shall never be less than ———, nor more than ———, but each State shall, after the first enumeration, have at least two Representatives; and prior thereto."

Thirdly. That in article 1st, section 6, clause 1, there be added to the end of the first sentence, these words, to wit: "But no law varying the compensation last ascertained shall operate before the next ensuing election of Representatives."

Fourthly. That in article 1st, section 9, between clauses 3 and 4, be inserted these clauses, to wit: The civil rights of none shall be abridged on account of religious belief or worship, nor shall any national religion be established, nor shall the full and equal rights of conscience be in any manner, or on any pretext, infringed.

The people shall not be deprived or abridged of their right to speak, to write, or to publish their sentiments; and the freedom of the press, as one of the great bulwarks of liberty, shall be inviolable.

The people shall not be restrained from peaceably assembling and consulting for their common good; nor from applying to the Legislature by petitions, or remonstrances, for redress of their grievances.

The right of the people to keep and bear arms shall not be infringed; a well armed and well regulated militia being the best security of a free country: but no person religiously scrupulous of bearing arms shall be compelled to render military service in person.

No soldiers shall in time of peace be quartered in any house without the consent of the owner; nor at any time, but in a manner warranted by law.

No person shall be subject, except in cases of impeachment, to more than one punishment or one trial for the same offence; nor shall be compelled to be a witness against himself; nor be deprived of life, liberty, or property, without due process of law; nor be obliged to relinquish his property, where it may be necessary for public use, without a just compensation.

Excessive bail shall not be required, nor excessive fines imposed, nor cruel and unusual punishments inflicted.

The rights of the people to be secured in their persons, their houses, their papers, and their other property, from all unreasonable searches and seizures, shall not be violated by warrants issued without probable cause, supported by oath or affirmation, or not particularly describing the places to be searched, or the persons or things to be seized.

In all criminal prosecutions, the accused shall enjoy the right to a speedy and public trial, to be informed of the cause and nature of the accusation, to be confronted with his accusers, and the witnesses against him; to have a compulsory process for obtaining witnesses in his favor; and to have the assistance of counsel for his defence.

The exceptions here or elsewhere in the Constitution, made in favor of particular rights, shall not be so construed as to diminish the just importance of other rights retained by the people, or as to enlarge the powers delegated by the Constitution; but either as actual limitations of such powers, or as inserted merely for greater caution.

Fifthly. That in article 1st, section 10, between clauses 1 and 2, be inserted this clause, to wit:

No State shall violate the equal rights of conscience, or the freedom of the press, or the trial by jury in criminal cases.

Sixthly. That, in article 3d, section 2, be annexed to the end of clause 2d, these words, to wit:

But no appeal to such court shall be allowed where the value in controversy shall not amount to ———— dollars: nor shall any fact triable by jury, according to the course of common law, be otherwise re-examinable than may consist with the principles of common law.

Seventhly. That in article 3d, section 2, the third clause be struck out, and in its place be inserted the clauses following, to wit:

The trial of all crimes (except in cases of impeachments, and cases arising in the land or naval forces, or the militia when on actual service, in time of war or public danger) shall be by an impartial jury of freeholders of the vicinage, with the requisite of unanimity for conviction, of the right of challenge, and other accustomed requisites; and in all crimes punishable with loss of life or member, presentment or indictment by a grand jury shall be an essential preliminary, provided that in cases of crimes committed within any county which may be in possession of an enemy, or in which a general insurrection may prevail, the trial may by law be authorized in some other county of the same State, as near as may be to the seat of the offence.

In cases of crimes committed not within any county, the trial may by law be in such county as the laws shall have prescribed. In suits at common law, between man and man, the trial by jury, as one of the best securities to the rights of the people, ought to remain inviolate.

Eighthly. That immediately after article 6th, be inserted, as article 7th, the clauses following, to wit:

The powers delegated by this Constitution are appropriated to the departments to which they are respectively distributed: so that the Legislative Department shall never exercise the powers vested in the Executive or Judicial, nor the Executive exercise the powers vested in the Legislative or Judicial, nor the Judicial exercise the powers vested in the Legislative or Executive Departments.

The powers not delegated by this Constitution, nor prohibited by it to the States, are reserved to the States respectively.

Ninthly. That article 7th be numbered as article 8th.

appendix b

Amendments Reported by House Select Committee,
July 28, 1789

In the introductory paragraph before the words, *"We the people,"* add, "Government being intended for the benefit of the people, and the rightful establishment thereof being derived from their authority alone."

Art. 1, Sec. 2, Par. 3—Strike out all between the words, *"direct"* and *"and until such,"* and instead thereof insert, "After the first enumeration there shall be one representative for every thirty thousand until the number shall amount to one hundred; after which the proportion shall be so regulated by Congress that the number of Representatives shall never be less than one hundred, nor more than one hundred and seventy-five, but each State shall always have at least one Representative."

Art. 1, Sec. 6—Between the words *"United States,"* and *"shall in all cases,"* strike out *"they,"* and insert, "But no law varying the compensation shall take effect until an election of Representatives shall have intervened. The members."

Art. 1, Sec. 9—Between Par. 2 and 3 insert, "No religion shall be established by law, nor shall the equal rights of conscience be infringed."

"The freedom of speech, and of the press, and the right of the people peaceably to assemble and consult for their common good, and to apply to the government for redress of grievances, shall not be infringed."

"A well regulated militia, composed of the body of the people, being the best security of a free State, the right of the people to keep and bear arms shall not be infringed, but no person religiously scrupulous shall be compelled to bear arms."

"No soldier shall in time of peace be quartered in any house without the consent of the owner, nor in time of war but in a manner to be prescribed by law."

"No person shall be subject, except in case of impeachment, to more than one trial or one punishment for the same offence, nor shall be compelled to be a witness against himself, nor be deprived of life, liberty, or property without due process of law; nor shall private property be taken for public use without just compensation."

"Excessive bail shall not be required, nor excessive fines imposed, nor cruel and unusual punishments inflicted."

"The right of the people to be secure in their person, houses, papers and effects, shall not be violated by warrants issuing, without probable cause supported by oath or affirmation, and not particularly describing the places to be searched, and the persons or things to be seized."

"The enumeration in this Constitution of certain rights shall not be construed to deny or disparage others retained by the people."

ART. 1, SEC. 10, between the 1st and 2d PAR. insert, "No State shall infringe the equal rights of conscience, nor the freedom of speech, or of the press, nor of the right of trial by jury in criminal cases."

ART. 3, SEC. 2, add to the 2d PAR. "But no appeal to such court shall be allowed, where the value in controversy shall not amount to one thousand dollars; nor shall any fact, triable by a Jury according to the course of the common law, be otherwise re-examinable than according to the rules of common law."

ART. 3, SEC. 2—Strike out the whole of the 3d paragraph, and insert—"In all criminal prosecutions the accused shall enjoy the right to a speedy and public trial, to be informed of the nature and cause of the accusation, to be confronted with the witnesses against him, to have compulsory process for obtaining witnesses in his favor, and to have the assistance of counsel for his defence."

"The trial of all crimes (except in cases of impeachment, and in cases arising in the land or naval forces, or in the militia, when in actual service in time of war or public danger) shall be by an impartial jury of freeholders of the vicinage, with the requisite of unanimity for conviction, the right of challenge and other accustomed requisites; and no person shall be held to answer for a capital, or otherwise infamous crime, unless on a presentment or indictment by a Grand Jury; but if a crime be committed in a place in the possession of an enemy, or in which an insurrection may prevail, the indictment and trial may by law be authorized in some other place within the same State; and if it be committed in a place not within a State, the indictment and trial may be at such place or places as the law may have directed."

"In suits at common law the right of trial by jury shall be preserved."

"Immediately after ART. 6, the following to be inserted as ART. 7."

"The powers delegated by this Constitution to the government of the United States, shall be exercised as therein appropriated, so that the Legislative shall never exercise the powers vested in the Executive or the Judicial; nor the Executive the powers vested in the Legislative or Judicial; nor the Judicial the powers vested in the Legislative or Executive."

"The powers not delegated by this Constitution, nor prohibited by it to the States, are reserved to the States respectively."

ART. 7 to be made ART. 8.

appendix c

*Amendments Passed by
House of Representatives, August 24, 1789*

ARTICLE THE FIRST.

After the first enumeration, required by the first Article of the Constitution, there shall be one Representative for every thirty thousand, until the number shall amount to one hundred, after which the proportion shall be so regulated by Congress, that there shall be not less than one hundred Representatives, nor less than one Representative for every forty thousand persons, until the number of Representatives shall amount to two hundred, after which the proportion shall be so regulated by Congress, that there shall not be less than two hundred Representatives, nor less than one Representative for every fifty thousand persons.

ARTICLE THE SECOND.

No law varying the compensation to the members of Congress, shall take effect, until an election of Representatives shall have intervened.

ARTICLE THE THIRD.

Congress shall make no law establishing religion or prohibiting the free exercise thereof, nor shall the rights of Conscience be infringed.

ARTICLE THE FOURTH.

The Freedom of Speech, and of the Press, and the right of the People peaceably to assemble, and consult for their common

good, and to apply to the Government for a redress of grievances, shall not be infringed.

ARTICLE THE FIFTH.

A well regulated militia, composed of the body of the People,
being the best security of a free State, the right of the People
to keep and bear arms, shall not be infringed, but no one
religiously scrupulous of bearing arms, shall be compelled to
render military service in person.

ARTICLE THE SIXTH.

No soldier shall, in time of peace, be quartered in any house
without the consent of the owner, nor in time of war, but in
a manner to be prescribed by law.

ARTICLE THE SEVENTH.

The right of the People to be secure in their persons, houses,
papers and effects, against unreasonable searches and seizures, shall not be violated, and no warrants shall issue, but
upon probable cause supported by oath or affirmation, and
particularly describing the place to be searched, and the persons or things to be seized.

ARTICLE THE EIGHTH.

No person shall be subject, except in case of impeachment, to
more than one trial, or one punishment for the same offense,
nor shall be compelled in any criminal case, to be a witness
against himself, nor be deprived of life, liberty or property,
without due process of law; nor shall private property be
taken for public use without just compensation.

ARTICLE THE NINTH.

In all criminal prosecutions, the accused shall enjoy the right
to a speedy and public trial, to be informed of the nature and
cause of the accusation, to be confronted with the witnesses
against him, to have compulsory process for obtaining wit-

nesses in his favor, and to have the assistance of counsel for his defence.

ARTICLE THE TENTH.

The trial of all crimes (except in cases of impeachment, and in cases arising in the land or naval forces, or in the militia when in actual service in time of War or public danger) shall be by an Impartial Jury of the Vicinage, with the requisite of unanimity for conviction, the right of challenge, and other accustomed requisites; and no person shall be held to answer for a capital, or otherways infamous crime, unless on a presentment or indictment by a Grand Jury; but if a crime be committed in a place in the possession of an enemy, or in which an insurrection may prevail, the indictment and trial may by law be authorised in some other place within the same State.

ARTICLE THE ELEVENTH.

No appeal to the Supreme Court of the United States, shall be allowed, where the value in controversy shall not amount to one thousand dollars, nor shall any fact, triable by a Jury according to the course of the common law, be otherwise re-examinable, than according to the rules of common law.

ARTICLE THE TWELFTH.

In suits at common law, the right of trial by Jury shall be preserved.

ARTICLE THE THIRTEENTH.

Excessive bail shall not be required, nor excessive fines imposed, nor cruel and unusual punishments inflicted.

ARTICLE THE FOURTEENTH.

No State shall infringe the right of trial by Jury in criminal cases, nor the rights of conscience, nor the freedom of speech, or of the press.

Appendix C

ARTICLE THE FIFTEENTH.

The enumeration in the Constitution of certain rights, shall not be construed to deny or disparage others retained by the people.

ARTICLE THE SIXTEENTH.

The powers delegated by the Constitution to the government of the United States, shall be exercised as therein appropriated, so that the Legislative shall never exercise the powers vested in the Executive or Judicial; nor the Executive the powers vested in the Legislative or Judicial; nor the Judicial the powers vested in the Legislative or Executive.

ARTICLE THE SEVENTEENTH.

The powers not delegated by the Constitution, nor prohibited by it, to the States, are reserved to the States respectively.

appendix d

ARTICLE THE FIRST.

After the first enumeration, required by the first article of the Constitution, there shall be one Representative for every thirty thousand, until the number shall amount to one hundred; to which number one Representative shall be added for every subsequent increase of forty thousand, until the Representatives shall amount to two hundred, to which number one Representative shall be added for every subsequent increase of sixty thousand persons.

ARTICLE THE SECOND.

No law, varying the compensation for the services of the Senators and Representatives, shall take effect, until an election of Representatives shall have intervened.

ARTICLE THE THIRD.

Congress shall make no law establishing articles of faith, or a mode of worship, or prohibiting the free exercise of religion, or abridging the freedom of speech, or of the press, or the right of the people peaceably to assemble, and to petition to the government for a redress of grievances.

ARTICLE THE FOURTH.

A well regulated militia, being necessary to the security of a free State, the right of the people to keep and bear arms, shall not be infringed.

Appendix D

ARTICLE THE FIFTH.

No soldier shall, in time of peace, be quartered in any house, without the consent of the owner, nor in time of war, but in a manner to be prescribed by law.

ARTICLE THE SIXTH.

The right of the people to be secure in their persons, houses, papers, and effects, against unreasonable searches and seizures, shall not be violated, and no warrants shall issue, but upon probable cause, supported by oath or affirmation, and particularly describing the place to be searched, and the persons or things to be seized.

ARTICLE THE SEVENTH.

No person shall be held to answer for a capital, or otherwise infamous crime, unless on a presentment or indictment of a Grand Jury, except in cases arising in the land or naval forces, or in the militia, when in actual service in time of war or public danger; nor shall any person be subject for the same offence to be twice put in jeopardy of life or limb; nor shall be compelled in any criminal case, to be a witness against himself, nor be deprived of life, liberty or property, without due process of law; nor shall private property be taken for public use without just compensation.

ARTICLE THE EIGHTH.

In all criminal prosecutions, the accused shall enjoy the right to a speedy and public trial, to be informed of the nature and cause of the accusation, to be confronted with the witnesses against him, to have compulsory process for obtaining witnesses in his favour, and to have the assistance of counsel for his defence.

ARTICLE THE NINTH.

In suits at common law, where the value in controversy shall exceed twenty dollars, the right of trial by Jury shall be preserved, and no fact, tried by a Jury, shall be otherwise re-examined in any court of the United States, than according to the rules of the common law.

ARTICLE THE TENTH.

Excessive bail shall not be required, nor excessive fines imposed, nor cruel and unusual punishments inflicted.

ARTICLE THE ELEVENTH.

The enumeration in the Constitution, of certain rights, shall not be construed to deny or disparage others retained by the people.

ARTICLE THE TWELFTH.

The powers not delegated to the United States by the Constitution, nor prohibited by it to the States, are reserved to the States respectively, or to the people.

appendix e

Amendments Passed by Congress, September 25, 1789 *

Article the first . . . After the first enumeration required by the first Article of the Constitution, there shall be one Representative for every thirty thousand, until the number shall amount to one hundred, after which, the proportion shall be so regulated by Congress, that there shall be not less than one hundred Representatives, nor less than one Representative for every forty thousand persons, until the number of Representatives shall amount to two hundred, after which the proportion shall be so regulated by Congress, that there shall not be less than two hundred Representatives, nor more than one Representative for every fifty thousand persons.

Article the second . . . No law, varying the compensation for the services of the Senators and Representatives, shall take effect, until an election of Representatives shall have intervened.

Article the third . . . Congress shall make no law respecting an establishment of religion, or prohibiting the free exercise thereof; or abridging the freedom of speech, or of the press, or the right of the people peaceably to assemble, and to petition the Government for a redress of grievances.

Article the fourth . . . A well regulated Militia, being necessary to the security of a free State, the right of the people to keep and bear Arms, shall not be infringed.

Article the fifth . . . No Soldier shall, in time of peace be quartered in any house, without the consent of the Owner, nor in time of war, but in a manner to be prescribed by law.

* Apart from the first two articles (which failed of state ratification), these amendments (renumbered to reflect the nonratification of the first two) now constitute the Federal Bill of Rights.

Article the sixth . . . The right of the people to be secure in their persons, houses, papers, and effects, against unreasonable searches and seizures, shall not be violated, and no Warrants shall issue, but upon probable cause, supported by Oath or affirmation, and particularly describing the place to be searched, and the persons or things to be seized.

Article the seventh . . . No person shall be held to answer for a capital, or otherwise infamous crime, unless on a presentment or indictment of a Grand Jury, except in cases arising in the land or naval forces, or in the Militia, when in actual service in time of War or public danger; nor shall any person be subject for the same offence to be twice put in jeopardy of life or limb, nor shall be compelled in any criminal case to be a witness against himself, nor be deprived of life, liberty, or property, without due process of law; nor shall private property be taken for public use without just compensation.

Article the eighth . . . In all criminal prosecutions, the accused shall enjoy the right to a speedy and public trial, by an impartial jury of the State and district wherein the crime shall have been committed, which district shall have been previously ascertained by law, and to be informed of the nature and cause of the accusation; to be confronted with the witnesses against him; to have compulsory process for obtaining witnesses in his favor, and to have the Assistance of Counsel for his defence.

Article the ninth . . . In suits at common law, where the value in controversy shall exceed twenty dollars, the right of trial by jury shall be preserved, and no fact tried by a jury shall be otherwise re-examined in any Court of the United States, than according to the rules of the common law.

Article the tenth . . . Excessive bail shall not be required, nor excessive fines imposed, nor cruel and unusual punishments inflicted.

Article the eleventh . . . The enumeration in the Constitution, of certain rights, shall not be construed to deny or disparage others retained by the people.

Article the twelfth . . . The powers not delegated to the United States by the Constitution, nor prohibited by it to the States, are reserved to the States respectively, or to the people.

notes

CHAPTER ONE

1. *Infra* p. 21.
2. *Infra* p. 67.
3. *Infra* p. 35.
4. *Infra* p. 46.
5. See McKechnie, *Magna Carta* 92-101 (2d ed. 1914). For the text of Magna Carta, see Stephenson and Marcham, *Sources of English Constitutional History* 115 (1937).
6. Coke, *The Second Part of the Institutes of the Laws of England* 1 (1797 ed.).
7. 1 Stubbs, *The Constitutional History of England* 595 (1880).
8. Quoted in McKechnie, *op. cit. supra* n. 5, at 107, n. 4.
9. 1 Churchill, *A History of the English Speaking Peoples* 255 (1956).
10. Compare McKechnie, *op. cit. supra* n. 5, at 115; Holt, *Magna Carta* 197 (1965).
11. Coke, *op. cit. supra* n. 6, at 45, 50.
12. Hallam, quoted in Schwartz, *The Roots of Freedom: A Constitutional History of England* 19 (1965).
13. Gough, *Fundamental Law in English Constitutional History* 15 (1955).
14. 1 Pollock and Maitland, *The History of English Law before the Time of Edward I* 152 (1895).
15. Churchill, *op. cit. supra* n. 9, at 256.
16. Bowen, *The Lion and the Throne* 487 (1957).
17. Jones, *Politics and the Bench* 45 (1971). The statistics on lawyers are from id. at 46.
18. Pocock, *The Ancient Constitution and the Feudal Law* 48 (1957).
19. Bowen, *op. cit. supra* n. 16, at 452–53.
20. Id. at 453.
21. 1 Barnett Smith, *History of the English Parliament* 375 (1892).

22. 5 Holdsworth, *A History of English Law* 449 (1937).
23. Bowen, *op. cit. supra* n. 16, at 484.
24. 3 Howell's *State Trials* 188. Coke did not, however, originate the idea of a petition. It was first suggested by Sir Dudley Digges, and subsequently taken up by Coke. Jones, *op. cit. supra* n. 17, at 73.
25. Gough, *op. cit. supra* n. 13, at 63.
26. 3 Howell's *State Trials* 193–94.
27. 3 Howell's *State Trials* 1 (1627).
28. Id. at 58–9.
29. Bowen, *op. cit. supra* n. 16, at 485.
30. 3 Howell's *State Trials* at 131.
31. 3 Howell's *State Trials* 230. For the text of the Petition of Right, see 5 *Statutes of the Realm* 23 (1819).
32. Six Members Case, 3 Howell's *State Trials* 235, 281 (1629).
33. Quoted in Jones, *op. cit. supra* n. 17, at 165.
34. Macaulay, *The History of England from the Accession of James II,* Chapter I.
35. Gough, *op. cit. supra* n. 13, at 69.
36. See *infra* p. 66.
37. See Pease, *The Leveller Movement* 194 (1916).
38. John Lilburne, quoted in Wolfe, *Leveller Manifestoes of the Puritan Revolution* 14 (1944) (italics omitted).
39. Id. at 113.
40. Quoted in id. at 13 (italics omitted).
41. "A Remonstrance of Many Thousand Citizens" (1646), id. at 117.
42. "The Case of the Army Truly Stated" (1647), id. at 212.
43. Brailsford, *The Levellers and the English Revolution* 255 (1961).
44. See id. at 256.
45. For its text, see Wolfe, *op. cit. supra* n. 38, at 337.
46. See id. at 331.
47. William Walwyn, "A Manifestation," quoted in Brailsford, *op. cit. supra* n. 43, at 526.
48. For its text, see Wolfe, *op. cit. supra* n. 38, at 400.
49. Compare Pease, *op. cit. supra* n. 37, at 199.
50. Gough, *op. cit. supra* n. 13, at 113.
51. See Wolfe, *op. cit. supra* n. 38, at 347.
52. Id. at 406 *et seq.*
53. Id. at 412.
54. 43 *Harvard Classics* 126 (1910).
55. *Reliquiae Baxterianae,* pt. 1, 7, quoted in 22 *Encyclopedia Britannica* 885 (1969). See Fraser, *Cromwell: The Lord Protector* 113 (1973).
56. Stirling Taylor, *Cromwell* 262 (1928).

57. 43 *Harvard Classics* 141–42.
58. Wolfe, *op. cit. supra* n. 38, at 349.
59. Id. at 410.
60. Compare Brant, *The Bill of Rights* 106 (1965).
61. For the text of the Instrument of Government, see Stephenson and Marcham, *op. cit. supra* n. 5, at 525.
62. Macaulay, *loc. cit. supra* n. 34.
63. Ibid.
64. So characterized in *Letter to the People of Pennsylvania* 25 (1760), in 1 Bailyn, *Pamphlets of the American Revolution* 266 (1965).
65. Quoted in Maier, *From Resistance to Revolution* 29 (1973).
66. For its text, see Stephenson and Marcham, *op. cit. supra* n. 5, at 599.
67. Quoted in Dicey, *Introduction to the Study of the Law of the Constitution* 186 (10th ed. 1967).
68. Ibid.
69. Id. at 206.
70. See id. at 260.
71. Compare id. at 268.
72. Macaulay, *Essay on Hallam* (1828).
73. Compare Dicey, *op. cit. supra* n. 67, at 207.

CHAPTER TWO

1. Van Tyne, *The Causes of the War of Independence* 23 (1922).
2. Smith, *Appeals to the Privy Council from the American Plantations* 483, n. 68 (1950).
3. 1 Commager, *Documents of American History* 56 (1934). For a similar 1764 assertion by Governor Thomas Fitch of Connecticut, see 1 Bailyn, *Pamphlets of the American Revolution* 387–8 (1965). It is not, however, true (despite later contrary assertions of the colonists themselves) that the common law alone was the measure of colonial law. See Goebel, "King's Law and Local Custom in Seventeenth-Century New England," 31 Columbia Law Review 416 (1931).
4. Van Tyne, *op. cit. supra* n. 1, at 25.
5. For the Virginia Charter's text, see Commager, *op. cit. supra* n. 3, at 8.
6. Id. at 56. See Smith, *op. cit. supra* n. 2, Chapter VIII, for discussion of the legal debate on the extension of English law and rights to the colonies.
7. See Perry, *Sources of Our Liberties* 35 (1952).
8. See Van Tyne, *op. cit. supra* n. 1, at 25.

9. Commager, *op. cit. supra* n. 3, at 23.

10. 1 Bryce, *The American Commonwealth* 429 (3d ed. 1895).

11. As the legislature was called following the Massachusetts prece-dent.

12. Compare Perry, *op. cit. supra* n. 7, at 118.

13. Van Tyne, *op. cit. supra* n. 1, at 218.

14. 10 *Works of John Adams* 359 (C. F. Adams ed. 1856).

15. Bailyn, *The Ideological Origins of the American Revolution* 192 (1967).

16. Kammen, *People of Paradox* 38 (1972).

17. Van Tyne, *op. cit. supra* n. 1, at 33, 34.

18. Maier, *From Resistance to Revolution* 187 (1973).

19. See Adams, *op. cit. supra* n. 14, at 48.

20. 2 Hart, *American History Told by Contemporaries* 131 (1914).

21. See Van Tyne, *op. cit. supra* n. 1, at 25–26.

22. See Rossiter, *The Seedtime of the Republic* 22 (1953).

23. See Van Tyne, *op. cit. supra* n. 1, at 40.

24. 2 *The Writings and Speeches of Edmund Burke* 124–25 (1931).

25. 2 Parkman, *Montcalm and Wolfe* 423 (1910).

26. For its text, see Commager, *op. cit. supra* n. 3, at 16.

27. For its text, see id. at 21.

28. Skeggs, *Roots of Maryland Democracy* 13 (1973). The same was true of all the proprietary charters except that of Pennsylvania. See Klein and Hoogenboom, *A History of Pennsylvania* 34 (1973).

29. Quoted in Craven, *The Colonies in Transition* 26 (1968).

30. See Andrews, *The Founding of Maryland,* Chapter VI (1933).

31. Browne, Archives of Maryland, *Proceedings and Acts of the Gen-eral Assembly of Maryland,* 1637–1664, 41 (1883).

32. 2 Channing, *A History of the United States* 223 (1916).

33. *Infra* pp. 42, 49.

34. Commager, *op. cit. supra* n. 3, at 16.

35. 1 Channing, *op. cit. supra* n. 32, at 330.

36. John Winthrop to Sir Nathaniel Rich, 1634. Original in private collection.

37. 2 Hosmer, *Winthrop's Journal* 290 (1908).

38. 1 id. at 323.

39. Massachusetts Body of Liberties, Preamble. Whitmore, *A Bibli-ographical Sketch of the Laws of the Massachusetts Colony* 33 (1890).

40. 1 Hosmer, *op. cit. supra* n. 37, at 151.

41. Whitmore, *op. cit. supra* n. 39, at 5.

42. 1 Hosmer, *op. cit. supra* n. 37, at 196.

43. Haskins, *Law and Authority in Early Massachusetts* 131 (1960).

44. 1 Hosmer, *op. cit. supra* n. 37, at 151.

45. The text of the Body of Liberties is given in Whitmore, *loc. cit. supra* n. 39. It contains the following divisions: Rites Rules and Liberties concerning Juditiall proceedings; Liberties more pecularlie concerning the free men; Liberties of Woemen; Liberties of Children; Liberties of Servants; Liberties of Forreiners and Strangers; Off the Bruite Creature; Capitall Laws; A Declaration of the Liberties the Lord Jesus Hath Given to the Churches.

46. Quoted in 1 Channing, *op. cit. supra* n. 32, at 252.

47. Commager, *op. cit. supra* n. 3, at 31.

48. Craven, *op. cit. supra* n. 29, at 277.

49. 4 Shurtleff, *Records of the Governor and Company of the Massachusetts Bay,* part 2, 25 (1853–54).

50. Quoted in Easton, *Roger Williams* 353 (1930).

51. 1 Osgood, *The American Colonies in the Seventeenth Century* 336 (1904).

52. Commager, *op. cit. supra* n. 3, at 25.

53. For the text of the Rhode Island Charter, see 2 Poore, *The Federal and State Constitutions, Colonial Charters and Other Organic Laws of the United States* 1595 (1878).

54. For its text, see id. at 1397.

55. These comic-opera titles were actually used by Locke throughout the Carolina constitutions.

56. 1 *The Colonial Laws of New York from the Year 1664 to the Revolution* xv (1894).

57. Id. at xiv.

58. See Lovejoy, *The Glorious Revolution in America* 113 (1972).

59. *Op. cit. supra* n. 56, at 111.

60. 4 Wall. 2 (U.S. 1866).

61. *Op. cit. supra n.* 56, at xvii.

62. Id. at 244. See Lovejoy, *op. cit. supra* n. 58, at 358.

63. Bailyn, *op. cit. supra* n. 15, at 195. For the text of the Concessions, see Leaming and Spicer, *The Grants, Concessions, and Original Constitutions of the Province of New Jersey* 393 (2d ed. 1881).

64. 1 Whitehead, *Documents Relating to the Colonial History of the State of New Jersey,* 1st ser., 228 (1880).

65. The quotes are from Chapter XIII of the Concessions. It is not certain whether William Penn or Edward Byllynge was the primary author of the Concessions. Perry, *op. cit. supra* n. 7, at 182, opts for Penn, while Craven, *op. cit. supra* n. 29, at 187 thinks Byllynge may have been principally responsible.

66. *Supra* p. 17.

67. I.e., the subtitle of Chapters XIII–XXIII of the Concessions.

68. Channing, *op. cit. supra* n. 32, at 110.

69. Pennsylvania Frame of Government, The Preface.
70. For its text, see 5 Thorpe, *The Federal and State Constitutions, Colonial Charters, and other Organic Laws* 3052 (1909).
71. 6 Howell's *State Trials* 999 (1670). See Schwartz, *The Roots of Freedom: A Constitutional History of England* 185–86 (1965).
72. See Channing, *op. cit. supra* n. 32, at 118.
73. Quoted in Craven, *op. cit. supra* n. 29, at 265.
74. Quoted in Perry, *op. cit. supra* n. 7, at 251.
75. For its text, see Commager, *op. cit. supra* n. 3, at 40.
76. 1 Anne c. 9.
77. See Plucknett, *A Concise History of the Common Law* 386 (2d ed. 1936).
78. Bailyn, *op. cit. supra* n. 3 at 661.
79. Quoted in Craven, *op. cit. supra* n. 29, at 5.
80. See Van Tyne, *op. cit. supra* n. 1, at 217–18.
81. *Supra* n. 13.

CHAPTER THREE

1. Wood, *The Creation of the American Republic* 293 (1969). The Cannon quotes are from ibid.
2. See Gough, *Fundamental Law in English Constitutional History* 12 (1955).
3. 8 Co. Rep. 113b, 118a (1610).
4. See 2 *Legal Papers of John Adams* 118 (Wroth and Zobel eds., 1965); Gough, *op. cit. supra* n. 2, at 34; 1 Bailyn, *Pamphlets of the American Revolution* 100, 412 (1965); Thorne, "Dr. Bonham's Case," 54 Law Quarterly Review 543 (1938).
5. Berger, *Congress v. The Supreme Court* 349 (1969).
6. Id. at 27.
7. 10 *Works of John Adams* 244–45 (C. F. Adams ed. 1856).
8. *Quincy Reports* 51 (Mass. 1761). The best account of the case is in Adams *op. cit. supra* n. 4, at 123 *et seq.*
9. Adams, *op. cit. supra* n. 4, at 141.
10. *Quincy Reports*, Appendix 521 (Mass.).
11. Adams, *op. cit. supra* n. 4, at 127–28.
12. *Quincy Reports*, Appendix 520–21 (Mass.).
13. Bailyn, *The Ideological Origins of the American Revolution* 178–81 (1967); Bailyn, *op. cit. supra* n. 4, at 101–3, 412–7. The quotation is from Otis, *The Rights of the British Colonies Asserted and Proved* 39 (1764), id. at 448. Compare Pole, *Foundations of American Independence* 46–7 (1972).
14. Bailyn, *op. cit. supra* n. 4, at 415.

15. Adams, *op. cit. supra* n. 4, at 128, n. 72.
16. Id. at 121. Compare Bailyn, *The Ordeal of Thomas Hutchinson* 84 (1974).
17. 9 Adams, *op. cit. supra* n. 7, at 386.
18. On Henry's "inadequacy as a legal scholar," see Beeman *Patrick Henry: A Biography* 9 (1974).
19. See Becker, *The Eve of the Revolution* 70, 71 (1918).
20. 2 Adams, *op. supra* n. 7, at 158. See 3 id. at 469.
21. *Quincy Reports,* Appendix 527 (Mass. 1769).
22. Id. at 527–28; 9 Adams, *op. cit. supra* n. 7, at 390.
23. Bailyn, *op. cit. supra* n. 16, at 111.
24. 1 Mays, *Edmund Pendleton, 1721–1803: A Biography* 170 (1952).
25. See McLaughlin, *A Constitutional History of the United States* 47 (1935). For two other cases, see Mays, *op. cit. supra* n. 24, at 172.
26. *Quincy Reports,* Appendix 441 (Mass. 1769). See the similar statement in a 1766 letter by Hutchinson quoted in Bailyn, *op. cit. supra* n. 16, at 70–71.
27. For its text, see 1 Commager, *Documents of American History* 58 (1934).
28. 2 *The Writings of Samuel Adams* 350–51 (Cushing ed. 1904).
29. For its text, see id. at 350 *et seq.*
30. Id. at 371.
31. Reply of the Town of Truro. At a Meeting of the Freeholders and Other Inhabitants of the Town of Truro legally Assembled by Adjournment on Monday the 24th day of January 1773. Original in private collection.
32. See 2 Hart, *American History Told by Contemporaries* 410 (1914).
33. See Wright, *The Fabric of Freedom* 70 (1961).
34. Samuel Adams to Richard Henry Lee, July 15, 1774. 3 Adams, *op. cit. supra* n. 28, at 139. Compare the statements by Gerry and Madison quoted in Maier, *From Resistance to Revolution* 245 (1973).
35. Extracts from the Votes and Proceedings of the American Continental Congress Held at Philadelphia, Sept. 5, 1774. Containing The Bill of Rights, a List of Grievances, etc. (New York 1774).
36. See 1 Journals of the Continental Congress 63–74 (Ford ed. 1904). For the Declaration's text, see Commager, *op. cit. supra* n. 27, at 82.
37. For its text, see *op. cit. supra* n. 36, at 105.
38. 1 Gordon and Trenchard, *Cato's Letters* 100 (3d ed. 1733).
39. 4 Adams, *op. cit. supra* n. 7, at 193.
40. Quoted in Schwartz, *The Reins of Power: A Constitutional History of the United States* 20–21 (1963).
41. 4 Adams, *op. cit. supra* n. 7, at 207.
42. Continental Congress, *op. cit. supra* n. 36, at 342.

43. See McLaughlin, *op. cit. supra* n. 25, at 107–08.
44. Journal of the Virginia Convention, 1776. 6 American Archives, Fourth Series 1523 (Force ed. 1846).
45. Adair, "James Madison's Autobiography," 2 William and Mary Quarterly, Third Series 199 (1945).
46. *Op. cit. supra* n. 44, at 1538.
47. Randolph, "Essay on the Revolutionary History of Virginia," 44 Virginia Magazine of History and Biography 43, 44 (1936).
48. Madison, *loc. cit. supra* n. 45.
49. The first ten articles in this draft are in Mason's hand, the last four (apparently after committee discussion) in that of Thomas Ludwell Lee. See Miller, *George Mason: Gentleman Revolutionary* 337 (1975); 1 *The Papers of George Mason* 279 (Rutland ed. 1970).
50. 1 Rowland, *The Life of George Mason* 436 (1892).
51. See Brant, *James Madison: The Virginia Revolutionist* 245–47 (1941). The term "free exercise" had first been used in the Maryland Toleration Act, 1649, *supra* p. 39.
52. 1 *The Papers of Thomas Jefferson* 361–64 (Boyd ed. 1950).
53. Grigsby, *The Virginia Convention of 1776,* 163–64 (1855; 1969 reprinting).
54. George Mason to Richard Henry Lee, May 18, 1776. Mason, *op. cit. supra* n. 49, at 271.
55. See id. at 274.
56. For its text, see Commager, *op. cit. supra* n. 27, at 103.
57. Levy, *Origins of the Fifth Amendment* 405–7 (1968).
58. Randolph, *supra* n. 47, at 47.
59. 3 Adams, *op. supra* n. 28, at 298.
60. The May 27 committee draft of the Virginia Declaration appeared in the Pennsylvania *Evening Post* on June 6, the Pennsylvania *Ledger* on June 8, and the Pennsylvanian *Gazette* on June 12. Mason, *op. cit. supra* n. 49, at 276.
61. 3 Adams, *op. cit. supra* n. 7, at 220.
62. For its text, see 5 Thorpe, *The Federal and State Constitutions, Colonial Charters, and Other Organic Laws* 3081 (1909).
63. Quoted in Rutland, *The Birth of the Bill of Rights* 54 (1955).
64. For its text, see 1 *Laws of the State of Delaware, 1700–1797,* Appendix, 79 (1797).
65. Randolph, *supra* n. 47, at 47.
66. See Rutland, *op. cit. supra* n. 63, at 49, 50. For a recent discussion of the Maryland Convention, see Skaggs, *Roots of Maryland Democracy,* Chapter 9 (1973).
67. For its text, see 3 Thorpe, *op. cit. supra* n. 62, at 1686.
68. Quoted in Rutland, *op. cit. supra* n. 63, at 50.
69. For its text, see 2 Poore, *The Federal and State Constitutions, Colonial Charters and Other Organic Laws of the United States* 1409 (1878).

70. See Rutland, *op. cit. supra* n. 63, at 64.
71. For its text, see 6 Thorpe, *op. cit. supra* n. 62, at 3737.
72. Though there had been a provision on the matter in the Massachusetts Body of Liberties, 1641, *supra* p. 37.
73. For its text, see 1 Poore, *op. cit. supra* n. 69, at 257.
74. For its text, see 2 id. at 1310.
75. *Supra* p. 49.
76. 2 *The Literary Diary of Ezra Stiles* 49 (Dexter ed. 1901).
77. For its text, see 2 Thorpe, *op. cit. supra* n. 62, at 777.
78. *Infra* p. 82.
79. For its text, see 5 Thorpe, *op. cit. supra* n. 62, at 2623.
80. For its text, see Poore, *op. cit. supra* n. 69, at 1620.
81. As the Massachusetts legislature was called.
82. For its text, see Parsons, *Memoir of Theophilus Parsons* 359 (1859).
83. Journal of the Convention for Framing a Constitution of Government for the State of Massachusetts Bay, 1779–1780, 22 (1832).
84. Id. at 23.
85. Quoted in Rutland, *op. cit. supra* n. 63, at 69.
86. For the text of the Massachusetts Declaration, see Commager, *op. cit. supra* n. 27, at 107.
87. *Supra* p. 37.
88. *Infra* p. 126.
89. For its text, see 4 Thorpe, *op. cit. supra* n. 62, at 2453.
90. See Schwartz, *Constitutional Law: A Textbook* 247 (1972).
91. *The Complete Works of Thomas Paine* 274 (Foner ed. 1945) (italics omitted).
92. *Infra* p. 200.
93. Miller, *Lectures on the Constitution of the United States* 71 (1893).
94. Compare Brant, *The Bill of Rights* 41 (1965).

CHAPTER FOUR

1. As summarized in Bailyn, *The Ordeal of Thomas Hutchinson* 102–3 (1974). For the text of Hutchinson's Dialogue see 9 *Perspectives in American History* 343 (Bailyn ed. 1975).
2. Bailyn, *The Ordeal of Thomas Hutchinson* 106.
3. Wood, *The Creation of the American Republic* 304 (1969).
4. See Corwin, *The President: Office and Powers* 18 (4th ed. 1957).
5. Quoted in Wood, *loc. cit. supra* n. 3.
6. Ibid.
7. Id. at 338–39.
8. Id. at 538.
9. Ibid.

10. Id. at 304.
11. Id. at 538.
12. The case was unreported and the best account of it is in Scott, *"Holmes vs. Walton:* The New Jersey Precedent: A Chapter in the History of Judicial Power and Unconstitutional Legislation," 4 American Historical Review 456 (1899).
13. Id. at 459–60; Goebel, 1 *History of the Supreme Court of the United States: Antecedents and Beginnings to 1801,* 124 (1971).
14. Particularly 2 Crosskey, *Politics and the Constitution in the History of the United States* 948–52 (1953).
15. Scott, *supra* n. 12, at 459.
16. Id. at 464. Even Crosskey assumes that the Morris statement refers to *Holmes v. Walton, op. cit. supra* n. 14, at 951.
17. *State v. Parkhurst,* 9 N.J.L. 427, 444 (1802).
18. 4 Call 5 (Va. 1782).
19. 4 Call at 20.
20. Wythe was the first holder of an American law professorship; among his students was John Marshall who was to elevate Wythe's view in the Caton case to the federal constitutional plane.
21. 4 Call at 8. Pendleton's notes were sketchy on Wythe's opinion, but they confirm the essentials of the Call account. 2 *The Letters and Papers of Edmund Pendleton* 426 (Mays ed. 1961). See Goebel, *op. cit. supra* n. 13, at 127–8.
22. Pendleton, *op. cit. supra* n. 21, at 422. See 2 Mays, *Edmund Pendleton 1721–1803: A Biography* 200 (1952).
23. Edmund Pendleton to James Madison, Nov. 8, 1782. Id. at 201.
24. Id. at 202. Such reliance on Caton did not, however, occur until after it was reported in 1827. See Berger, *Congress v. The Supreme Court* 103, n. 263 (1969).
25. So characterized in Goebel, *op. cit. supra* n. 13, at 131.
26. The best account is in 1 Goebel, *The Law Practice of Alexander Hamilton* 282–419 (1964).
27. Berger, *op. cit. supra* n. 24 at 42.
28. Varnum, *The Case, Trevett against Weeden* (Providence 1787).
29. So characterized in Wood, *op. cit. supra* n. 3, at 460.
30. Quoted ibid.
31. Newport Mercury, October 6, 1786, quoted in Crosskey, *op. cit. supra* n. 14, at 966.
32. 1 N.C. 5 (1787).
33. Id. at 7.
34. 2 McRee, *Life and Correspondence of James Iredell* 169, 172–3 (1858).
35. 4 Call. 135 (Va. 1788).
36. Id. at 142, 146. The Remonstrance received wide distribution. It

was read by Chief Justice Pendleton in open court, printed in full in the newspapers, and laid before the legislature by Governor Randolph. Mays, *op. cit. supra* n. 22, at 273.

37. 1 Cranch 137 (U.S. 1803).
38. 21 Journals of the Continental Congress, 1774–1789, 669–72 (Ford ed. 1904). For Jefferson's Ordinance see 6 *The Papers of Thomas Jefferson* 604 (Boyd ed. 1951).
39. It is in the handwriting of Nathan Dane, who later wrote, "I drew the ordinance (which passed, a few words excepted, as I originally formed it)." Quoted in Rutland, *The Birth of the Bill of Rights* 103 (1955).
40. The italicized words were omitted from the final version. See 32 *op. cit. supra* n. 38, at 317. For the Northwest Ordinance's text, see 1 Commager, *Documents of American History* 128 (1934).
41. Quoted in Rutland, *loc. cit. supra* n. 39.
42. 2 Marshall, *Life of George Washington* 92 (2d ed. 1850).
43. 3 Farrand, *The Records of the Federal Convention of 1787*, 13 (1911).
44. Pole, *Foundations of American Independence* 196 (1972).
45. 2 Farrand *op. cit. supra* n. 43, at 588.
46. Id. at 587–88.
47. Id. at 588.
48. Id. at 341.
49. Id. at 617–18.
50. James Madison to George Washington, September 30, 1787. 5 *The Writings of James Madison* 4–7 (Hunt ed. 1904).
51. 3 *The Papers of George Mason* 993 (Rutland ed. 1970) states that September 16 was the probable date.
52. For the text of Mason's objections, see id. at 991–93. For a summary see Miller, *George Mason: Gentleman Revolutionary* 262–63 (1975).
53. George Mason to Thomas Jefferson, May 26, 1788. Mason, *op. cit. supra* n. 51, at 1045.
54. As shown by his letter of October 7, 1787, sending a copy to Washington. Id. at 1001. This led a correspondent to write Washington, "I think he might have been satisfied with the publication of his objections, without taking the pains to lodge them at every house." Id. at 1047.
55. Id. at 1003.
56. Ford, *Pamphlets on the Constitution of the United States* 156 (1888).
57. Ford, *Essays on the Constitution of the United States* 163–64 (1892).
58. Ford, *op. cit. supra* n. 56, at 336.
59. Ford, *op. cit. supra* n. 56, at 290–91, 318, 320. A recent article questions Lee's authorship of the Farmer Letters. See Wood, "The Authorship of the *Letters from the Federal Farmer*,"

30 William and Mary Quarterly, Third Series 299 (1974).
60. Ford, *op. cit. supra* n. 57, at 185.
61. Id. at 363, 365.
62. Id. at 373.
63. Id. at 96.
64. *United States v. Darby,* 312 U.S. 100, 124 (1941).
65. *Debates and Proceedings in the Convention of the Commonwealth of Massachusetts Held in the Year 1788,* 381, 383 (1856).
66. *Infra* p. 127.
67. Ford, *op. cit. supra* n. 57, at 121.
68. Id. at 314.
69. *Supra* p. 107.
70. Ford, *op. cit. supra* n. 57, at 220.
71. Ford, *op. cit. supra* n. 56, at 184, 186.
72. Sullivan, "Letters of Cassius," Ford, *op. cit. supra* n. 57, at 5: Hanson, "Address on the Proposed Plan of a Federal Government," Ford, *op. cit. supra* n. 56, at 221; Williamson, "Remarks on the New Plan of Government," Ford, *op. cit. supra* n. 57, at 397.
73. Id. at 398.
74. Warren, in *The Great Rights* 89 (Cahn ed. 1963).
75. *Infra* p. 146.
76. See 5 *The Papers of Alexander Hamilton* 702, 714 (Syrett ed. 1962).
77. Ford, *op. cit. supra* n. 56, at 83.
78. Id. at 91–3.
79. *Infra* p. 146.
80. *Infra* p. 137.
81. Madison, *op. cit. supra* n. 50, at 34.
82. 12 Jefferson, *op. cit. supra* n. 38, at 440.
83. Id. at 569.
84. Id. at 571.
85. Madison, *op. cit. supra* n. 50, at 271–74.
86. 14 Jefferson, *op. cit. supra* n. 38, at 650.
87. Id. at 659.
88. *Infra* p. 168.

CHAPTER FIVE

1. *Barron v. Mayor of Baltimore,* 7 Pet. 243, 250 (U.S. 1833).
2. Alexander Hamilton to James Madison, June 25, 1788, 5 *The Papers of Alexander Hamilton* 80 (Syrett ed. 1962); June 8, 1788, id. at 3.
3. James Madison to Thomas Jefferson, August 10, 1788. 5 *The Writings of James Madison* 244 (Hunt ed. 1904).

4. James Madi/,on to G. L. Turberville, November 2, 1788. Id. at 300.
5. *Infra* p. 163.
6. Ferguson, *Early Western Pennsylvania Politics* 83 (1938), quoted in Rutland, *The Birth of the Bill of Rights* 138 (1955).
7. 2 Elliott, *The Debates in the Several State Conventions on the Adoption of the Constitution* 435 (1836).
8. *Supra* p. 104.
9. Elliott, *op. cit. supra* n. 7, at 436, 454.
10. McMaster and Stone, *Pennsylvania and the Federal Constitution* 261, 256 (1888).
11. Elliott, *op. cit. supra* n. 7, at 454.
12. McMaster and Stone, *op. cit. supra* n. 10, at 471.
13. For their text, see id. at 421.
14. James Madison to Thomas Jefferson, February 19, 1788. Madison, *op. cit. supra* n. 3, at 101.
15. See Rutland, *The Birth of the Bill of Rights* 144 (1955).
16. *Supra* p. 81.
17. James Madison to George Washington, February 11, 1788. Madison, *op. cit. supra* n. 3, at 99.
18. Elliott, *op. cit. supra* n. 7, at 131, 154.
19. Id. at 161, 162.
20. *Debates and Proceedings in the Convention of the Commonwealth of Massachusetts Held in the Year 1788,* 87 (1856).
21. Elliott, *op. cit. supra* n. 7, at 177.
22. P. J. Van Berckel, quoted in Miller, *George Mason: Gentleman Revolutionary* 278 (1975).
23. February 3, 1788. Op. cit. supra note 20, at 44.
24. For their text, see Elliott, *op. cit. supra* n. 7, at 177.
25. James Madison to George Washington, February 15, 1788. Madison, *op. cit. supra* n. 3, at 100.
26. Thomas Jefferson to Edward Carrington, May 27, 1788. 13 *The Papers of Thomas Jefferson* 208 (Boyd ed. 1956).
27. Elliott, *op. cit. supra* n. 7, at 548–49.
28. See Dumbauld, *The Bill of Rights and What It Means Today* 18 (1957).
29. For their text, see Elliott, *op. cit. supra* n. 7, at 550–52.
30. For their text, see id. at 552–53.
31. *Supra* p. 105.
32. 4 Elliott, *op. cit. supra* n. 7, at 315–16.
33. The other South Carolina amendments related to control of congressional elections, direct taxes, and religious tests. For their text, see 2 *Documentary History of the Constitution of the United States* 139 (1894).
34. For their text, see id. at 142.

35. Madison, *op. cit. supra* n. 3, at 121.
36. *Supra* n. 25.
37. Madison, *op. cit. supra* n. 3, at 119.
38. Hamilton, *op. cit. supra* n. 2, at 61.
39. The extracts from the Virginia debates are from 3 Elliott, *op. cit. supra* n. 7.
40. 3 *The Papers of George Mason* 1140 (Rutland ed. 1970). See Beeman, *Patrick Henry: A Biography* 147 (1974).
41. Madison, *op. cit. supra* n. 3, at 240.
42. *Supra* p. 117.
43. See James Madison to Edmund Randolph, July 2, 1788. Madison, *op. cit. supra* n. 3, at 235.
44. 1 Cranch 137 (U.S. 1803).
45. *Supra* p. 96.
46. Henry's amendments were based upon a George Mason draft, as revised by an Antifederalist committee. Mason, *op. cit. supra* n. 40, at 1054, 1068.
47. These were essentially Henry's declaration of rights and amendments which he had moved as prior amendments. Mason, *op. cit. supra* n. 40, at 1788.
48. June 27, 1788. Madison, *op. cit. supra* n. 3, at 234. See, similarly, James Madison to Alexander Hamilton, June 27, 1788. Hamilton, *op. cit. supra* n. 2, at 91.
49. For the text of the Virginia-proposed bill of rights and additional amendments, see 3 Elliott, *op. cit. supra* n. 7, at 657, 659.
50. June 8, 1788. Hamilton, *op. cit. supra* n. 2, at 2. See, similarly, James Madison to Thomas Jefferson, July 24, 1788. Madison, *op. cit. supra* n. 3, at 242. On the results of the election for the New York Convention, see De Pauw, *The Eleventh Pillar: New York State and the Federal Constitution* 184 (1966).
51. June 25, 1788. Hamilton, *op. cit. supra* n. 2, at 80.
52. Clinton, somewhat unfairly, referred to Hamilton's speeches as "a second edition of Publius well delivered." See Goebel, 1 *History of the Supreme Court of the United States: Antecedents and Beginnings to 1801,* 398 (1971).
53. The extracts from the New York debates, which are not stated to be from other sources, are from Elliott, *op. cit. supra* n. 7, at 205–413.
54. This is the account referred to in the last note. It is from the shorthand record made by Francis Childs, editor of a New York newspaper. See Hamilton, *op. cit. supra* n. 2, at 11.
55. Now in the Gilbert Livingston Papers, New York Public Library. Their full text is printed, with permission, in 2 Schwartz, *The Bill of Rights: A Documentary History* 881 (1971).
56. Hamilton, *op. cit. supra* n. 2, at 147.

57. Id. at 156.
58. Id. at 157.
59. Gilbert Livingston Notes, id. at 164.
60. Id. at 166–67.
61. Id. at 167, from notes made by John McKesson.
62. Gilbert Livingston Notes.
63. Hamilton, *op. cit. supra* n. 2, at 177.
64. Gilbert Livingston Notes, id. at 182.
65. Opinion on the Constitutionality of an Act to Establish a Bank, February 23, 1791, 8 Hamilton, *op. cit. supra* n. 2, at 97.
66. 5 id. at 187.
67. Gilbert Livingston Notes.
68. For its text, see Elliott, *op. cit. supra* n. 7, at 413.
69. Madison, *op. cit. supra* n. 3, at 249.
70. For their text, see 2 *op. cit. supra* n. 33, at 190.
71. For their text, see id. at 196.
72. George Mason to John Mason, September 2, 1788. Mason, *op. cit. supra* n. 40, at 1130.
73. 28 Edward III c. 3.
74. *Supra* p. 7.
75. See Mott, *Due Process of Law* 97 (1926).
76. *Supra* p. 43.
77. *Gopalan v. State of Madras* (1950), 13 Supreme Court Journal 174. See Schwartz, "A Comparative View of the Gopalan Case," 4 Indian Law Review 276 (1950).
78. 2 Laws of the State of New York 344.
79. New York Assembly Journal, January 13, 16, 17, 1787. New York Senate Journal, January 19, 1787.
80. 4 Hamilton, *op. cit. supra* n. 2, at 35.
81. At least before the Bill of Rights was passed by Congress. Rhode Island voted ratification with recommendatory amendments on May 29, 1790—too late to influence the Bill of Rights debate (which explains why the Rhode Island proposals are not discussed in this volume).
82. The extracts from the North Carolina debates are from 4 Elliott, *op. cit. supra* n. 7, at 1–252.
83. For their text, see id. at 249.
84. For the text of the North Carolina Declaration of Rights and amendments, see id. at 243–47.
85. *Supra* p. 104.
86. See Dumbauld, *op. cit. supra* n. 28, at 32.
87. See id. at 33.
88. Thomas Jefferson to John Paul Jones, March 23, 1789. 14 Jefferson, *op. cit. supra* n. 26, at 688.
89. Ibid.

90. James Madison to Thomas Jefferson, December 8, 1788. Madison, *op. cit. supra* n. 3, at 311.
91. Id. at 312.

CHAPTER SIX

1. 1 Annals of Congress 441, 448–50.
2. James Madison to Thomas Jefferson, December 8, 1788. 5 *The Writings of James Madison* 312 (Hunt ed. 1904).
3. James Madison to George Washington, January 14, 1789. Id. at 319–20.
4. January 2, 1789. Id. at 319.
5. See Brant, *James Madison: Father of the Constitution* 14 (1950).
6. Id. at 249.
7. See 1 Beveridge, *The Life of John Marshall* 394 (1916).
8. Brant, in *The Great Rights* 30 (Cahn ed. 1963).
9. *Loc. cit. supra* n. 7.
10. 1 Annals of Congress 29.
11. Id. at 257.
12. Ibid.
13. Id. at 257, 281.
14. 15 *The Papers of Thomas Jefferson* 154 (Boyd ed. 1958).
15. 1 Annals of Congress 442.
16. Id. at 444.
17. Id. at 445.
18. Madison's June 8 speech is printed id. at 448–59.
19. James Madison to Samuel Johnston, June 21, 1789. Madison, *op. cit. supra* n. 2, at 409; James Madison to Edmund Randolph, August 21, 1789. Id. at 418.
20. Madison sent a copy of this pamphlet with his letter to Jefferson of October 17, 1788. Id. at 271.
21. See Dumbauld, *The Bill of Rights and What It Means Today* 36 (1957).
22. For their text, see Appendix A.
23. Madison *op. cit. supra* n. 2, at 372.
24. Id. at 389–90.
25. 5 *Documentary History of the Constitution of the United States* 93 (1905), quoted in Rutland, *The Birth of the Bill of Rights* 191 (1955).
26. His proposed seventh amendment provision on civil jury trial retained "ought" instead of "shall." This was probably an oversight on Madison's part.
27. *Supra* p. 91.

28. See Cahn in *op. cit. supra* n. 8, at 5.
29. 6 Madison, *op. cit. supra* n. 2, at 83.
30. Compare *op. cit. supra* n. 8, at 4–5.
31. 4 *The Papers of Alexander Hamilton* 35 (Syrett ed. 1962). *Supra* p. 153.
32. 1 Annals of Congress 685.
33. Id. at 690.
34. Id. at 686.
35. Id. at 699.
36. For the text of the amendments reported by the select committee, see Appendix B.
37. 1 Annals of Congress 770.
38. The August 13–24 House debate is contained in id. at 730–809. The quotes in the text are from the debate as reported in the Annals.
39. As late as 1886, however, Sir Henry Maine could refer to the Federal Bill of Rights as "a certain number of amendments on comparatively unimportant points." Maine, *Popular Government* 243 (1886).
40. Brant, *op. cit. supra* n. 5, at 268.
41. See "The People's Ancient and Just Liberties Asserted in the Trial of William Penn and William Mead (1670)," 1 *The Select Works of William Penn* 179 (4th ed. 1825).
42. August 21, 1789. Madison, *op. cit. supra* n. 2, at 417–18.
43. August 16 was a Sunday, so there was no debate on that day.
44. The committee had inadvertently left out the words "against unreasonable searches and seizures."
45. *Infra* p. 207.
46. Opinion on the Constitutionality of an Act to Establish a Bank, February 23, 1791. 8 Hamilton, *op. cit. supra* n. 31, at 97.
47. 4 Wheat. 316 (U.S. 1819).
48. Brant, *op. cit. supra* n. 5, at 271.
49. *Supra* p. 69.
50. August 24, 1789. Madison, *op. cit. supra* n. 2, at 418.
51. For the text of the amendments as passed by the House, see Appendix C.
52. *Journal of William Maclay* 134 (Maclay ed. 1890), quoted in Rutland, *op. cit. supra* n. 25, at 211.
53. *Journal of William Maclay* 142–156.
54. 7 Pet. 243 (U.S. 1833), *infra* p. 203.
55. Senate Legislative Journal, 1 *Documentary History of the First Federal Congress of the United States* 150–51 (De Pauw ed. 1972).
56. Id. at 151.
57. Id. at 151, 153.
58. September 14, 1789. Madison, *op. cit. supra* n. 2, at 420.

59. *Op. cit. supra* n. 55, at 153–68.
60. For the text of the Senate amendments, see Appendix D.
61. 1 Annals of Congress 939.
62. James Madison to Edmund Pendleton, September 23, 1789. Madison, *op. cit. supra* n. 2, at 424.
63. Brant, *op. cit. supra* n. 5, at 272.
64. For the text of the amendments passed by Congress, see Appendix E.
65. 1 Annals of Congress 90.
66. President Washington to Samuel Huntington, Governor of Connecticut, October 2, 1789. Original in private collection. Identical letters were sent to the other Governors.
67. *Harper's* 43 (June, 1963).
68. 5 Hamilton, *op. cit. supra* n. 31, at 517.
69. Hardin Burnley to James Madison, November 5, 1789. 5 *Documentary History of the Constitution of the United States* 214 (1905).
70. New York *Journal and Weekly Register,* January 7, 1790.
71. D. Stuart to President Washington, December 13, 1789. *Op. cit. supra* n. 69, at 220.
72. James Madison to President Washington, December 5, 1789. Madison, *op. cit. supra* n. 2, at 429.
73. January 4, 1790. *Op. cit. supra* n. 69, at 230–31.
74. Journal of the Senate of the Commonwealth of Virginia Begun and Held in the City of Richmond On Monday, the 19th day of October, in the Year of Our Lord 1789, 62–64 (1828).
75. Edmund Randolph to George Washington, December 15, 1789. *Op. cit. supra* n. 69, at 225.
76. New York *Journal and Weekly Register,* January 28, 1790.
77. Id. January 14, 1790.
78. Maryland *Gazette,* January 22, 1790.
79. New York *Journal and Weekly Register,* January 26, 1790.
80. Maryland *Journal & Baltimore Advertiser,* December 4, 1789.
81. New York *Journal and Weekly Register,* December 10, 1789; March 25, 1790.
82. Id. December 10, 1789.
83. United States *Chronicle,* February 4, 1790; New York *Journal and Weekly Register,* February 11, 1790.
84. Id. February 18, 1790.
85. Maryland *Journal & Baltimore Advertiser,* November 13, 1789.
86. United States *Chronicle,* March 25, 1790.
87. Myers, *Massachusetts and the First Ten Amendments* 10 (1936).
88. 10 Massachusetts Senate and House Journals (May 1789–March 1790).
89. Myers, *op. cit. supra* n. 87, at 8.
90. For the official ratifications, see History of Congress Exhibiting

a Classification of the Proceedings of the Senate and House of Representatives from March 4, 1789 to March 3, 1793, 174–87 (1843).

CHAPTER SEVEN

1. The CBS News Poll, Ser. 70, No. 1, Rpt. 2, March 20, 1970.
2. Warren, *A Republic, If You Can Keep It* 110–11 (1972).
3. Bartlett, *Familiar Quotations* 597 (14th ed. 1968).
4. *Supra* p. 12.
5. 3 Howell's *State Trials* 1, 45 (1627).
6. Warren, *op. cit. supra* n. 2, at 32.
7. See Dicey, *An Introduction to the Study of the Law of the Constitution* 189–90 (10th ed. 1967).
8. Compare Warren, *op. cit. supra* n. 2, at 112.
9. Compare Dicey, *op. cit. supra* n. 7, at 190.
10. Quoted in Brant, *The Bill of Rights* 242 (1965). For a comparable, though little known, New York seditious libel case just before Independence, see Maier, *From Resistance to Revolution* 192–93 (1973).
11. Dicey, *op. cit. supra* n. 7, at 243.
12. 2 May, *The Constitutional History of England since the Accession of George the Third* 106–07 (1863).
13. Rex v. Cuthell, 27 Howell's *State Trials* 642, 675 (1799), quoted in Dicey, *op. cit. supra* n. 7, at 246.
14. See May, *op. cit. supra* n. 12, Chapter X.
15. Though most of the restrictions against Protestant dissenters had been removed, virtually all of them were still enforced against Catholics and non-Christians.
16. *Supra* p. 153.
17. Brennan, J., dissenting, in *Lopez v. United States,* 373 U.S. 427, 454 (1963).
18. Notably in Entick v. Carrington, 19 Howell's *State Trials* 1029 (1765).
19. See Plucknett, *A Concise History of the Common Law* 386, 388 (2d ed. 1936).
20. See Blackstone's *Commentaries,* Book IV, Chapters 1 and 6.
21. *Supra* p. 177.
22. See Brant, *The Bill of Rights* 64 (1965).
23. Compare id. at 218.
24. Rawls, *A Theory of Justice* 61 (1971).
25. See Schwartz, *The Law in America: A History* 90 (1974).
26. Except for New York, which used the "due process" language, *Supra* p. 151.

27. See Schwartz, *Constitutional Law: A Textbook* 286 (1972).
28. Compare Frankfurter, J., concurring, in *Adamson v. California,* 332 U.S. 46, 63 (1947).
29. Compare Black, J., dissenting, in *Griswold v. Connecticut,* 381 U.S. 479, 520 (1965).
30. *Supra* pp. 182.
31. 7 Pet. 243 (U.S. 1833).
32. Id. at 247, 250–51.
33. See 2 Crosskey, *Politics and the Constitution* 1056 *et seq.* (1953).
34. 1 Stat. 596 (1798).
35. Quoted in Smith, *Freedom's Fetters: The Alien and Sedition Laws and American Civil Liberties* 184 (1956).
36. Id. at 226.
37. Id. at 270–71, 274.
38. Id. at 186.
39. Quoted id. at 178.
40. Quoted in *New York Times Co. v. Sullivan,* 376 U.S. 254, 276 (1964).
41. 3 Story, *Commentaries on the Constitution of the United States* §1886 (1833).
42. *New York Times Co. v. Sullivan,* 376 U.S. 254, 276 (1964).
43. Id. at 273.
44. McMaster and Stone, *Pennsylvania and the Federal Constitution* 308–09 (1888).
45. See Smith, *op. cit. supra* n. 35, at 139.
46. But see Schwartz, *From Confederation to Nation: The American Constitution 1835–1877,* 92–104 (1973).
47. Brant, *op. cit. supra* n. 22, at 318.
48. See Schwartz, *op. cit. supra* n. 46, at 74–6.
49. Wharton, *State Trials of the United States during the Administrations of Washington and Adams* 712 (1849).
50. 1 Cranch 137 (U.S. 1803).
51. *Supra* n. 31.
52. Black, J., dissenting, in *Adamson v. California,* 332 U.S. 46, 74 (1947).
53. See 1 Schwartz, *A Statutory History of the United States: Civil Rights* 306 (1970).
54. *Supra* p. 182.
55. Compare *The Mind and Faith of Justice Holmes* 18 (Lerner ed. 1954).
56. For a fuller discussion, see Schwartz, *op. cit. supra* n. 25, at 109.
57. Maine, *Popular Government* 243 (1886).
58. *Children's Hospital v. Adkins,* 284 Fed. 613, 622 (D.C. Cir. 1922).
59. 332 U.S. 46 (1947).
60. Id. at 71–72.

61. 16 Wall. 36 (U.S. 1873).
62. Id. at 79.
63. See Corwin, *The Constitution of the United States of America: Analysis and Interpretation* 965 (1953).
64. 110 U.S. 516 (1884).
65. 211 U.S. 78 (1908).
66. Id. at 106–07.
67. Virginia, New York, North Carolina, and Rhode Island (which proposed its amendments after the Bill of Rights had been passed by Congress, which is why they have not been dealt with in this volume).
68. 211 U.S. at 118.
69. See Brant, *op. cit. supra* n. 22, at 381.
70. Compare Frankfurter, J., concurring, in *Francis v. Resweber,* 329 U.S. 459, 467 (1947).
71. Douglas, *We the Judges* 264 (1956).
72. Holmes, *The Common Law* 1 (1881).
73. Douglas, *loc. cit. supra* n. 71.
74. *Malinski v. New York,* 324 U.S. 401, 415 (1945).
75. Compare Frankfurter, J., concurring, in *Adamson v. California,* 332 U.S. at 63.
76. 211 U.S. at 106.
77. *Palko v. Connecticut,* 302 U.S. 319, 325 (1937).
78. Harlan, J., dissenting, in *Williams v. Florida,* 399 U.S. 78, 130 (1970).
79. *Palko v. Connecticut,* 302 U.S. 319, 326 (1937).
80. Id. at 325.
81. *Duncan v. Louisiana,* 391 U.S. 145, 212 (1968), per Fortas, J.
82. Id. at 150.
83. *Hurtado v. California,* 110 U.S. at 535.
84. 332 U.S. at 69.
85. Id. at 90.
86. Black, J., concurring, in *Rochin v. California,* 342 U.S. 165, 177 (1952).
87. *Supra* n. 31.
88. *Supra* n. 64.
89. *Supra* n. 65.
90. Venable, "Growth or Evolution of Law," 23 American Bar Association Reports 278, 299 (1900).
91. Brandeis, *Business—A Profession* liv (1914).
92. *Gitlow v. New York,* 268 U.S. 652 (1925); *Pierce v. Society of Sisters,* 268 U.S. 510 (1925).
93. *Palko v. Connecticut,* 302 U.S. 319, 327 (1927).
94. *Moore v. Dempsey,* 261 U.S. 86 (1923).
95. *Wolf v. Colorado,* 338 U.S. 25 (1949).

96. *Brown v. Mississippi*, 297 U.S. 278 (1936).
97. *In re Oliver*, 333 U.S. 257 (1948).
98. *Norris v. Alabama*, 294 U.S. 587 (1935).
99. *Powell v. Alabama*, 287 U.S. 45 (1932); *Betts v. Brady*, 316 U.S. 455 (1942).
100. *Francis v. Resweber*, 329 U.S. 459, 463 (1947).
101. *Wolf v. Colorado*, 338 U.S. 25 (1949).
102. *Palko v. Connecticut*, 302 U.S. 319 (1937).
103. *Adamson v. California*, 332 U.S. 46 (1947).
104. See *Palko v. Connecticut*, 302 U.S. 319, 324 (1937).
105. *Betts v. Brady*, 316 U.S. 455 (1942).
106. Warren, "The Law and the Future," *Fortune* 106, 126 (November 1955).
107. *United States v. Carolene Products Co.*, 304 U.S. 144, 152, n. 4 (1938).
108. Letter of Justice Stone, April 12, 1941. Quoted in Mason, "The Core of Free Government, 1938–40: Mr. Justice Stone and 'Preferred Freedoms,' " 65 Yale Law Journal 597, 626 (1956).
109. See Jackson, J., dissenting, in *Brinegar v. United States*, 338 U.S. 160, 180 (1949).
110. Compare Frankfurter, J., concurring, in *Kovacs v. Cooper*, 336 U.S. 77, 95 (1949).
111. See *Benton v. Maryland*, 395 U.S. 784, 794 (1969).
112. See Harlan, J., dissenting, in *Williams v. Florida*, 399 U.S. 78, 130 (1970).
113. 367 U.S. 643 (1961).
114. 372 U.S. 335 (1963).
115. *Benton v. Maryland*, 395 U.S. 784 (1969).
116. *Malloy v. Hogan*, 378 U.S. 1 (1964).
117. *Duncan v. Louisiana*, 391 U.S. 145 (1968).
118. *Klopfer v. North Carolina*, 386 U.S. 213 (1967).
119. *Pointer v. Texas*, 380 U.S. 400 (1965).
120. *Pilkinton v. Circuit Court*, 324 F. 2d 45 (8th Cir. 1963).
121. *Supra* p. 217.
122. 406 U.S. 356 (1972).
123. 391 U.S. 145 (1968).
124. See Schwartz, *op. cit. supra* n. 27, at 210.
125. Powell, J., concurring, in *Johnson v. Louisiana*, 406 U.S. at 369.
126. Id. at 375.
127. Compare *United States v. Wood*, 299 U.S. 123, 143 (1936).
128. Dissenting, in *New State Ice Co. v. Liebmann*, 285 U.S. 262, 311 (1932).
129. Powell, J., concurring, in *Johnson v. Louisiana*, 406 U.S. at 375.
130. 394 U.S. 618 (1969).
131. 410 U.S. 113 (1973).

132. Id. at 153.
133. Id. at 155.
134. Compare Harlan, J., dissenting, in *Shapiro v. Thompson*, 394 U.S. at 661.
135. See Schwartz, *The Supreme Court: Constitutional Revolution in Retrospect* 23–4 (1957).
136. 1 Farrand, *The Records of the Federal Convention of 1787*, 533 (1911).
137. 6 *The Works of John Adams* 280 (C.F. Adams ed. 1851).
138. Pius XII, in Bartlett, *Familiar Quotations* 941 (14th ed. 1968).
139. Compare Chafee, *How Human Rights Got into the Constitution* 2 (1952).
140. *Merchant of Venice*, Act IV, scene 1.
141. Compare Warren, "The Bill of Rights and the Military," 37 New York University Law Review 181, 200 (1962).
142. John F. Kennedy, in message calling for civil rights legislation, New York *Times*, June 20, 1963, p. 16.
143. 3 Pound, *Jurisprudence* 332 (1959).
144. *Lynch v. Household Finance Corp.*, 405 U.S. 538, 552 (1972).
145. Compare Gunther, Foreword: "In search of Evolving Doctrine on a Changing Court," 86 Harvard Law Review 1, 38 (1972).
146. See Schwartz, *op. cit. supra* n. 25, at 153–57.
147. Slaughter-House Cases, 16 Wall. 36, 78 (U.S. 1873).
148. Lochner v. New York, 198 U.S. 45 (1905).
149. Rehnquist, J., dissenting, in *Roe v. Wade*, 410 U.S. at 174.
150. *The Great Rights* 148 (Cahn ed. 1963).
151. 4 *The Collected Essays, Journalism and Letters of George Orwell* 75 (1968).
152. *Loc. cit. supra* n. 150.
153. Fortas, J., quoted in Schwartz, *The Fourteenth Amendment Centennial Volume* 34 (1970).
154. 2 Tocqueville, *Democracy in America* 147 (Bradley ed. 1954).
155. Compare Tawney, *Equality* 125 (1931).
156. Compare 3 Pound, *op. cit. supra* n. 143, at 321.
157. Bell, "On Meritocracy and Equality," 29 *The Public Interest* 29, 40 (1972).
158. Rawls, *op. cit. supra* n. 24, at 303.
159. Id. at 100.
160. *Lochner v. New York*, 198 U.S. 45, 75 (1905).
161. See Schwartz, *The Law in America: A History* 108–13 (1974).
162. *The Words of Justice Brandeis* 121 (Goldman ed. 1953).
163. Compare Lewis, "The Future of Equality," New York *Times*, November 27, 1972, p. 35, col. 5.
164. Compare Bell, *op. cit. supra* n. 157, at 50.
165. Bickel, *The Morality of Consent* 20 (1975).

index

271

Privileges and immunities, 78, 100, 105, 209-10
Privileges, legislative, 10, 23, 31-32
Property vs. personal rights, 216-19, 223-24
Protestation, 1621, 10-11, 15
Public office, right to, 201
Public records, access to, 38
Public trial, 45, 47, 51, 73, 88, 125, 148, 158, 166, 192, 199, 217
Punishment. *See* Cruel and unusual punishment
Puritans, 35-37, 39, 40
Purse, power of, 32, 43, 103

Quakers, 41, 46-48, 175
Quartering soldiers, 11, 23, 44, 51, 61, 64, 75, 76, 83, 84, 87, 105, 131, 132, 133, 134, 140, 141, 148, 157, 158, 166, 176, 183, 198
Quebec, Address to, 64-65
Quebec, fall of, 33

Randolph, Edmund, 68, 72, 75, 135-37, 176, 189
Rational basis test, 223
Rawls, John, 201, 228-30
Read, George, 74
Redress, principle of, 228-29
Religion, establishment of, 39, 61, 73, 79, 80, 82, 85, 87, 90, 131, 132, 140, 141, 147, 157, 158, 166, 174-75, 180, 182, 183, 184, 185-86, 189, 194, 195, 198, 218
Religion, free exercise of, 18, 38-42, 44, 45, 47, 49, 51, 61, 68, 69, 71, 76, 77, 79, 80, 84-85, 87, 103, 108, 116, 117, 123, 125, 127, 129, 132, 134, 137, 140, 141-42, 147, 157, 158, 166, 168, 169, 174-75, 177, 180, 182, 183, 184, 185-86, 194, 195, 198, 201, 203, 207, 217, 218
Religious Freedom, Bill for Establishing, 79

Religious test, 73, 105
Remonstrance, Virginia judges, 99-100
Representatives, House of, 121, 124, 128, 129, 140, 148, 149, 150, 160-86
Republican government guaranty, 103
Reserved powers, 83, 90, 100, 107, 109, 114, 117, 128, 129, 132, 140, 142, 146, 147, 155, 158, 167, 178, 180, 184, 199
Residence requirement, 222
Result, equality of, 228-30
Retained rights, 86, 158, 172, 177, 199
Rhode Island Charter, 27, 40-41, 42, 45, 51, 67, 78
Rhode Island Ratifying Convention, 156
Rich, Sir Nathaniel, 36
Rights of Man, 194
Rights of the Colonists, 61-62
Roe v. Wade, 222
Rule of law, 47
Rump Parliament, 18
Rutgers v. Waddington, 97

Scutage, 5
Searches and seizures, 24, 61, 73, 75, 77, 83, 84, 88, 90, 124, 127, 139, 141, 148, 157, 158, 166, 183, 192, 196, 198, 199, 201, 217
Second constitutional convention, 114, 121, 147, 163
Secret trials, 192
Sedgwick, Theodore, 175
Sedition Act, 204-06
Seditious libel, 194-95
Selden, John, 8
Select Committee, 171-72, 173, 174, 176, 178
Selective incorporation, 213-15, 219
Self-incrimination, 18, 24, 71, 73, 75, 77, 83, 88, 123, 125, 139, 141, 148,

Index

Self-incrimination (*continued*)
157, 166, 177, 184, 192, 196, 198,
210-11, 218, 220
Senate, 141, 150, 161, 162, 177, 181-
86, 203, 207
Separation of powers, 70, 80, 82, 83,
84, 124, 139, 167, 169, 178, 183
Shapiro v. Thompson, 222
Sherman, Roger, 104, 105, 112, 164,
171, 173, 179, 180, 185
Slaughter-House Cases, 209
Slavery, 37, 77, 101, 102, 133
Smilie, John, 94
Smith, Melancton, 114-15, 142, 145,
146
Social Statics, 229
Sons of Liberty, 60
South Carolina Constitution, 80
South Carolina proposed amend-
ments, 133, 142, 156, 165
South Carolina Ratifying Conven-
tion, 133
Spaight, Richard Dobbs, 99
Speech, freedom of, 23, 24, 37, 51, 71,
73-74, 76, 77, 82, 83, 84, 87, 124,
125, 129, 139, 141, 157, 158, 166,
172, 175-76, 177, 182, 183, 184, 192,
195, 198, 201, 204-06, 217, 218
Speedy trial, 71, 73, 75, 76, 88, 90,
125, 148, 158, 166, 199, 220
Spencer, Herbert, 229
Spencer, Samuel, 154
Stamp Act, 56, 58-60, 62, 63
Stamp Act Congress, 60, 64
Star Chamber, 24
States, restrictions on, 166, 168, 169,
172, 177, 182, 183, 202-03, 207-25
Stiles, Ezra, 79
Stone, Harlan F., 218
Story, Joseph, 205
Stubbs, William, 4
Sullivan, James, 112
Supremacy Clause, 20, 45, 97
Supreme Court, 129, 140, 150, 154,
166, 182, 183, 185, 202, 205, 209-25,
227
Suspending power, 23, 139
Sydney, Algernon, 48, 70
Sydney Letters, 111

Taxes, 103, 124, 128, 131, 132, 149,
150, 180, 189
Testify, right to, 47-48, 196
Tocqueville, Alexis de, 23, 227
Torture, 38
Treason Act, 96
Treaties, 97, 103, 124, 131, 140, 149
Tredwell, Thomas, 143, 144
Trevett v. Weeden, 97-98
Triennial Act, 23
Truro, letter from, 62
Tucker, Thomas, 175-76, 178
Twain, Mark, 208
Twining v. New Jersey, 210-17

Unconstitutionality, 20, 45, 54-60,
63-64, 92-100

Vane, Sir Henry, 18-19
Varnum, James M., 97
Vermont Declaration of Rights, 77-78
Vice President, 148, 149
Vining, John, 172, 173, 178, 185
Virginia Charter, 27, 28, 30, 34, 35
Virginia Constitution, 67-69, 99
Virginia Convention, 1776, 67-72, 75
Virginia Court of Appeals, 96, 99
Virginia Declaration of Rights, 1, 64,
67-72, 73, 74, 76, 79, 91, 104, 107,
135, 170, 180
Virginia House of Delegates, 188
Virginia proposed amendments,
132, 138-42, 151, 155-56, 165, 169,
170, 183
Virginia Ratifying Convention, 119,
134-42, 151, 155-56, 162
Virginia Senate, 188-89

278